The Common Place of Law

Patricia Ewick &
Susan S. Silbey

The Common Place of Law

Stories from Everyday Life

THE UNIVERSITY OF CHICAGO PRESS / CHICAGO AND LONDON

The University of Chicago Press, Chicago 60637
The University of Chicago Press, Ltd., London
© 1998 by The University of Chicago
All rights reserved. Published 1998
Printed in the United States of America
14 13 12 11 10 09 08   5 6 7 8
ISBN: 0-226-22742-1 (cloth)
ISBN: 0-226-22744-8 (paper)

Library of Congress Cataloging-in-Publication Data

The common place of law : stories from everyday life / Patricia Ewick and
    Susan S. Silbey.
       p. cm.—(Language and legal discourse)
    Includes bibliographical references and index.
    ISBN 0-226-22742-1 (cloth : alk. paper).—ISBN 0-226-22744-8
    (pbk. : alk. paper)
    1. Culture and law.   2. Sociological jurisprudence.   3. Law—United
States—Case studies.   4. Law—New Jersey—Case studies.   I. Ewick,
Patricia.   II. Silbey, Susan S.   III. Series.
K487.C8C657   1998
340'.115—dc21   97-45760
                                                                       CIP

For Benjamin, Nicholas, Anna, and Jessica

Law, say the gardeners, is the sun,
Law is the one
All gardeners obey
To-morrow, yesterday, to-day.

Law is the wisdom of the old
The impotent grandfathers shrilly scold;
The granchildren put out a treble tongue,
Law is the senses of the young.

Law, says the priest with a priestly look,
Expounding to an unpriestly people,
Law is the words in my priestly book,
Law is my pulpit and my steeple.

Law, says the judge as he looks down his nose,
Speaking clearly and most severely,
Law is as I've told you before,
Law is as you know I suppose,
Law is but let me explain it once more,
Law is The Law.

Yet law-abiding scholars write:
Law is neither wrong nor right,
Law is only crime
Punished by place and by times,
Law is the clothes men wear
Anytime, anywhere,
Law is Good-morning and Good-night.

Others say, Law is our Fate:
Others say, Law is our State;
Others say, others say
Law is no more
Law has gone away.

W. H. AUDEN (1939)

CONTENTS

American society is filled with signs of legal culture. Every package of food, piece of clothing, and electrical appliance contains a label warning us about its dangers, instructing us about its uses, and telling us to whom we can complain if something goes wrong. Every time we park a car, dry-clean clothing, or leave an umbrella in a cloakroom, we are informed about limited liabilities for loss. Newspapers, television, novels, plays, magazines, and movies are saturated with legal images, while these same cultural objects display their claims to copyright. Moreover, the pervasiveness of law is not a new phenomenon. More than 150 years ago, Alexis de Tocqueville observed that in America all issues eventually become legal matters. We began this book with the hope of understanding the basis of this American romance with law.

The Common Place of Law uses stories of everyday life to discover the different ways in which people use and think about law. What are the different conceptions of law that encourage some people to call a lawyer if their neighbor's dog disturbs their trash, and others to accept the losses and pain that may be caused by defective products, unsuccessful surgery, or discrimination? To what degree do Americans understand their lives through legal concepts and processes? We explore the meanings of law in American lives, including the degree to which Americans may be enthusiastically using law; we also explore people's resistance to using law. In short, we want to know what legality means in the daily lives of Americans.

This book began with a request from the New Jersey Supreme Court Task Force on Minority Concerns for help in trying to find out whether, and in what ways, there might be racial discrimination in the New Jersey courts. Specifically, the task force had suggested that one of the most important and detrimental forms of racial variation might be the differential voluntary use of law and courts by minority populations. It seemed plausible to the task force that when faced with the option of using legal procedures (calling the police, filing a grievance, or initiating a lawsuit), minorities were more likely than nonminorities to refrain. Put differently, if Americans have a romance with law, it is not a universal attraction.

The court's request seemed to be an opportunity to put our professional skills to the service of a political project to which we are totally committed—racial equality. Agreeing to design a research project for the task force was the beginning of a seven-year involvement during which the project was transformed from a relatively circumscribed set of policy questions to an exploration of fundamental problems in social theory and legal culture. We convinced the task force that we could answer their questions about differential use of courts only if we could understand the taken-for-granted place of law in the lives of New Jersey citizens. To do so, we had to look at more than the courts, or even legal disputes and problems.

We decided to collect stories of everyday experiences from a large number of people, and in the course of these conversations to see if we could locate the place of law in American culture. "Collecting stories" and "having conversations" is not the usual way of describing social science research. But this is not, we hope, a usual project of either qualitative or quantitative social science. Rather, we have self-consciously attempted to combine several different methods and to work at the intersections of several fields of scholarship in response to contemporary controversies in sociology, cultural studies, and legal theory. We have combined aspects of textual interpretation with survey research to mediate debates about the place of subject and observer, authorship and representation, as well as reliability and accuracy in social research. We also hope to contribute to the growing field of cultural studies by focusing not only on the symbols and representations embedded in legal materials, but on the production and reception of legal culture by citizens. Finally, we have interwoven sociological theories of social structure and human agency with theories of social construction to develop a model of the lived experiences of legality, its varieties and dimensions. Thus, this book sits at the intersection of several literatures and should be of interest to scholars in most social sciences, as well as socio-legal studies, legal theory, and cultural studies.

In the end, we were able to respond to the court's concerns and at the same time identify the various ways in which legality is understood and enacted in the daily lives of ordinary citizens. Once we had mapped the complex and contradictory fabric of legality, we also observed the continuity between popular and professional legal consciousness. In this sense, our analysis of popular legal consciousness confirms what other observers find when they look at professional legal practices and the ways in which formal legal institutions work: a persistent contradiction between the ideal and the actual in the law. One of the themes of this book is how this gap sustains rather than undermines legality.

Another theme of this book is the relationship among text, meaning, and authority. People write letters, save receipts, document events, and sign contracts because they know that "getting it in writing" makes a difference. It makes what they say more emphatic, more permanent, and more important (some say more "legal"). During our interviews people also reported loss and frustration associated with putting their words into writing. Sometimes their words were unread, filed away, or misinterpreted. In some cases, people decided later that they wanted to take some words back or change their minds, but couldn't.

We have spent many years "getting this in writing," as some respondents said. And for us there is the same pleasure and loss that they spoke of. Years of conversations have now assumed this final form. All of those spoken words, scribbled notes, cut and pasted text do seem more definitive as they appear here. They certainly have greater authority (being protected by copyright law and the conventions of social science citation practices). But for all that, there are the typical dangers and losses. Having assumed this form, the hundreds of interviews, conversations, half-formed as well as deliberate lines of analysis now have a life of their own. We can no longer change them and must live with our errors, omissions, the awkward phrases, undeveloped points, and misplaced commas.

But here is the place in the text where we can keep the process of writing (ongoing, tentative, always collaborative) alive. Here we can document the help, contributions, and support that we have received from many people over many years. We are grateful for the lively collegiality and the generous and supportive responses to urgent inquiries and uncertainties. The irony of our efforts to document and concretize this vital human process and these relationships in writing is not, however, lost on us. But in this instance we want to be loud and emphatic in our thanks, and we are confident we will not change our minds.

There are a number of people for whom we feel great affection and to whom we owe debts of many kinds. Marc Steinberg has been a penetrating reader and unfailing friend for many years. He is a master teacher, and we have benefited greatly from his gentle instruction. Ronen Shamir has been an intellectual provocateur who always has time for a hundred visions and revisions. His reading of earlier drafts helped to give shape and sophistication to our ideas. From the beginning, we were inspired by Rick Fantasia's groundbreaking work on class consciousness and cultures of solidarity. More generally, we have been enriched, both personally and professionally, by Rick's energy and passionate convictions. Austin Sarat has been a friend, collaborator, and thoughtful critic; his prodigious intellect, affection, and loyalty are unfailing and for all of these we are grateful.

One research assistant has been with us in this project from the very beginning. Although she served as interviewer, coder, and reader, Elizabeth Schuster McGeveran was as much a companion and collaborator, an all-purpose conscience keeping us focused and reliable throughout. One of the special joys has been to work with such an imaginative and capable student.

In large part, the impetus for framing the question of differential use of law as part of a broader question about the place of law in everyday life grew out of a fourteen-year-long conversation in the Amherst Seminar on Legal Ideology and Legal Process. For us, *The Common Place of Law* is the culmination of those discussions, bringing together diverse threads that preoccupied the seminar: power, ideology, resistance, social practice, and interpretation. Thus, we are particularly indebted to our colleagues in the Amherst Seminar: John Brigham, Kristin Bumiller, Sara Cobb, Christine Harrington, Sally Merry, Brinkley Messick, Ron Pipkin, Austin Sarat, Adelaide Villmoare, Barbara Yngvesson, and Larry Zacharias.

We would also like to thank Frank Munger, David Engel, and Bryant Garth, with whom we have been engaged for years in an ongoing discussion about legal consciousness and narrative. Joel Handler has kept us intellectually and politically honest. For nearly three decades, Egon Bittner and David Greenestone provided Susan unselfish instruction and unfailing wisdom for which she is particularly grateful. Many others have read various drafts of this work, engaged us in helpful conversations, and contributed ideas and insights. We have tried to learn from their suggestions: Estelle Lau, Dirk Hartog, Martha Minow, Alice Hearst, Keith Bybee, Jill Frank, Martha Umphrey, Vicky Spellman, Carroll Seron, Karen Orren, Owen Flanagan, John

Conley, Mack O'Barr, Lauren Edelman, Kim Scheppelle, Marianne Constable, Gary Marx, and Yves Dezalay.

Both of us are lucky to work in intellectually congenial and supportive institutions. We would like to thank especially our colleagues in the Sociology Departments at Clark University (Bruce London, Deborah Merrill, Bob Ross, and Shelly Tenenbaum) and Wellesley College (Lee Cuba, Jonathan Imber, and Tom Cushman) for all of their help. Jens Kruse, Vernon Shetley, and Caroline Webb were all conscripted into the project at one time or another.

We also accumulated debts from the beginning of the project in New Jersey. We collaborated with Bill Chambliss and Howard Taylor when we began working for the New Jersey Supreme Court. Robert Joc Lee's and Sylvia Breau's competence at managing such a large project was instrumental in contributing to its success. John Blazer was one of the most skillful interviewers we have ever known.

One of the expected difficulties of taking on a project of this size is the continual need for assistance; one of the unexpected pleasures was the people who helped us. We are particularly indebted to their willingness to work unpredictable hours, sometimes at short notice, and too often with insufficiently specific instructions. We had many research assistants, some of whom enthusiastically taught us about resistant practices: Lisa Kaunelis, Tara Kominiak, Bethany Hoffman, Shanna Connor, Kathryn Hudak, Linda Puls, Rachel Onanian, Shanna Whitehead, Christy Agor, Ling Tang, Frances Ramberg, Ted Rooney, Laura Melbin, Jeremy Rudd, Diane Merians, Anna Silbey, Jessica Silbey, and Zachary Deutch.

We appreciate the financial support we received and without which this work would not have been possible. We were supported by grants from Clark University, Wellesley College, the State Justice Institute (A-89-081), the New Jersey Administrative Office of the Courts, and the National Science Foundation (SES 9123561). Portions of the book were written while on leaves supported by our institutions and by the American Association of University Women, Harvard Law School, and the American Council of Learned Societies. Susan is most grateful for the sparkling intellectual communities of the Villa Serbelloni, Bellaggio, Italy (Rockefeller Foundation) and the Maison Suger of the Maison de Sciences de l'Homme, Paris, which provided stimulation and challenge while she worked on portions of the book.

We are also grateful for permission to reprint some materials.

Portions of chapter 1 originally appeared in Patricia Ewick and Susan S. Silbey, "Conformity, Contestation and Resistance: An Account of Legal Consciousness," *New England Law Review* 26 (1992): 731–49; © Copyright New England School of Law 1992; all rights reserved; reprinted by permission. Portions of chapter 2 originally appeared in Susan S. Silbey, "Making a Place for a Cultural Analysis of Law," *Law and Social Inquiry* 17 (1992): 39–48; © Copyright 1992 by The American Bar Foundation; all rights reserved; reprinted by permission of the University of Chicago Press. Portions of chapter 3 originally appeared in Patricia Ewick and Susan S. Silbey, "Subversive Stories and Hegemonic Tales: Toward a Sociology of Narrative," *Law and Society Review* 29, no. 2 (1995): 197–226; reprinted by permission of the Law and Society Association. Portions of chapter 7 originally appeared in Patricia Ewick, "Postmodern Melancholia," *Law and Society Review* 26, no. 4 (1992): 755–63; reprinted by permission of the Law and Society Association.

Finally, as we clean the files and save the disks, we know that we must declare the work done even as the relations, affections, and memories remain. We were friends before we were colleagues, and colleagues before we were official collaborators, and it does not end here. We say official collaborators because from the very beginning of our connection, there was a conspiracy between the two of us. Our professional lives had followed similarly irregular paths, and we often found ourselves observing from the peripheries of whatever group or institution we joined. We found that we not only shared a passion for sociology but for teaching it as well. Thus when we came to do this research together (from a combination of opportunity, political commitment, and financial inducement) we found a place to join our pleasure in gabbing about sociology and life with more professional but no less compelling desires. This book has been produced in our offices, on the beaches of West Falmouth, in a garden in Worcester, and a good part of it on the New Jersey Turnpike and at the Newark Airport. We pushed baby carriages while discussing Goffman and Giddens, and grounded ourselves literally (in our first joint sailing effort) as we found ourselves metaphorically beached on the shoals of narrative scholarship. We made heavy demands on our families—not so much for the time away, which was considerable, but because the time at home was often colonized by the endless talk about structures and schemas, Nikos and Bess. We want to thank our families. We owe them much. Thanks to Lee Cuba, friend for life, for things unimaginable. Thanks to Marion Ewick and Barbara Trocki for joyfully and generously becoming "nannies," or whatever else they needed to be, at a moment's notice. Thanks to Alma and Dick Merians for their help in more ways than we can possibly acknowledge. Thanks to Annie and Jess for being willing to join the corps. And, thanks to Bobby for being, always.

PART ONE
Introduction

CHAPTER ONE

Millie Simpson

Our sense of being a person can come from being drawn into a wider social unit; our sense of selfhood can arise through the little ways in which we resist the pull. Our status is backed by the solid building of the world, while our sense of personal identity often resides in the cracks.

ERVING GOFFMAN, *Asylums*

[T]here is no single locus of great Refusal, no soul of revolt, source of all rebellions, or pure law of the revolutionary. Instead there is a plurality of resistances, each of them a special case; . . . resistances . . . are distributed in irregular fashion: the points, knots, or focuses of resistance are spread over time and space in varying densities, inflaming certain points of the body, certain moments in life, certain types of behavior . . . Just as the network of power relations ends by forming a dense web that passes through apparatuses and institutions, without being exactly localized in them, so too the swarm of points of resistance traverses social stratifications and individual unities.

MICHEL FOUCAULT, *The History of Sexuality*

For close to nine years, Millie Simpson drove each weekday from her apartment in the South Ward section of Newark to Carol and Bob Richards's ten-room stone-fronted colonial house in suburban Short Hills, where she worked as a housekeeper. Although Millie couldn't afford to buy a new car, nor to service her old one regularly, an automobile was nonetheless important for traveling the ten miles to and from work. It was, in addition, necessary for the work she performed for the Richards family—picking up groceries and dry cleaning, and in recent years transporting Mr. Richards's elderly parents around town. During these nine years, Millie Simpson had owned seven older, gas-guzzling, American-made clunkers. Her cars regularly fell victim to accidents, breakdowns, and thefts. There were several times in the nine years when she was without an automobile. With great difficulty and time, she would take a bus and then a train from Newark, or have a friend drive her to the Richardses' home and then use one of the family cars to do the household errands.

In late October 1989, Millie Simpson arrived at work by train, cleaned the house, and left a note for Carol Richards saying that she could not drive and would be unable to do errands for a while. Carol and Millie had found that notes left on the kitchen table were the most reliable means of communication between them. Face-to-face and telephone conversations were rare. Carol left for work before Millie arrived in the morning, returning home after Millie left, and they had never gotten into the habit of telephoning because Millie's number was often changed and the service was sometimes disconnected. Millie spoke regularly, however, with the younger Richards child, Judy, a teenage girl who was often at home in the afternoons. This is the story, as Millie Simpson told it to Judy, then to Carol Richards, and later to us.

Several months earlier, for a period of two to three weeks, Millie had parked her 1984 Mercury in front of her apartment building and had been having a friend drive her to and from work. She was short of cash and didn't have the money to make an insurance payment; she needed time to collect the cash and she didn't want to use the car while it was uninsured. Early one morning, the police arrived and served her with summonses for leaving the scene of an accident and driving an uninsured vehicle. Millie was incredulous and explained that she had not been using the car because it was uninsured. The summonses were served nonetheless. Frustrated that the police would not investigate her claims, Millie began making inquiries and found that a friend of her son's, who had been staying with her, had taken the keys to the car without her permission. After backing into the car parked behind Millie's, he then went for a ride and returned the car before the police arrived or Millie noticed that it had been miss-

ing. The car had been returned to the same spot where Millie had left it, but now with a dent in its rear end.

Millie Simpson appeared in court on the day noted on the summonses. When asked by the judge whether she wished to plead guilty, she replied no, she was not guilty. Surprised, the judge asked whether her car was insured and whether she had left the scene of an accident. She answered that it was true that the car had not been insured, so she must be guilty of that; but she had not been driving it and therefore was not involved in nor did she leave any accident. She explained to the judge that her car had been used without permission by her son's friend, and the young man had been in the accident. According to Millie, the judge said that he would mark her plea "not guilty because she was not driving the car" and that he would set another date for a hearing. (Here there is some disagreement between Millie Simpson's account and the official record, which indicates that Millie did plead guilty.) The judge also asked whether she wanted a public defender. Millie said yes and, after filling out some papers in another office in the courthouse, was assigned a lawyer.

A few weeks later, never having heard from her public defender, Millie Simpson appeared in court, once again without an attorney. The judge had a packet of papers in front of him, which Millie believed contained the information she had reported during her first appearance. As a result, Millie did not explain at this second appearance, as she had at the first, what had happened to her car. Without any discussion, she claims, the judge found her guilty and told her that her license was being suspended for a year, that she would have to pay three hundred dollars in fines and serve fifteen hours of community service. The public defender showed up at this point, Millie says, after the judge had finished with her.

Upon hearing Millie Simpson's story from their daughter, and filling in details about the whereabouts of the car, the involvement of Millie's son's friend, Millie's actions and responsibility, and the lack of involvement of the public defender, Bob and Carol Richards decided to have an attorney see if anything could be done for Millie. Bob Richards referred the matter to the law firm that was counsel to his company. A litigator

*for the firm met with Millie. After investigating the status of
the case in the court records and discovering that the record
indicated that Millie Simpson had pleaded guilty, the attorney,
David Stone, filed a motion to have the case reopened and to
withdraw the plea. Stone then appeared before the court, on
the record, and asserted that Millie Simpson had appeared in
court a few weeks prior, without a lawyer, and although she
had stated that she understood what was going on, she, in
fact, did not recognize the seriousness of the charges nor the
implications of being found guilty. Stone also spoke with the
prosecutor's office, which said that it would take no position
and would have no problem if the judge was willing to reopen
the case, which indeed he was.*

*Four to five weeks later, attorney David Stone and Millie
Simpson again appeared before Judge Tyler, the same judge
who had found Millie Simpson guilty and with whom David
Stone had met to reopen the case. At this final appearance,
Stone presented the facts, the same facts that Millie Simpson
had been reporting from the outset—that she wasn't operating
the car and had not been using it because it was uninsured;
that someone had stolen it and had been in an accident and
had left the scene, but not her. No witnesses were called, no
corroborating evidence was offered, and Millie was not asked
to testify. The court found her not guilty and dismissed the
charges. She was repaid that amount of the fine that had
already been paid, and her license was reinstated.*

*Millie Simpson's story, as she told it to us and as we
learned more about it by interviewing her employers and her
attorney, illustrates the varied and contingent character of
legal consciousness. Millie's story also illustrates the power of
institutionalized authority and the constraints and opportunities such authority presents for the construction of legality. In
this case, and critical to its interpretation, Millie Simpson is
an African American woman, supplementing her $18,000
annual income as a domestic with several part-time jobs. Her
employers, the Richardses, are white. Bob Richards owns a
nationwide service company that he built, and Carol Richards
is an academic administrator; their combined income exceeds
$350,000 a year, making them, at least with regard to income,*

*atypical Americans. In many ways, Millie Simpson and Bob
and Carol Richards represent opposite extremes of wealth and
status. They represent as well the range of people whom we
interviewed, a sample that approximates the racial and economic composition of the state of New Jersey.*

*When we first heard Millie Simpson describe her experi-
ence to us, we were struck by how she accepted the interpretations and conformed to the instructions of each of the legal actors she encountered. Although knowing she was not
guilty of driving an uninsured vehicle or leaving the scene
of an accident, she dutifully fulfilled the obligations imposed
by the summonses, accepted her legal guilt, and immediately
began taking responsibility for the penalties the court imposed, arranging to pay her fine and fulfill her community
service.*

*Millie Simpson's interventions during her first appearance
conformed to the script offered by the court. When asked, she
denied leaving the scene of the accident and explained herself
to the judge.*

> *Then, I go to court and the judge asks me do I plead guilty? I am
> not guilty. Then he says to me "Your car without insurance?" My
> car didn't have any insurance on it so I said "I plead guilty." So
> I was explaining to him what happened but he finds out that I
> wasn't driving the car. . . . So then he said, after I explained it to
> him, he tells me, he said "Okay, I can't put down guilty because
> you weren't driving the car," right? So he said "I'll put down not
> guilty and make another date for you to come back."*

*Millie Simpson assumed the judge had been persuaded by
her story when he seemed to record her explanation, appointed
a public defender, and set a date for a second hearing. Her
intervention in this first court appearance was verbal and
timely, but it was, she thought, transformed by writing and
authorized into something else. She believed her account had
entered and become part of the court's institutional territory.
Paper, after all, occupies space. It concretizes and makes both
visible and intransigent otherwise fleeting and temporal interventions. By occupying paper, Millie Simpson believed that
she could enter the realm of strategic power. Her case, as she*

properly understood it, was spatialized and rendered visual: recorded, filed, and placed on a docket. She believed that this physical rendering of her story would provoke the judge's memory when he read "the paper." "When you go to court," she said, "they remember you, you know, you haven't been gone that long. I wasn't gone that long, you know, a lot will remember you because they read the paper."

An outsider, inexperienced in the ways of the court, Millie Simpson assumed that her second appearance would be continuous with her first. Thus, when she returned to the court she thought there was no need to repeat herself by introducing the same details about not driving the car, and therefore not leaving the scene, that she had revealed in her first court appearance.

> *I didn't tell the story because he, he had the paper there in front of him, I assumed . . . I assumed that he knew what the deal was.*

In fact, rather than the continuity provided by shared interaction and memory, Millie Simpson's interactions within the court, by being embodied by "the paper" in physical rather than temporal space, were transformed into two distinct and unconnected points—court appearance one and court appearance two. The rules, taxonomies, and operating procedures of the court flattened and froze time into these separate occasions. The spatialized modes of knowledge abstracted the actors from continuing interactions and arranged them in static impersonal roles, moments, and unconnected performances. The court drama—the meanings and interpretations of both the events and Millie Simpson's legal identity—derived from impersonal standards, forms, and records, rather than the experience of repeated encounters and relationships. The human interaction that Millie believed was to be embodied in the paper was instead preempted by it.

For Millie Simpson, the spatialization of her story in the form of paper also endowed it with authority. For nine years, Millie had received written instructions from her employer. What groceries to buy, what rooms to clean, whom to pick up, all of her duties as a housekeeper were recorded daily in notes left on the kitchen table. These instructions gave shape, content, and direction to Millie's day. Arriving every morning, she simply had to do what the paper said. The same was true, she said, for the judge who "just had to read the paper and do what it said."

Upon entering the court, Millie Simpson believed in the process. She followed its rules and deferred to its procedures. Even the form of her story revealed her submissiveness and deference to the law. Millie's accounts were presented in the form of what historians call an annal. She described events juxtaposed, statements made, even actions observed, in a world conspicuously absent human agency or will. Continuity, cause and effect are absent from her account. This is a world in which things happen to people, rather than one in which people do things. This is not, however, because Millie recognizes no moral realm, nor is it because she is oblivious to agency or causality. For Millie Simpson, the central ordering principle was so obvious, so necessary, so present as not to require articulation. For Millie, the order of things, the power of the court, the comfort and ease with which rich white folks negotiated these matters was simply there, it didn't need to be stated.

During our interviews with Millie Simpson, she expressed skepticism for the first time when telling about her second court appearance.

> Some of them probably don't even read the paper, they just read what they need to read to find out why you are there . . . that second judge, he acted like he didn't know why I was even back there, you know.

Here Millie acknowledged the limits of the paper to order and organize human interaction, as well as the opportunities these limits afford for human agency. Millie entered the terrain of the court frightened and confused, she said, momentarily spotlighted by the foreign and powerful order. She hoped to exit quickly; she left, she told us, disappointed, but somewhat more experienced in the ways of the institution.

Emphasizing her conformity before the law, Millie's tale can be read as an illustration of the power of law. She never

missed nor came late to a court appearance. This is a remark-
able fact since the majority of participants in lower court-
processes—defendants as well as lawyers—routinely come late
or miss hearings entirely. The system seemed to work as she
had heard about it from friends. Before her court appearance,
Millie had asked friends and neighbors about what it would be
like when she got to court. They had talked about the long
waits, the high bench behind which the judge sat, and how the
court was filled with lots of people milling around. The defen-
dants sat in rows in the back of the room. The police congre-
gated in what seemed to be a special place in the court. It was
a regular courtroom, she commented to us. It looked the same
as courts did on TV. This was how things were supposed to be.
She recognized it and went along.

But Millie Simpson did not simply stand before the law,
submitting to an external and powerful authority; she also con-
tested its findings. Millie returned to the court several weeks
later, this time with an experienced attorney. Armed with the
Richards family's assistance, Millie returned to engage the
court on its own terms, within the law's terrain. Part of this
challenge involved redefining and recharacterizing the persons
and events Millie had related in her terms. Millie's account of
how her son's friend had taken her car without permission
was translated by her attorney into testimony before the court
about an automobile theft. A misunderstanding became a
crime. Millie Simpson was identified not as a mother whose
house guest misunderstood her hospitality, but as a victim of
crime. The fact that the public defender had shown up late for
Millie's trial was no longer just a mix-up and bad timing but,
in the appeal to the court, evidence of a failure of due process
and grounds for a new trial.

These interventions mobilized carefully crafted legal con-
structions to achieve specific objectives. Less concerned with
moral rectitude, biography, identity, or sensibility, Millie Simp-
son's contestation, during her second appearance, was articu-
lated explicitly within the discursive space of the law. It was a
public engagement and an official victory, yet Millie seemed
mystified by and almost indifferent to the contest waged on
her behalf.

I met him there and waited for them to call me, and they called me and we went up, you know, to the table. And I don't even know what the judge said, I couldn't even understand what he was saying. And the lawyer told me, he said "okay," he said "that's it, it's all over." I was right there and I don't even know . . . I didn't even know what he was talking about.

For the lawyers, for the Richardses, and for many of those who regularly operate within the space of the law, the legal engagement is enacted with a sense of entitlement and routine, one of a variety of experiences used to establish social position, defend personhood, and construct identity. Millie Simpson's contestation relied, in the end, on her access to the Richardses' greater resources. Acting as her patrons, Bob and Carol Richards extended the reach of their habitual participation in a market of expensive professional services to include Millie.

In receiving help from Bob and Carol Richards, Millie Simpson successfully mobilized extralegal resources to challenge the court's findings. Millie Simpson won her appeal in spite of, not because of, due process protections. Legal processes may have vindicated Millie, but her vindication was not a result of the universalistic rights American citizenship supposedly guarantees. Rather, Millie's vindication depended upon her participation in an approximation to that feudal order that liberal law has historically opposed. Liberalism has claimed, after all, to enable every citizen to be equal before the law, without regard to master-servant relations. Yet this case, Carol Richards said, was "the typical story of American racism." She went on, "To get justice the poor black woman needs a rich white lady."

In this telling of the story, Millie Simpson is reinscribed in a system of domination from which the law provides no exit. Her engagement with law confirmed her subordination elsewhere. Only by relying on her dependent position in one realm—employment—was Millie Simpson able to escape her subordination in another—law. That Millie was able successfully to contest the law makes hers an unusual story. The contest was premised, however, upon her particular and affectionate relationship with a relatively powerful employer.

For most of those without power or position, the only

alternative to conformity is resistance: poaching, appropriation, or silence. That is the third story embedded in Millie Simpson's account. From this third perspective, Millie Simpson's story is neither one of total subordination nor one of surrogate contestation. It is also a story of resistance. Millie's resignation and submission before the law was mediated by a tactical maneuver some recognize as a form of resistance. In telling us about arranging for her community service (required as one of the three penalties for conviction on the two charges), Millie Simpson paused, laughed, and informed us conspiratorially that she had suggested to the court officer that she work at a church where she had, for a number of years, been doing volunteer work.

> *I do it anyway, [small laugh]. I do it anyway, you see? So it wasn't no problem, you know. So he signed the paper and said it would be all right for me, you know, to work, but I do it anyway.*

By suggesting her church work as fulfillment of her legal obligation to perform community service, Millie Simpson successfully insinuated her life into the space of the law and, in doing so, reversed for a moment the trajectory of power. She combined heterogeneous elements of her biography—churchgoer, volunteer, defendant—to create and seize an opportunity to enter the space of the law, making it "habitable." Moreover, her victory was more than momentary. As Millie took the trouble to note, "he signed the paper." Thus, with her ruse, she succeeded, where earlier she had failed, to infiltrate the dominant text.

In the transcript of our interview with Millie, there is a second, distinctive moment of laughter and pleasure. Millie described to us how she caught the law out; she discovered an institutional vulnerability, a crack in the seamless institutional facade. When she was leaving the court, arranging the schedule for paying her fines and performing her community service, Millie Simpson was not asked to turn in her license. She left the court, license in hand. She concluded that although she had been convicted, they had forgotten to enact this penalty. Since she had the license, she believed that she could still drive, but, she told us, she chose not to. Millie Simpson enacted and reclaimed her vision of being a good woman and a good citizen, even though the court had decided otherwise.

Arranging to do community service and paying the fine, Millie Simpson submitted to the law's authority and accepted the burden it imposed, but did so without having to bear its full weight. She deflected the law's power, without challenging it. She "escaped" it, without leaving it. Michel Foucault used the word esquiver, meaning to dodge or feint as in fencing, to describe forms of resistance such as Millie Simpson's. These tactics are a sort of antidiscipline, which, like the professional power they oppose, are dispersed and invisibly distributed throughout everyday life. Successful dodges, ruses, and feints such as these rarely leave a structural imprint. Neither the law nor the sentencing practices of New Jersey were changed or challenged by Millie's evasive tactics. Still, they were not inconsequential. For, with the successful dodge, the sword, too, misses its mark and leaves no imprint. For a moment, through fortuity and guile, power, from Millie's point of view, was rendered impotent. Millie took immense pleasure in the ruse she played on the court. While she was relatively disengaged in the legal contestation orchestrated by the Richardses and her attorney, Millie Simpson savored her private victory won within the cracks of the institution.

Over the course of months, engaged in different sorts of interactions with various players, Millie Simpson at times followed generally predictable pathways, as directed by the law. At times, however, she avoided these paths. Embedded in Millie Simpson's account are stories of conformity, contestation, and resistance. Forged out of the play of choice and constraint, Millie's legal consciousness reflected both the institutionalized strategies practiced by the court and her tactical resistances. Millie Simpson's race, class, and gender, expressed in the specific elements of her biography, shaped her experience within the court and enabled the particular forms of her consciousness. Her conformity, including her faith in and deference to the legal papers, echoed her experiences as a domestic, in which she daily received and followed written instructions, and drew on her faith in and observance of religious scripture. Her tactical evasions relied on her membership in a church and her history of volunteering. Her contest was condi-

tioned by her dependent relationship to her wealthy and more legally experienced employers.

Millie Simpson's different experiences of law—her initial submissiveness before the law; her contest over her conviction; her acts of resistance—are all part of the project of describing legality. The discernible variations in legal consciousness represent the ambivalent and shifting experiences and understandings of men and women as they move through legal institutions and other arrangements of power. Regardless of their political significance, these "hidden transcripts,"[2] these "tales of the unrecognized,"[3] stand as important in their own right. They remind us that "our practical daily activity contains an understanding of the world—subjugated, perhaps, but present."[4] And, as Millie's story illustrates, the moments of resistance are often the most memorable parts of the journey. To ignore Millie's tactics because they are momentary and private is to reinscribe the relations of power they oppose. To overlook these interventions is to deny their meaning within Millie Simpson's particular biography and her relationships with the law, church, and employer. To dismiss these momentary feints and ruses is to deny the varieties of Millie Simpson's legal consciousness.

CHAPTER TWO

The Common Place of Law

Commonplace? The commonplace is just that light, impal-
pable, aerial essence which they've never got into their con-
founded books yet.
                      WILLIAM DEAN HOWELLS, *The Rise of Silas Lapham*

Everyday things represent the most overlooked knowledge.
                                    DON DELILLO, *Underworld*

Commonplace experiences and images of law vary. At times, the law
appears as a magisterial, remote, and transcendent force governing
human affairs from some high and distant plane. At other times, the
law seems like an all-too-human arena in which people struggle with
one another in serious and playful encounters, more or less skillfully,
for all sorts of sublime and petty purposes. Most of the time, though,
people don't think of the law at all.

As we go about our daily lives, we rarely sense the presence or
the operation of the law. We pay our bills because they are due; we
respect our neighbor's property because it is theirs; we drive on the
right side of the street because it is prudent. We rarely consider
through what collective judgments and procedures we have defined
"coming due," "theirs," or "prudent driving." If we trace the source
of these meanings to some legal institution or practices, the legal
origin is fixed so far away in time and place that circumstances of
their invention have been long forgotten. As a result, contracts, property, or traffic rules seem not only necessary but natural and inevitable parts of social life. In other words, for most of us the law generally sits on a distant horizon of our lives, remote and often irrelevant
to the matters before us.

Occasionally, however, the law seems to intrude into the "law-
less" everyday world, often displacing our very experience of mun-

danity. Normal appearances are shattered when our motives, relationships, obligations, and privileges are explicitly redefined within
"legal" constructs and categories. The taken-for-granted practices of
parents' materially providing for their children are transformed, in
the context of divorces, into contracts that are purposively negotiated
and then monitored and enforced by attorneys, mediators, social
workers, and judges. The tragic, but sadly commonplace, aspects of
life become strangely refigured through law: harsh words between
feuding coworkers become harassment, or the brutal violence committed by a husband against his wife is euphemistically labeled a
domestic dispute. In short, when we confront our own lives trans-
posed within the legal domain, we often find ourselves subject to a
mighty power that can render the familiar strange, the intimate public, the violent passive, the mundane extraordinary, and the awesome banal.

Although the law may appear remote from our taken-for-granted
world, it also has a commonplace materiality pervading the here and
now of our social landscape. The material forms of the law include
such things as courthouses; parking meters; marriage, birth, death,
and mortgage certificates; weapons hanging from the belts of police
officers; and the signs that warn us against trespassing, loitering,
right turns, or smoking.

The law seems to have a prominent cultural presence as well,
occupying a good part of our nation's popular media, providing grist
for both news and entertainment. We watch real and fictitious trials
on television, often unable to distinguish fact from fiction. We share
jokes about lawyers. We hear reports of crimes and criminals on the
nightly local news. And, if the success of authors like John Grisham
is any indication, millions of us devote hours of our leisure time to
reading stories about crime, courts, lawyers, and law.

Thus the law is experienced as both strange and familiar; an episodic event and a constant feature of our lives; deadly serious and a
source of humor and entertainment; irrelevant to our daily lives and
centrally implicated in the way those lives are organized and lived.
That the law can operate in these various ways may appear contradictory. To some critics, this variety is a sign of the erosion of the rule
of law: what had once been understood and experienced as a noble
gift of reason and justice is now treated as just one more place where
avarice, selfishness, and competition hold sway. To other observers,
law's commonplace variety signals the fragmentation of the public

culture. Where once Americans could view themselves as participants in a grand democratic experiment, empowered and protected
by constitutional rights, it appears to some that social heterogeneity
has fractured the binding legal covenant. Another observer, however,
might notice that these contradictory views each provide only partial
accounts of legality. The apparent contradiction—and the source of
much lament—is resolved once we abandon an understanding of the
law as a single, coherent entity. If we set to one side for a moment
the emblematic imagery of unity and consistency as hallmarks of law,
we see that the law is a complex structure.

The law incorporates countless, varied, and often ambiguous
rules. It refers to a host of official actors and organizations—ranging
from the Supreme Court to the local building inspector—each operating with different purposes and with vastly different material and
symbolic resources. The law also includes institutionalized procedures that range from licensing practices and rational filing systems
to forensic science and abstract rhetorical argumentation. So it is
not surprising that the law appears to us in varied and sometimes
contradictory ways.

This book attempts to map and understand this variety of law's
presence in everyday life. Using stories and accounts of ordinary
people, we describe how Americans interpret and make sense of the
law. We trace the ways in which commonplace transactions and relationships come to assume (or not assume) a legal character. By illus-
trating the diversity of law's uses and interpretations, we hope to
demonstrate that legality is an emergent feature of social relations
rather than an external apparatus acting upon social life. As a constituent of social interaction, the law—or what we will call legality—
embodies the diversity of the situations out of which it emerges and
that it helps structure. Because legality is embedded in and emerges
out of daily activities, its meanings and uses echo and resonate with
other common phenomena, specifically bureaucracies, games, or
"just making do." Legality is not sustained solely by the formal law
of the Constitution, legislative statutes, court decisions, or explicit
demonstrations of state power such as executions. Rather, legality is
enduring because it relies on and invokes commonplace schemas of
everyday life. Finally, we argue that the multiple and contradictory
character of law's meanings, rather than a weakness, is a crucial component of its power.

From Legal Organizations to Commonplace Legality

Our analysis of commonplace legality builds on a tradition of research on the social construction of law.[1] This "law and society" tradition provides abundant evidence of law's variable and complex character. In general, socio-legal investigations have focused on routine practices in specific organizational settings: the Supreme Court, local trial courts, regulatory agencies, insurance offices, law firms, and mediation and arbitration hearings. In these studies of legal practice—litigations, public regulation, legal profession, and crime control—research has shown how social networks, organizational resources, and local cultures shape both the written content and behavioral enactment of legality.

These accounts describe how legal actors respond to particular situations and demands for service, rather than follow universal principles. Although law claims to be a distinctive arena of general rationality, it is, like most other work, operating on the basis of variable rules. Legal practice proceeds on a case-by-case basis. And, because legal action emerges from specific situations, it is shaped by many extralegal factors. In exercising their discretion (e.g., to file a complaint, sue, negotiate, or settle) legal actors respond to situations and cases on the basis of recurrent features of social interactions rather than from criteria provided in law or policy. For example, Sudnow shows that in exercising their prosecutorial discretion, district attorneys construct and rely on models of "normal" crimes.[2] What makes a crime "normal" (and thus subject to routine processing) is often influenced less by its statutory definition than by such mundane features as the time or location of its occurrence or the social characteristics of the victim or defendant. These "folk" categories are used to sort and channel legal work. Thus, by relying on ordinary social logics and local cultural categories and norms, legal action reflects, and also reproduces, nonlegal features of daily life. Although we can talk about the law as if it were a singular and distinct entity, we have learned that we cannot observe it outside of its particular, and thus variable, material and historical manifestations.

Moreover, when researchers have looked at the mobilization of law—the ways in which citizens initiate legal action—they have discovered that most legal activity takes place outside the purview of official legal agents and without the invocation of formal legal doctrine. Very few legal matters become cases, trials, or appeals. This is true for criminal law, regulatory administration, and civil litigation. For instance, many people suffer injuries and losses that they overlook, even when they hold others responsible; and in those instances in which claims are made, few of these exchanges lead to litigation. It turns out that although almost any social interaction could, in theory, become a matter of contest and dispute, few do.[3] Even when people hire an attorney and then file suit, less than 3 percent of all civil filings in federal or state courts go to trial; of all the criminal and civil cases decided, less than 5 percent are appealed.[4] The cases at trial and appeal, and certainly the fewer than one to two hundred cases decided annually by the U.S. Supreme Court,[5] represent the minuscule top of a giant pyramid of legal engagements. Even those few interactions that become formal cases—cases that are sifted and winnowed, and shaped and pushed, into the form of trials and appeals and thus to the top of the pyramid—are a product of informal as well as official considerations.

Rather than imagining law as existing apart from social relations (i.e., so-called natural law), or conceiving of it as produced solely by groups of powerful law "makers" (i.e., the positive law of legislatures, and common law of appellate courts), much law and society research portrays law from the "bottom up" as a continuing production of practical reason and action. This research provides a view of law emerging from the routine, often discretionary, encounters among professional and nonprofessional actors. It depicts a legal system with numerous actors, involved in diverse projects, employing different legitimating discourses, material resources, and political power to achieve a wide range of goals. Emerging from these interactions, the practices and ideals to which the term "law" might be applied are understandably variable, complex, and sometimes contradictory.

Although this tradition of law and society research fractures the imagined coherence of the law, it rarely challenges the boundary that presumably encompasses it. In other words, the so-called bottom from which the law emerges and from which it radiates "out toward" society is treated as fixed by an institutional boundary, albeit an elusive one. Although much socio-legal research demonstrates that the law has no center and little uniformity, it is often implicitly assumed that the law is still recognizably, and usefully, distinguishable from that which is not law. This assumption is revealed by an empirical focus on official legal institutions and their relationship to some other domain of social life, for example lawyers and clients in the process of divorce,[6] trial court responses to family violence,[7] or neighbor and family disputes in clerk's hearings.[8] Nonprofessional actors are recognized to be part of this project of law making only when they engage official legal actors. Consequently, citizens have been theoretically interesting to sociologists of law only when they pass through that institutional boundary to lodge their complaints, voice their grievances, seek their rights, or demand justice.

The most serious limitation of this institutionally centered law-first perspective is that, by reckoning the boundary of law to correspond neatly to its formal institutional location, we drastically narrow our vision. By focusing our scholarly eye on exchanges across that boundary, we fail to ask how people get to that hypothesized boundary. We exclude from observation that which needs yet to be explored and explained: how, where, and with what effect law is produced in and through commonplace social interactions within neighborhoods, workplaces, families, schools, community organizations, and the like. How do our social roles and statuses, our relationships, our obligations, prerogatives, and responsibilities, our identities, and our behaviors bear the imprint of law? Having just asked how social relations become marked by law, we want to hasten to add, of course, that the law does not simply work on social life (to define and to shape it). Legality also operates through social life as persons and groups deliberately interpret and invoke law's language, authority, and procedures to organize their lives and manage their relationships. In short, the commonplace operation of law in daily life makes us all legal agents insofar as we actively make law, even when no formal legal agent is involved.

Recognizing the importance of broadening their empirical scope, some scholars have begun to examine aspects of social life not conventionally included within traditional socio-legal studies. This research has uncovered the operation of law in everyday life, as well as the operation of everyday life in law. This is not an easy task. In moving beyond the institutional boundaries, we are forced to abandon, or at least question, the conceptual categories the official institution provides. To discover the law outside of formal legal settings, we must tolerate a kind of conceptual murkiness. Instead of relying on the doctrinal definitions of, for instance, private property (purchased, titled, and receiving the protection of the state), we must acknowledge and try to fathom the significance of "property" as it is claimed, used, protected, and fought over in the social spaces outside of official agencies of law.

We have found, for instance, that during the winter in certain neighborhoods, an old chair placed in a recently shoveled parking spot on a public street is often understood to endow the chair's owner with use rights in the space. The chair signals to the neighborhood a type of ownership. In doing so, it often elicits the same sorts of deference or respect accorded more conventional types of property (i.e., the neighbors park elsewhere). Similarly, the violation or transgression of this property may lead to conflicts and disputes more commonly associated with property as it is formally defined by the legal system (i.e., informal claims of trespass). Without naming the concepts of constructive or adverse possession, the person placing the chair in a clearing among mounds of snow implicitly invokes conventional justifications for property on the basis of investment and labor. In this example, the formal legal idea of private property is appropriated along with many of the rights associated with it (such as exclusive use). Yet property here is construed very differently than its doctrinal sense demands or would allow. Even without registered deeds and titles, stamps and seals, the law is both present and absent in organizing social interactions on a New Jersey street around this particular construction of the concept of private property.

An example of research that has systematically explored the presence of law in everyday life is Hendrik Hartog's analysis of the eighteenth-century diary of Abigail Bailey.[9] Hartog's reading of Abigail Bailey's diary reveals how this woman, over the course of many years, struggled to make sense of her marriage, her husband's sexual abuse of their daughter, and their separation and eventual divorce, as well as her own religious beliefs regarding her duties as a wife and mother. Hartog demonstrates that this narrative of personal tragedy and change is incomprehensible without reference to legal categories such as the prevailing law of coverture (a woman's loss of legal rights or personality upon marriage). Abigail Bailey's perception and assessment of her situation, and her daughter's experiences, were conditioned upon her understanding of the legitimacy of a husband's desires and the priority of his rights. Because the law established a husband as a virtual sovereign within his family, it was difficult to question or oppose openly her husband's actions as inappropriate. Equally important, however, the events of Abigail Bailey's narrative are incomprehensible when viewed only through the lens of formal law.

> Abigail Bailey's thoughts, prayers, and arguments were filled with law; legal facts, remedies, strategies, and institutions were constantly present. Yet the nature of her consciousness was not determined by law. She bargained in the shadow of law. Yet the law in whose shadow she bargained was a complex and contradictory structure: experienced as an external control and constraint, reconstructed regularly in conversations and arguments, intertwined in significant tension with religious beliefs and norms.[10]

Because law is both an embedded and an emergent feature of social life, it collaborates with other social structures (in this case religion, family, and gender) to infuse meaning and constrain social action. Furthermore, because of this collaboration of structures, in many instances law may be present although subordinate. To recognize the presence of law in everyday life is not, therefore, to claim any necessarily overwhelming power for law.

Hartog's excavation of law in the diary of Abigail Bailey suggests that the formal practices of official legal actors and agencies do not fully account for law's operation in and through social life. Legal institutions do not, it would appear, have a monopoly over the cluster of concepts and procedures that we might recognize as legal. Abigail Bailey's identity, her relationships, and her behavior were partially, but only partially, forged out of her invocation and interpretation of the law. Significantly, her reliance on the law occurred outside of any formal legal setting, without the advice or action of any legal agent.

To examine law uncoupled from legal institutions demands some conceptual clarification and linguistic innovation. Rather than "law," we will use the word "legality" to refer to the meanings, sources of authority, and cultural practices that are commonly recognized as legal, regardless of who employs them or for what ends. In this rendering, people may invoke and enact legality in ways neither approved nor acknowledged by the law. Even as we recognize a sense of the legal that exists independently of its institutional manifestation, we will also acknowledge institutionalized forms of legality. Because the designation of some actors or actions as "official" and others as "lay" is an important cultural distinction, one drawn and respected by people we studied, we will retain the conceptual distinction. We will use the word "law" specifically to refer to aspects of legality as it is employed by or attributed to formal institutions and their actors.

In sum, we conceive of legality as an emergent structure of social life that manifests itself in diverse places, including but not limited to formal institutional settings. Legality operates, then, as both an interpretative framework and a set of resources with which and through which the social world (including that part known as the law) is constituted.

Studying Legality in Everyday Life

Reconceptualizing legality as an internal and emergent feature of social life requires that we shift our empirical focus away from law to "events and practices that seem on the face of things, removed from law, or at least not dominated by law from the outset."[11] The necessity of this shift in focus has certain methodological implications, that is, implications for where and how we go about studying legality in everyday life.

We designed the empirical research upon which this book is based to allow us to analyze daily life and legality. Each of our methodological decisions was intended to expand our capacity to capture legality as it might operate in the most mundane settings, out of view of more conventional legal research. While we did not want to eliminate the possibility of examining formal legal events, we understood these to be only a subset of possibly relevant events and practices. Decisions regarding sampling, sequencing of questions, organization of the interview, and eventually coding and analysis of data were deliberately made to ensure that our empirical gaze would encompass those phenomena "that seem on the face of things removed from law." Additional description of these methodological issues, including the forms of data collection and the analytic strategies we employed, appears in appendix A.

A Methodological Sketch

Millie Simpson was one of 430 persons whom we interviewed for this study. Rather than interview only persons with legal experience, or persons found within some legal setting such as a welfare office, law firm, mediation program, or local court, we sought a broad representative sample. Because we were attempting to study everyday law, we decided to talk to a random sample of New Jersey adults in the contexts of their everyday lives. It was our expectation, borne out by the data, that we would find substantial variation in the legal experiences of our respondents. For some, the law was conspicuously absent. For others, experience in formal legal settings was a frequent, ongoing feature of their lives and relationships. Most of the people with whom we spoke fell somewhere in between, having had some legal experience.[12] This wide variation suggests that had we attempted to locate respondents through any specific legal site (a local court or police department, for instance), we would have ended up with a considerably less diverse sample. Biographical information on those informants who are quoted in this book appears in appendix B.

The interview itself was also designed to capture a picture of legality unmoored from official legal settings and actors. This part of the methodological design proved to be the most challenging. Because we were interested in mapping the variation in legality in common everyday experiences, we needed to reach a broad and diverse population. For this reason, we decided to conduct a survey rather than, for instance, an ethnography of a community or organization. The chief strength of survey research is its capacity to provide a picture of range and variation. Its usefulness in this regard is, however, counterbalanced by methodological constraints. In comparison to participant observation and ethnography, in which observations are made over months or even years, surveys are limited in terms of the amount of time and the forms of interaction that occur between researcher and respondent. Two or three hours spent with a single respondent is considered a fairly lengthy and involved interview. Because the time is limited, survey researchers must be more active in shaping and focusing the conversation with respondents. Typically this is done by asking questions designed to elicit information about a person's activities and views in relation to the specific set of research questions. Conventional methodological wisdom, moreover, dictates that the clearer and more direct the questions are, the more reliable and valid the data.

These constraints are particularly troublesome given our interest in the often unarticulated (indeed, unexamined) aspects of daily life. The problem we faced in shaping and focusing the interview arose because we did not want our questions to imply or enforce a conventional definition of law and legality. We did not want to ask people about their legal problems or needs, since it was the respondents' own understandings and definitions of these concepts—as they might be expressed in their words, revealed in their actions, or embedded in their stories and accounts—that we wanted to hear about. How then were we to focus the interview to be able to elicit talk about these issues without projecting our own hypotheses regarding legality and its construction? Our solution to this problem was to design an unusually lengthy interview consisting of three parts distinguished from one another in terms of how focused and structured they were. In this way, we hoped to reach a large number of diverse respondents and yet create opportunities for the respondents to shape the discussion.

We told respondents the interview was about community, neighborhood, work, and family issues. Given our theoretical perspective this description seemed to describe accurately our approach, while it also served the practical purpose of decoupling legality from formal institutional law. The initial part of the interview consisted of a series of questions concerning the respondents' community and neighborhood. We asked how long they had lived there; what they liked most and least about their neighborhood; and how they saw themselves in relation to their neighbors. We also inquired about the number and strength of social ties they had in the community: how many friends and family members lived nearby and how often and in what capacity they interacted with others.

This turned out to be an effective way of beginning. We are extremely grateful to the hundreds of people who accepted our request for an interview, most often from curiosity rather than anything else, who very quickly settled into what turned out to be not only informative but often very personal and heart-wrenching accounts of anguish, wrath, and pleasure. These first questions about neighborhoods, friends, and family seem to have eased the transition from formal interview to open conversation because the questions were obviously nonthreatening and because they allowed the respondents to name the topics and issues of interest to them. Although we were asking the questions, respondents were setting the boundaries of privacy and exposure. Interestingly, people would often use these opening questions to initiate stories that were elaborated and enriched as the interview continued. More often than not, we could look back at the transcripts and see how the subjects that filled the next few hours were forecast in these opening exchanges. We had a script we followed, a sequence of topics and questions, but we allowed our respondents to set the pace and emphases; we encouraged diversions.

This portion of the interview was followed by a series of open-ended questions that asked respondents about a wide range of events and practices that might have "troubled or bothered" them at some point. If a respondent asked what we meant by trouble or bother, we defined these as "[a]nything that was not as you would have liked it to be, or thought it should be." In presenting the topics for discussion to the respondents we avoided any allusion to these events or problems as legal or legally related, hoping instead to discover their definitions of the situations. Whenever a respondent mentioned that they had experienced a particular problem, they were asked to describe the situation in greater detail: when and how often it occurred, who was involved, how they experienced it and how they responded to it, and how, if at all, it ended.

The particular situations about which we asked were intentionally varied and comprehensive. The list included the sorts of events that are not unusual for people to define as legal problems or to seek a legal remedy (such as vandalism in neighborhoods, property disputes, and work-related accidents). The list also included events and situations that seem less obviously connected to traditional legal categories or remedies, such as the division of household labor, medical care, or curricular issues in schools. Thus, in choosing the topics for discussion and in presenting these to respondents, we sought to create, rather than foreclose, opportunities for diverse interpretations.

This part of the interview was followed by a more in-depth conversational portion focusing on one event. This conversation was initiated by asking respondents to speak further about any event of their choice. They were asked to describe the event in greater detail, to elaborate upon their experience of and reaction to it. They were also asked to discuss issues of responsibility, cause, and motive, their own as well as others'. The questions we posed in this part of the interview were considerably less structured than those we posed initially. They were intended to elicit a narrative of the event, rather than to collect specific information regarding its occurrence. This strategy also reflected our understanding that a person's interpretations and experiences of legality may assume forms that would be difficult to anticipate, and thus would be difficult to capture using more structured interview formats.

In order to collect information that would allow us to make comparisons with existing surveys regarding people's interpretations and perceptions of law, we included a series of closed-ended questions at the end of the interview. These questions addressed such issues as the respondent's formal legal knowledge, formal legal experiences, and perception of the effectiveness and legitimacy of legal procedures. Whereas, up to this point, the topic of law and legality was deliberately vague, these final questions moved law to the foreground. Because these questions were posed at the end of the interview, they could not influence the earlier responses.

Finally, at the end of the interview, we discussed the general outlines of the project with respondents. We did not want to leave people uneasy about our purposes and interests. Only two persons told us that they were uncomfortable with portions of the interview, and most respondents said that they found the experience interesting. It gave them an opportunity to vent concerns, some said, but also put some things in focus.

In addition to a written record of the interview, each of the interviews was also tape-recorded. This was done in order to preserve a verbatim account of the interaction. The transcriptions of 141 of these interviews serve as the empirical basis for this book.[13] In addition to examining the particular words, metaphors, and figures of speech that people used to make and convey meaning, we considered the role and characterization of law and legality within their narratives. At times law and legality were characterized explicitly; at times their meanings were elusive. We also read these transcripts to discover what people found funny about situations and what they found tragic. We looked for moments when people presented themselves as active participants in constructing or challenging legality and moments when they expressed a feeling of powerlessness. In short, conceiving of legality as present in and through our everyday lives, we anticipated that we would find its presence in and through the stories and accounts of our respondents.

Our decision to collect people's interpretations of legality by asking about problematic situations requires further explanation. This strategy appears to contradict our understanding that the law operates, perhaps most powerfully, in rendering the world unproblematic. Indeed, in organizing and giving meaning to the most routine everyday events—such as buying groceries or driving down the street—the law may be most present in its conspicuous absence. In organizing much of our interview around problems, then, we confronted the apparent contradiction between this conceptualization of legality and our method of studying it. We nonetheless opted for a problem-focused interview. We did so after concluding that the most effective way of initiating a conversation that would reveal the quotidian character of law and legality would be to inquire about those moments when the routine and the mundane seemed to break down. Not only are people more likely to recall such events and situations, but they are more likely to have spent time making sense of such situations. Finally, we believed that people's interpretations and accounts of these problems would reveal their unarticulated understanding of the mundane; in short, that the taken-for-granted would reveal itself in its breach.[14]

A Word about Stories

> The reality that lends itself to narrative is the conflict between desire and the law.
>
> HAYDEN WHITE, *The Content of the Form: Narrative Discourse and Historical Representation*

The Common Place of Law describes how residents in one American state define, think about, and use law. People tell three stories. In one story, legality is imagined and treated as an objective realm of disinterested action, removed and distant from the personal lives of ordinary people. In this story, law is majestic, operating by known and fixed rules in carefully delimited spheres. The law exists in times and places that put it outside of, rather than in, the midst of everyday life. But people also tell a second story where legality is depicted as a game, a terrain for tactical encounters through which people marshal a variety of social resources to achieve strategic goals. In this game, people see themselves and others bound by a set of rules that they may also try to change. Rather than existing outside of daily life, this second story describes legality as operating simultaneously with commonplace events and activities. People also told us a third story of legality. In this account, the law is a product of power. Rather than objective, legality is understood to be arbitrary and capricious. Unwilling to stand before the law and unable to play with law, people act against the law. In this third story, people talk about the ruses, tricks, and subterfuges they use to appropriate part of law's power.

We use the language of stories and narrative to describe what we found and what we are doing with what we found.[15] We adopted the concept of narrative because people tend to explain their actions to themselves and to others through stories.[16] Rather than offering categorical principles, rules, or reasoned arguments, people report, account for, and relive their activities through narratives: sequences of statements connected in such a way as to have both a temporal and a moral ordering.[17] As a form of social action, stories thus reflect and sustain institutional and cultural arrangements, bridging the gap between daily social interaction and large-scale social structures.[18] In other words, stories people tell about themselves and their lives both constitute and interpret those lives; the stories describe the world as it is lived and is understood by the storyteller.

Narratives can enter scholarly research as either the object, the method, or the product of inquiry.[19] In this book, we use stories as a lens to study law in everyday life and as a metaphor to represent what we have discovered. We collected stories of events and relationships from 430 people. From those reports, we abstracted three accounts of legality. For most of the book, we try to bracket our own understanding of legality, allowing our protagonists' notions to develop in ways that put the question of law and legality in a new light. Finally, we provide our own explanation of how the three stories constitute the structure of legality.

In the following chapters, we describe these stories of law as expressions and forms of legal consciousness. We use the words and accounts of the people whom we interviewed to illustrate how the stories are emplotted. Each of the three stories or types of consciousness portrays legality as a particular configuration of capacity and constraint organized to achieve a normative ideal: objectivity, interested representation, or power. Each also locates legality differently in time and space. In the stories of law we identified, legality is portrayed as a space in which subjectivity is confined, enabled, or suppressed. Woven together, however, the three stories collectively constitute the lived experience of legality as a struggle between desire and the law, social structure and human agency.

Each of the three stories is complex, varying from one another along these dimensions of normativity, capacity, constraint, and time-space. As we outline the various dimensions and axes along which legality is constructed and experienced, we suggest but do not specify the exact distribution of these stories among the population. The proportions and relations among these dimensions and stories are precisely the materials out of which cultural distinctions are made and that we try to identify without specifically measuring.

By using the language of narrative, we wish to underscore the point that stories do more than simply reflect or express existing structures and ideologies. Through their telling, people's stories help constitute whatever hegemony may in turn shape social lives and conduct. The taken-for-granted world of legality—in all its forms and experiences—gets produced and reproduced within individual, seemingly unique and discrete personal narratives. Thus, by telling stories of our lives, we not only report, account for, and relive portions of those lives, we participate in the production of legality.

In the chapters of part 2—"Before the Law," "With the Law," and "Against the Law"—we seem to treat the three stories as separate phenomena, purposely disaggregating what is experientially integrated. We do so, however, for didactic purposes, as a deliberate act of abstraction and possible violation, to identify the processes from which legality emerges as a durable social structure. The heuristic device of abstraction and disconnection is repaired, we hope, in part 3 (conclusions), as we reweave the separate elements to explore the seams of connection and tension among the stories. Of course, telling three separate stories runs the risk of ignoring the ways these forms of consciousness are entwined. To mitigate this possibility, we call attention here to our method of proceeding and our intention to re-plait in part 3 the threads we pull apart in the central portions of the book.

The book is organized into eight chapters with seven somewhat longer accounts of distinct individuals. Although most accounts are presented within the boundaries of analytic chapters, we want to emphasize what may be sacrificed by this organization: legal consciousness is variable, and individuals may express within their own lives and experiences the full range of variation. In the final chapters, we examine how the three stories or varieties of legal consciousness intersect and relate to one another, comprising the commonplace experience and power of legality.

We hope to show how legality's durability and strength derive directly from this schematic complexity and from the contradictions among and within legality's cultural representations. We believe that this storytelling is enabled, and thus legality strengthened, by the contradictions that exist within and among the forms of legal consciousness we call "before" and "with the law." We argue that in order for legality to remain vital, it must lay claim to the multiple and contradictory experiences of law. In short, a single account of law as ahistorical, transcendent, and impartial would eventually prove inadequate in the face of evidence that the law is partial, concrete, and flawed. Alternatively, a single account of law as venal would fail to secure the loyalty and legitimacy necessary to maintain its power. The cynicism and pessimism expressed in a view of law as a game level our aspirations and set realistic expectations. "The haves come out ahead,"[20] or "the rich always win," becomes what everybody knows and thus familiarizes the law. At the same time, the majestic removal of law from everyday life inspires allegiance. "A government of laws and not of men" becomes a source of commitment. Thus, "before the law" and "with the law" work in tandem by offering a story of law as both everyday and eternal even while it effaces the connection between them.

The same contradictions that underwrite the power of legality as a structure of social action also make resistance, or counterhegemonic accounts of legality, possible. Stories told "against the law" recognize the dual strands of legality as a general ideal of objective and impartial deliberation and as a particular space of privilege and power. As John Dewey has observed, these resistant readings are possible because of the character of social events. "[E]vents have their own distinctive indifferencies, resistances, arbitrary closures and intolerances, they also have their peculiar openness, warm responsiveness, greedy seekings, and transforming unions."[21] Resistance exposes legality's contradictions and exploits the openings in both its institutional and discursive fretwork to forge moments, if not lives, of respite from legality's power. If legality's power relies, in part, on its unarticulated duality (before and with the law), resistance recognizes and reveals this duality.

To understand how legality has presence in a culture, we need first to consider some conceptions of law and legal institutions. Toward this end, the next chapter introduces sociological theory about how institutions, including legal institutions, operate. This cultural or constructivist understanding sees legality as an ongoing human production. Legality is a pattern in relationships that is enacted daily in the interpretive schemas people invoke to make sense of their own and others' actions and in the human and material resources, capacities, and assets that make action possible. Rather than something outside everyday social relations, legality is a feature of social interaction that exists in those moments when people invoke legal concepts and terminology, associating law with other social phenomena.

CHAPTER THREE

The Social Construction of Legality

[We need to] unfreeze the world as it appears to common
sense as a bunch of more or less objectively determined
social relations and to make it appear as (we believe) it
really is: people acting, imagining, rationalizing, justifying.
ROBERT GORDON, "New Developments in Legal Theory"

How do people experience and interpret law in the context of their
daily lives? How do commonplace transactions and relationships
come to assume or not assume a legal character? And in what ways is
legality constituted by these popular understandings, interpretations,
and enactments of law?

These sorts of questions concerning the ordinary presence of legality derive from a much more general and long-standing question
about the role of law in social relations. Over the years, interest in
the relationship between "law" and "society" has led scholars to examine how and with what effect law is made, enforced, violated, and
avenged. It has motivated their empirical investigations tracing the
trajectories of law from legislatures, courtrooms, police departments,
and regulatory agencies into the streets, homes, and workplaces and
back again. For some, this question has been pursued with the goal
of assessing the effectiveness of a law, that is, the success of a specific
rule (e.g., a reduced speed limit), or a change in legal procedures
(e.g., abolishing the death penalty) or in the organization of legal
actors (e.g., increasing police personnel). For others, the objective of
these investigations has been to observe the effects, rather than the
effectiveness, of law: what law does and how it behaves, regardless
of the intention or purposes of its framers. Whatever the variations,
most of the empirical research that now constitutes the sociology of
law has been animated in one way or another by this question of the
relationship between law and society.

Even as it has opened up some lines of inquiry, the "law and society" question has necessarily foreclosed others. This question, like all questions, presupposes a set of meanings and analytic relationships. It relies for its intelligibility on a horizon of certainty: a set of terms that are accepted as self-evident and that frame the central problem. For instance, the ontology implied in the pairing of "law and society" assigns to the law a distinctive, coherent, and recognizable form, independent of something called society. Similarly the conjunction "and" assumes a more or less clear boundary demarcating the two spheres of social life. Finally, the surface question regarding the relationship between law and society instructs us, if we want to learn about this relationship, to focus on events and interactions that occur across or at that boundary. Each of these assumptions, however, might be challenged, generating with each challenge a new line of inquiry.

In this chapter, we describe recent reformulations of the relationship between law and society. We show how these reformulations of the law and society question entail a radical reconceptualization of law, culture, and society and a redirection of empirical attention away from formal law toward commonplace interpretations and relationships in which and through which legality circulates. We end the chapter by describing legality as a socially constructed phenomenon, both a precondition for and product of social action.

Law in Society: Legal Culture and Consciousness

Because the term "law" names assorted social acts, organizations, and persons, including lay as well as professional actors, and encompasses a broad range of values and objectives, it has neither the uniformity, coherence, nor autonomy that is often assumed. It is increasingly clear that to know the law we should expand rather than narrow the range of material and social practices and actors that constitute it. We need to discover not only how and by whom the law is used, but also when and by whom it is not used. We need, for that matter, to reassess what we define as using the law. Moving away from a focus on use as exclusively the mobilization of formal or official legal actors, we must consider legal use in other contexts, within families and neighborhoods, workplaces, and for purposes unintended by formal lawmakers.[1] Thus, we turn to commonplace events and transactions to seek the web of legality, conceiving of law not so much operating to shape social action but *as* social action. Finally, we want to understand how the law emerges from these local settings and interactions with the ontological integrity it claims for itself and that socio-legal scholars have for so long attributed to it.

Obviously, the most significant consequence of reconceptualizing the law in this way is that it renders the old "law and society" question incoherent. Its incoherence derives from the fact that the question presupposes the very thing that is now understood to be problematic: how is it that the law emerges out of, or is constituted within, local, concrete, and historically specific situations? If the law is now understood to be an internal feature of social situations, rather than simply an autonomous force acting upon them, we also need to understand how and in what ways these very same situations are constructed by something we call law. In other words, in denying legality the conceptual distinctiveness that is linguistically implied in the phrase "law and society," our theoretical question shifts away from tracking the causal and instrumental relationship between law and society toward tracing the presence of law *in* society.[2]

In order to discover the presence and consequences of law in social relations, we must understand how legality is experienced and understood by ordinary people as they engage, avoid, or resist the law and legal meanings. This is the study of legal consciousness. Of course, attention to lay or popular understandings of law has always been a part of socio-legal research. Surveys have been conducted to measure people's attitudes toward specific laws, their perception of legal institutions, their support for legal innovations, and their knowledge of legal procedures. This long-standing empirical attention to popular understandings of law, however, encompasses divergent theoretical formulations of the role of popular consciousness in relation to legality. Therefore, before discussing our own interpretation of consciousness and the theoretical foundation on which it rests, we will review two alternative definitions of legal consciousness.

Legal Consciousness as Attitude

Some scholars conceptualize consciousness as the ideas and attitudes of individuals that, when taken together, determine the form and texture of social life. An expression of the classical liberal tradition in political and legal theory, this conception of consciousness suggests that social groups of all sizes and types (families, peer groups, work groups, corporations, communities, legal institutions, and societies) emerge out of the aggregated actions of individuals. According to this approach, "political society is . . . an association of self determining individuals who concert their will and collect their power in the state for mutually self-interested ends."[3] Here, consciousness consists of both reason and desire. According to liberal ideology, desire, which remains unexplained, is "the moving, active, or primary part of the self . . . What distinguishes men from one another is not that they understand the world differently, but that they desire different things even when they share the same understanding."[4]

Relying on this "attitudinal" conception of legal consciousness, much American social science has attempted to document the variation in beliefs, attitudes, and actions among American citizens as a means of explaining the shape of American political and legal institutions. Lind and Tyler, for example, have documented Americans' attachment to these same ideals of fairness and due process and to what they call procedural justice. Lind and Tyler demonstrate that people commonly evaluate their legal experiences in terms of the processes and forms of interaction rather than the outcomes of those interactions. In other words, attitudes about the law correlate strongly with judgments about the fairness of procedures used by legal authorities, rather than with whether the person won or lost in that process. People care about having neutral, honest authorities who allow them to state their views and who treat them with dignity and respect.[5]

Ironically, despite the central focus on the capacity of individual desires, beliefs, and attitudes to shape the world, this research describes not individual variation but a deep, broad-based normative consensus. While people express persistent skepticism about the fairness of legal institutions, they appear to be committed to both the desirability and possibility of realizing legal ideals of equal and fair treatment.

Legal Consciousness as Epiphenomenon

At the other end of a continuum of conceptualizations, some scholars regard consciousness as a by-product of the operations of social structures rather than the formative agent in shaping structures and history. Structural anthropology, for instance, understands social actors as located in complex webs of patterned social relationships that determine their perceptions and actions. Similarly, some Marxist structuralism treats ideas, including cultural symbols and narratives, as a superstructural residue of material conditions that serves the interests of elites. Thus, within these theoretical paradigms, individuals are the bearers rather than agents of social relations. Consequently, social relations, not individuals, are the proper objects of analysis.

Following from this perspective, law and legal consciousness are epiphenomena because a particular social and economic structure is understood to produce a corresponding or appropriate legal order, including legal subjects. Work in this tradition often describes how the needs of capitalist production and reproduction mold legal behavior and consciousness. Studies focus on the production and practice of law, its accommodation to class interests, and the inequities that result.

Some research in this structuralist perspective complicates the proposed relationship between law and structure by suggesting that the legal order develops in response to conflicts and inconsistencies generated by the capitalist mode of production rather than as a direct instrument of particular class interests.

> To legitimize the inconsistencies and irrationalities born of the contradictions of the economy the legal order constitutes myths, creates institutions of repression and tries to harmonize exploitation with freedom, expropriation with choice, inherently unequal contractual agreements with an ideology of free will.[6]

An alternative view within the structuralist tradition looks at legal consciousness as one of the ways in which social organizations produce the means of authorizing, sustaining, and reproducing themselves. By focusing on the legitimating functions of law, research describes the ways in which law helps people see their worlds, private and public, as both natural and right. Balbus, for example, argues that certain features of liberal law, such as the highly prized claims to formal equality and what we earlier described as procedural justice, serve to buttress and legitimate the inequality of the existing economic order. The formal equality instantiated in due process rights provides "a stable and apparently neutral framework from which bourgeois class interests in accumulation and profit maximization can flourish"; but due process and formal equality also help convince "the 'propertyless' that they have the legal right and, hence, the real opportunity of rising into the bourgeoisie."[7]

Despite these alternative conceptualizations, structuralist and Marxist formulations often cast law and legal consciousness as products rather than producers of social relations.[8]

Consciousness as Cultural Practice

In contrast to these perspectives, we develop a cultural analysis that integrates human action and structural constraint. We identify and specify the mediating processes through which social interactions and local processes aggregate and condense into institutions and powerful structures.

We have found that the stories people tell us about events in their lives, about their neighborhoods, about buying and selling goods, about dealing with public officials in schools and government agencies, about their interactions with professionals and their encounters with modern bureaucracies, reveal a complexity that belies either the attitudinal or epiphenomenal approaches to consciousness. A notion of consciousness as determined solely by forces beyond the individual renders the thinking, knowing subject absent. Within this perspective there is no way to account for the rich interpretive work, the ideological penetrations, and the inventive strategies related to us by the persons with whom we spoke. On the other hand, a notion of legal consciousness that focuses solely on individual ideas (as attitudes or opinions) fails to connect people's accounts with their lived experiences, including the constraints operating within those particular locations. It fails to provide a coherent report of the finite and limited range of options available to people in either fashioning their interpretations or choosing their behaviors.

More important than the particular limitations of the attitudinal and structural conceptualizations of consciousness is the fact that they share an analytic strategy that limits each model's theoretical range. By emphasizing alternative wings of a dualistic conception of human life and experience, each model is able to imagine only part of what, at least conditionally, might be imagined as a process of ongoing mutual causation. The dualism illustrated by these two conceptualizations opposes idealist with materialist models of thought and action. Since Plato first attempted to distinguish what was real and true from what was illusory and false by differentiating a concrete and incomplete world of senses from an immutable and true world of ideas, this theoretical duality has persisted.

As modern sociological theory developed, it reproduced these oppositions between ideal and material phenomena in a series of dichotomies that reinstated the philosophical dilemmas. Thus, sociological theory and research have been struggling to resolve what at different times has been referred to as the problem of free will and determinism, subject and object, individual and society, or agency and structure. Each of these dyads describes opposing positions concerning the locus of agency in social relations. Voluntaristic theories see the individual subject's ideas, intentions, and motivations as critical variables in shaping the world. More deterministic, structural theories emphasize the power of society and material constraints in shaping the behavior and beliefs of persons.

In legal theory and scholarship, the dualisms that consumed philosophy and sociological theory were reproduced in the terminology and topics relevant to law. Seeking to identify the real (material) workings of the legal system, rather than the ideal (ideational) of a rule of law, socio-legal scholars created their own particular duality between the law on the books and the law in action. Research became preoccupied with dichotomies between law and state, equality and hierarchy, and its own version of agency and structure in debates about consent and coercion. In order to understand *how* individual action and understanding are implicated in the production of legality, we have sought an approach to legal consciousness that would mediate these opposing positions.[9]

Schemas and Resources as Media for Social Construction

We draw on a recent and growing body of literature in sociology that attempts to bridge these dualisms by redefining the relationship between the individual and social structure, reconfiguring what was understood to be an oppositional relationship as one that is mutually defining.[10] Within this framework, consciousness is understood to be part of a reciprocal process in which the meanings given by individuals to their world become patterned, stabilized, and objectified. These meanings, once institutionalized, become part of the material and discursive systems that limit and constrain future meaning making.

In other words, through its organization, society provides us with specific opportunities for thought and action. Through language, society furnishes images of what those opportunities and resources are: how the world works, what is possible and what is not. These schemas, as William Sewell[11] refers to them, include cultural codes, vocabularies of motive, logics, hierarchies of value, and conventions, as well as the binary oppositions that make up what he calls a society's "fundamental tools for thought." Examples of schemas include the interactive rules of a criminal trial, the concepts of guilt or innocence, and the obligation born of a promise or a contract, in addition to the commonplace proverbs and aphorisms asserting such truths as "possession is nine-tenths of the law" or the insistence that "this is a free country." It is on the basis of the enactment of these symbolic constructs that social action is largely (although not entirely) premised, and it is through the invocation or application of these schemas in particular settings and interactions that we actively make, as we make sense of, the world.

As cultural codes used for interpretations, schemas function as "generalizable procedures applied in the enactment/reproduction of social life."[12] Schemas are transposable; they can be invoked in many settings. By applying schemas from one setting in another, people are able to make familiar what may be new and strange; moreover, they can appropriate the legitimacy attached to the familiar to authorize what is unconventional. In this way the concept of the schema points to the power of naming as a fundamental aspect of social action. For example, in his study of unionism in early nineteenth-century England, Steinberg notes the absence of any discourse concerning labor exploitation and economic oppression that might have been deployed by the striking cotton spinners of Ashton-Stalybridge.[13] Examining the speeches and newspaper editorials of the emerging labor movement during this period, Steinberg finds that without a ready arsenal of appropriate interpretive schemas, the spinners drew from other available discourses forging what he calls a "poignant heterogloss." Borrowing from the abolition movement, the spinners invoked images of slavery. Appropriating from the Bible, the spinners conjured images familiar to middle-class Christianity. Finally, relying on a discourse of revolution, the spinners deployed potent images of political oppression. Through these inventive borrowings and appropriations, the spinners were able to suggest common ground with conventional practices and thus "convey the virtuousness of their cause, the necessity of commitment, and perhaps even the importance of violence and sacrifice to their peers and kindred factory hands."[14]

In addition to providing these schemas, societies also produce and distribute resources, material assets, and human capacities used to maintain or enhance power.[15] Resources include such diverse objects and abilities as legal knowledge, capital, property, political "connections," and even physical strength. Of course, resources require cultural schemas in order to invest them with their power-generating capacity. For instance, the modern trial as a cultural schema renders the verbal acuity, but not the physical strength, of a trial lawyer as a resource. This is not to say, as Sewell cautions us, that resources are reducible, and thus secondary, to schemas. In fact, schemas are equally dependent on resources in order to remain manifest and viable. Having only a virtual existence, schemas must find articulation in the resources that instantiate them. As Sewell observes, "schema not empowered or regenerated by resources would eventually be abandoned and forgotten, just as resources without cultural schema to direct their use would eventually dissipate and decay."[16]

The differential distribution of resources, together with the differential access to schemas, underwrites variations in social power and agency. In this way, the dual operation of schemas and resources account for the reproduction of social life, imperfect though it is. It is this tendency toward reproduction that has underwritten traditional notions of structure as pattern or constraint. The same duality of structure, however, is what also accounts for social change and historicity. The possibilities of invoking schemas in a wide variety of settings opens up the potential for generating new resources and thus the ability to challenge or revise cultural meanings and the distribution of resources.

What is crucial to this perspective is the claim that social structures, while they confront us as external and coercive, do not exist apart from our collective actions and thoughts as we apply schemas to make sense of the world and deploy resources to affect people and things. Accordingly, as Sewell notes, "human agency and structure, far from being opposed, in fact presuppose each other."[17] In this way, structures both determine and, at the same time, are highly contingent upon social practice. Finally, to the extent that social practice involves borrowings as well as inventiveness and a measure of unpredictability, structures are more appropriately understood as ongoing processes rather than as sets of immutable constraints.

Of course, by describing the world as immutable, inevitable, or natural, schemas often deny the very openness they allow. By obscuring the ongoing construction, structures appear to have an existence apart from their continuing production. However, the appearance of objectivity is not an illusion. Much like a rock that lies in our path, the constructed world cannot be ignored. If we proceed as if we can ignore the social world, we stumble or fall. We know the rock is real by the resistance it presents; the same is true of social structures (schemas and resources). To the extent that they establish expectations, limits, and contingencies for human thought and action that cannot be merely wished away, they too are real.

By rendering the world as made rather than in the making, the socially constructed world becomes impervious to our merely wishing or willing it away. Similarly, the fact that the world has not always been this way, or that it can be shown to be different elsewhere, does not undermine the reality of the socially constructed world here and now. By way of an example of the social construction of reality, consider the general belief in witches that characterized European societies during the Renaissance.[18] From a twentieth-century point of view, this belief, along with the customs, bodies of expert knowledge, and practices that sustained it, was illusory. Practicing our own rationalized worldview, we may seek to understand why Europeans at that time believed in and acted on their belief in the existence of witches. But even in our efforts to explain that historical experience, most of us would reject the reality of the world constructed around the presence of witches, prickers, inquisitors, Satan, and hell.

Such a casual rejection is possible, of course, because we do not happen to live in that world. That particular rock does not lie in our path. However, the belief in witches was a monstrous boulder in the paths of many seventeenth-century citizens[19] of Spain and England. It shaped how people saw one another, how they interpreted one another's, as well as their own, behavior. It informed how they responded to conflicts and how they worshipped God. It was a source of public identity, insofar as some people were labeled as witches, and personal identity, insofar as some people thought themselves to be witches.

Thus, despite our confidence in the unreality of witches, the social world of Renaissance Europe constructed around the presence of witches was undeniably real and consequential. Any person born into that world confronted a society that, among other things, believed in witches. They could ignore those beliefs, choose to act and to talk as if there were no witches, no inquisitors, no prickers, no hell, no devil. But if they did, and some people certainly did, it would be tantamount to walking into a rock. For in acting and talking as if there were no witches, people would confront the belief as a fact, would meet resistance, and would have to work hard, and most likely unsuccessfully, to sustain the idea that there are no witches. They might be accused, shunned, hanged, or burned. Those people would encounter the reality of the belief in witches by the consequences of that belief.[20]

Legality as Social Structure

We claim that legality is a structural component of society. That is, legality consists of cultural schemas and resources that operate to define and pattern social life. At the same time that schemas and resources shape social relations, they must also be continually produced and worked on—invoked and deployed—by individual and group actors. Legality is not inserted into situations; rather, through repeated invocations of the law and legal concepts and terminology, as well as through imaginative and unusual associations between legality and other social structures, legality is constituted through everyday actions and practices.

For example, David Engel's work on the intersection of law and everyday life reflects this view of law and legality. In his study of the Education for All Handicapped Children Act of 1975,[21] Engel rejects the kind of traditional analysis that would have traced the ways in which this legislation unilaterally constrained or defined the educational experiences of children, the meaning of their physical conditions, or the interactions that occurred between parents and educators. Instead, he examines how this legislation and everyday life within this community are interdependent and mutually shaped this social domain.

At times, Engel notes, the law reinscribed "commonsense" images of disability and difference, constituting the meaning and content of those social categories as they operated within the community. Even though the intended effect of the legislation was to challenge the community's perception of these students as different—by mandating educational inclusion or mainstreaming—the law's challenge to common prejudices was only partial. Engel observes, for instance, that in order to receive the benefits of educational inclusion guaranteed under this legislation, the law required an initial determination by educational experts that a child was different, in other words, disabled or abnormal, and thus subject to the law's protection. He also shows that the operation of the law in marking differences did not itself go unchallenged. Parents resisted this requirement, with varying degrees of vigor and success, by rejecting the holistic terms "disabled" or "multiply handicapped" and insisting upon more restricted and limited descriptions of their child's condition. By substituting more specific designations—for instance, "speech impairment" or "cerebral palsy"—for the global term "disability," parents were able to claim, within the constraints imposed, a degree of sameness for their children. This type of parental resistance was possible, moreover, because the legislation did not simply reinstate existing power relations within the community. The statute, by prescribing parental participation in decision making, unsettled the authority of teachers and experts, making such forms of challenge possible. The legal rights of handicapped children emerged as a product of a complex array of social relations— part legislation, part community conceptions of difference, part parental desires for children's inclusion.

Borrowing a very different illustration from marine biology, Stuart Henry offers another example of this conception of structure as an emergent property of social action.[22]

It has been observed by marine biologists, that whale songs have a characteristic form for each school of whales; that if whale songs are recorded on one day and then another, the same school has the same song. However, when biologists return to record that school's song say one year later, the song is completely different. The explanation for this change is that the characteristic song is the result of individual whales hearing and sharing in singing each other's song; each rendition is shaped by the social structure that is the whale song. But at the same time each individual has enough autonomy to add small variations and innovations to the main theme; the continuously produced whale song is a resource and medium through which each individual and unique whale can creatively reproduce the song. This creative interpretation and selection is not enough to completely transform the song, that is and remains the total medium, but it is enough to change the song just a little. Other whales in the school pick up the general song, incorporating as it now does, the slight modifications of those whales who have been singing. The result is that after a period of time the micro-contributions of the individual whales transform the very totality of the whale song which has given and continues to give shape and general direction to their individual action.[23]

Varieties of Legal Consciousness

With this conception of legality as a structural feature of society in place, we use the phrase "legal consciousness" to name participation in the process of constructing legality. This formulation of consciousness as cultural practice and specifically as participation in the construction of social relations attempts to keep alive the tension between structure and agency, constraint and choice. It seeks to capture people's sense of purposes, stakes, and constraints within a broad ethnographic domain. To reconcile the tensions in this formulation would defeat the theoretical work of focusing attention on the fulcrum precariously mediating self and society. Just as each whale's participation in the singing reproduces the song at the same time as it alters it ever so slightly, each person's participation sustains legality as an organizing structure of social relations. Every time a person interprets some event in terms of legal concepts or terminology— whether to applaud or to criticize, whether to appropriate or to resist—legality is produced. The production may include innovations as well as faithful replication. Either way, repeated invocation of the law sustains its capacity to comprise social relations.

Millic Simpson's various encounters with the law, described in chapter 1, enacted and produced legality. In the different episodes and encounters that Millie Simpson had with the court, the judge, the lawyers, the clerks, her employers, and her friends with whom she consulted, she displayed three forms of legal consciousness: conformity *before* the law, engagement *with* the law, and resistance *against* the law. Clearly, her passive obedience in the first two hearings collaborated in a manifest display of the law's powers and impenetrability. By contrast, the subsequent appeal orchestrated by the Richardses and the attorney David Stone contested the law in the ways that acknowledged, and took advantage of, formal legal procedures. The procedural problems regarding her guilty plea and the no-show public defender opened the way for a reversal of her sentence. Having received the Richardses' attention and through them access to legal representation, Millie Simpson was able to use available resources of legality—such as the rules regarding procedural accountability, the informal social networks produced by the organization of the court, and the lawyer's professional skill and experience—to reverse the sentence. Finally, Millie Simpson's resistance, by arranging to do community service at her own church and by deciding not to drive when she thought she could, represented instances in which the law was neither deferred to nor openly contested. In these moments of resistance, Millie was most engaged in confronting and understanding the legal forms and demands. In order to find a way to lessen the burden of their consequences, Millie reconstructed legal concepts and processes through aspects of her life and identity that were unrecognized by the court.

In this theoretical framing of legal consciousness as participation in the construction of legality, consciousness is not an exclusively ideational, abstract, or decontextualized set of attitudes toward and about the law. Consciousness is not merely a state of mind. Legal consciousness is produced and revealed in what people *do* as well as what they *say*. In this sense, consciousness is "an essential component of the full reality of the social world"[24] constituted and expressed in the practical knowledge individuals have of social life. Consciousness is discursively deployed as reflective consideration about day-to-day activities; it is also tacitly enacted as competent social action.[25] Although a product, in part, of desire and will, consciousness is not entirely individual or subjective. Legal consciousness is always a collective construction that simultaneously expresses, uses, and creates publicly exchanged understandings, what earlier we called schemas. Although individual consciousness expresses collective understandings, those meanings and interpretations are not perfect reproductions of an existing template. The enactment of collective understandings is variable, locally shaped and situated, involving improvisation and invention as well as appropriation and replication. We understand consciousness to be formed within and changed by social action. It is "less a matter of disembodied mental attitude than a broader set of practices and repertoires,"[26] inventories that are available for creative and banal uses.[27]

Although legal consciousness is emergent, complex, and moving, it nonetheless has shape and pattern. The possible variations in legal consciousness are developed within historically defined contexts and encounters. One would not expect, for example, the varieties of legal consciousness among the seventeenth-century residents of New Jersey to correspond to those of twentieth-century residents, since the available repertoires of action and interpretation and ensembles of resources are quite different. Similarly, we would not expect a wife's diary written in 1995 to express the same understandings of the obligations of marriage and the opportunities and constraints of law as Abigail Bailey's did in the eighteenth century. While acknowledging the work of social action, we should not ignore the power and contribution of what is given.[28]

Based on our conversations with the 430 residents of New Jersey whom we interviewed during the years 1990–93, we have identified three predominant types of legal consciousness, three ways of participating in the construction of legality. Each variety of consciousness invokes a particular cluster of cultural schemas and resources that position the law and the individual in relation to one another. People describe their relationships to law as something *before* which they stand, *with* which they engage, and *against* which they struggle.

Before the Law

In what we call "before the law," legality is envisioned and enacted as if it were a separate sphere from ordinary social life: discontinuous, distinctive, yet authoritative and predictable. In this form of consciousness, the law is described as a formally ordered, rational, and hierarchical system of known rules and procedures. Respondents conceive of legality as something relatively fixed and impervious to individual action. In a sense, respondents tell the law's story of its own awesome grandeur, something that transcends by its history and processes the persons and conflicts of the moment. It is often regarded as somewhere else, a place very different from everyday life. Objective rather than subjective, the law is defined by its impartiality. Imagining the law as a realm removed from ordinary affairs by its objectivity, people turn to law only when they can imagine their personal problems as having general import, as affecting others as well as themselves. Law is understood to be a serious and hallowed space in which the mundane world is refigured in importance and consequence. Often in these situations people express loyalty and acceptance of legal constructions; they believe in the appropriateness and justness provided through formal legal procedures, although not always in the fairness of the outcomes. Sometimes, however, finding themselves before the law, people express frustration, even anger, about what they perceive as their own powerlessness. Those who find themselves before the law acknowledge and, through their actions and interpretations, defer to the law's claim to autonomy.

With the Law

In other situations, facing different contingencies, we observed a second form of consciousness in which the law is described and "played" as a game, a bounded arena in which preexisting rules can be deployed and new rules invented to serve the widest range of interests and values. It is an arena of competitive tactical maneuvering where the pursuit of self-interest is expected and the skillful and resourceful can make strategic gains. The boundaries thought to separate law from everyday life are understood to be relatively porous. The law as game involves a bracketing of everyday life—different rules apply, different statuses and roles operate, different resources count—but it is a bracketing that can be abandoned if need be. Rather than being discontinuous from everyday life and its concerns, the law is enframed by everyday life. Respondents describe acceptance of formal legal constructions and procedures only for specified objectives and limited situations. Here respondents display less concern about the legitimacy of legal procedures than about their effectiveness for achieving desires. These stories describe a world of competitive struggles; they seem less concerned about law's power than about the power of self or others to successfully deploy and engage with the law.

Against the Law

Finally, we observed a third way of participating in legality when people revealed their sense of being caught within the law, or being up against the law, its schemas and resources overriding their own capacity either to maintain its distance from their everyday lives or to play by its rules. Finding themselves in such a position, people described their attempts at "making do," using what the situation momentarily and unpredictably makes available—materially and discursively—to fashion solutions they would not be able to achieve within conventionally recognized schemas and resources. People exploit the interstices of conventional social practices to forge moments of respite from the power of law. Foot-dragging, omissions, ploys, small deceits, humor, and making scenes are typical forms of resistance for those up against the law. In resisting, people seek diverse goals. For some it is to retain a sense of dignity and honor. For others it is to exact revenge. And for yet others the purpose of their momentary resistance or subterfuge is indeed instrumental: to avoid, if only for that moment, the law and its costs. Rarely, however, are such efforts to resist the power of law cynical; more often, people undertake small subterfuges, deceits, and other violations of conventional and legal norms with a strong sense of justice and right. Finally, these instances of resistance are recounted with humor and passion so that part of the resistance inheres in the telling of the story and passing on the message that legality can be opposed, if just a little.[29]

Constructing Legality

In part 2 we describe, through the words and stories of our respondents, these three forms of legal consciousness. Through the stories of law, we map the varieties of legal consciousness as both individual and collective participation in the process of constructing legality. Before turning to these stories, we conclude this chapter by suggesting four theoretical points that are important to keep in mind in order to appreciate the relationship of these stories to the production of legality.

   (1) *The particular interpretive schemas and resources that constitute legality and are expressed in these stories are not, for the most part, exclusively legal.* Societies are collections of many practices and multiple structures that draw upon common schemas and resources. In short, legality shares schemas and resources with other social structures.

   Many aspects of the game, as a cultural schema, appear in various institutional spheres. Notions of competition, winning, teamwork, "rules of the game," and "level playing fields" are an important part of capitalism (playing the market), education (graduating first in one's class), and even courtship ("all's fair in love and war"). Similarly, the idea of a transcendent, nonhuman, and autonomous source of power finds expression in religion (supernatural being, God), the economy (the invisible hand of the market), and courtship (true love).

   This overlap in interpretive schemas among various structures and within different institutions reflects what we earlier referred to as the transposability of schemas: the fact that they may be invoked and applied in unpredictable ways in diverse settings. This possibility is, as we pointed out, a source of change. The meaning of situations and relationships may be revised and new resources generated in light of new and different schemas being borrowed from one structure and applied in another. Thus while the market is often likened to a game, with winners and losers, determined by the human and material resources one brings to the game, it is also depicted as a transcendent structure (the invisible hand). This shift in the interpretive schema reconfigures the moral status of markets and capitalism. Perceiving the market, or capitalism, as a realm apart from politics and power according to an ahistorical logic connects capitalism with universal morality, justice, and perhaps even religion.

The same quality of transposability is also, however, a source of constraint and structural durability. To the degree that a particular interpretive schema finds expression, and legitimation, in multiple overlapping structures it derives a power and depth from these multiple expressions. Much like a fun-house hall of mirrors, each reflecting one another, it becomes increasingly difficult to perceive or imagine a way out. The intersection between legality and other social structures thus provides legality with supplemental meanings and resources that do not derive from legal practices alone. This surplus of meaning and resources can be appropriated for diverse legal projects and strategies.Thus, structures such as gender, economy, and legality are mutually constitutive because they share some schemas and resources.

(2) *The forms of consciousness do not neatly correspond to actors.* In other words, some people cannot be said to be "before" the law and others "against" the law. In describing and analyzing the various forms of legal consciousness, we employ an analytic language of relationship rather than one of persons.[30] Legal consciousness is not a permanent or essential aspect of a person's identity or life, although it may end up being empirically stable. Because people's legal actions and interpretations are situationally specific, an individual might, in the context of various interactions or events, express all three forms of consciousness, as Millie Simpson did. To the extent that consciousness is forged in and around situated events and interactions (a dispute with a neighbor, a criminal case, a plumber who seemed to work few hours but charged for many), a person may express, through words or actions, a multifaceted and possibly contradictory consciousness. As we use the term, then, legal consciousness is neither fixed nor necessarily consistent; rather, it is plural and variable across contexts, and it often expresses and contains contradiction.

While the variation that exists across a sample of individual sub-jects lies at the heart of social-scientific research (the goal of which is to describe it, partition it, and explain it), variation and contradiction within a single person have traditionally been ignored or dismissed by social science. They are typically characterized as either a method-ological problem regarding the reliability of our indicators ("why are we getting different, maybe even contradictory, answers to the same question?") or attributed to some sort of deficiency within the subject ("some individuals lack the intellectual capacity to maintain a coher-ent worldview"). More often than not, the contradictions within the stories and accounts have not received sufficient, if any, theoretical attention.

In the face of overwhelming evidence that individuals do not ex-press a "single cognitive framework" or invoke "a ready-made inter-pretation for every situation,"[31] it has become necessary to rethink our traditional expectations of coherence, unity, or what political sci-entists used to call "ideological constraint."[32] In fact, commonsense and popular consciousness (with which the day-to-day life of individ-uals is negotiated and the longue durée of institutions contemplated) contain multiple elements that "pull in contrary directions" through a series of dilemmas laid down by centuries of ideological sedimenta-tion.[33] This social and cognitive heterogeneity produces what Bakh-tin[34] calls "heteroglossia"—variable meaning—in situations when people invoke alternative interpretations within the same utterance and switch among what he called "different registers of voice."

It turns out that people express different understandings, values, and expectations, depending on the situation in which they are speaking and what they imagine accomplishing through their talk, whether it is to amuse, persuade, claim a right, demonstrate camara-derie, or avoid censure.[35] Such discursive variability and rhetorical maneuvering are accomplished by invoking alternative interpreta-tions from among the culturally available repertoires or ideologies.[36] Thus the contradictions do not reflect the cognitive deficiencies of individual speakers, but inhere in the availability of multiple inter-pretive schemas.

(3) *Legality is composed of several strands of consciousness that are expressed simultaneously within popular culture.* The contrary themes that exist within these schemas, and their commonsense articulation, should not be interpreted as something that needs to (or could) be adjusted to produce coherence. The contradictions do not represent

a flaw at the social level, as social scientists had previously interpreted such contradiction at the individual level. In fact, quite the
opposite is the case. Contradiction among cultural schemas is inevitable since each theme requires the imagining of another for its own
intelligibility. According to Billig, "An ideology is [always] against another ideology."[37] Consequently, the meaning of one depends upon
the meaning assigned to its counterpoint. In order for something to
be meaningful at all, it must contain, at least implicitly, an opposing
or contrasting meaning. These alternative meanings and multiple interpretive schemas simultaneously sustain each other in symbiotic
tension. Furthermore, as one meaning or schema changes, it trans-
forms the meaning of the other.

For example, in her analysis of *Sears Roebuck v. EEOC*,[38] Joan
Scott has demonstrated the political consequences of these schematic couplings. In this landmark case the EEOC charged that Sears
discriminated against women in hiring for its commissioned sales
force. Sears's defense in the face of statistical underrepresentation of
women was that men and women had different interests in pursuing
such high-pressured and demanding sales jobs. Women were, Sears
claimed, less competitive and less willing to sacrifice time away from
home and family.

Scott's analysis of Sears's legal argument demonstrated that its
persuasiveness rested on an unexamined cultural understanding that
opposed gender difference to gender equality. Within the context of
this opposition, each concept—difference and equality—derived its
specific meaning: men and women are either the same and should be
treated equally, or they are different and thus equal treatment is not
necessary. Scott points out, however, that there is nothing necessary
about this particular opposition. In fact, demands for equality (and
for the social devices that ensure its realization) are most likely only
when social differences are perceived. Thus equality functions as a
commitment to ignore as irrelevant, for particular purposes, those
very differences.

The polyvocality of legality, that is, the varieties of legal consciousness and the multiple schemas of and by which it is constituted, permit individuals wide latitude in interpreting social phenomena, while at the same time still deploying signs of legality. Thus
those who see the law as an autonomous external force almost sacred
in its distinctiveness and those who use legal devices as one of the

many resources with which they negotiate their day-to-day affairs join in the construction of legality as a structure of social relations.

(4) *While we describe a legal culture layered with the sediment of diverse interpretive schemas, the variability that an individual might express is neither limitless, random, nor arbitrary.* The culturally available schemas, or repertoires of interpretation, as well as the availability of social and material resources, including education, experience, money, and access to legal representation, create contingencies that make the expression of one type of consciousness more likely than others. Millie Simpson's expression of three types of consciousness over the course of her various interactions can be understood as reflecting these contingencies. Her initial interaction reflected her lack of experience, money, and legal representation, as well as her understanding of legality as depicted in mass culture and neighborhood conversation. Her contestation of the charges was tied to her job as a full-time housekeeper, an occupation socially constructed around gender, race, and paternal domesticity. Finally, her resistance reflected the fortuity of circumstance and, as important, her ability to import her experience as a churchwoman into the legal domain. Her social relations enabled and limited the ways she participated in the construction of legality. Thus, legal consciousness varies across time (to reflect learning and experience) and across interactions (to reflect opportunity, different objects, relationships or purposes, and the differential availability of schemas and resources). We turn more explicitly to these contingencies in legal consciousness in part 3. But before that, in part 2, we present the stories of legal consciousness—the interpretive schemas we call "before the law," "with the law," and "against the law."

PART TWO

Stories of Legal Consciousness: Constructing Legality

CHAPTER FOUR

Before the Law

Rita Michaels

*Rita Michaels is a middle-aged, white, divorced woman work-
ing sixty hours a week as an office manager to support two
sons in college. Rita Michaels is Catholic and attends mass
several times a week. Divorced since her children were in
grade school, Rita Michaels has never received child support
from her husband. Her income, at the time of this interview in
1991, was just at the national median of $34,000.*

*She lives in a meticulously neat and well-maintained
house in a lower-middle-class section of a generally more
affluent suburb in northern New Jersey. Amid the postage
stamp front lawns, many littered with toys and garden orna-
ments, Rita Michaels's lawn stood out. Green and cropped, it
was disturbed only by a short walkway that led to an enclosed
porch. The porch was freshly painted and empty, with none of
the debris that tends to accumulate: no cast-off shoes, unre-
trieved newspapers, or garden tools.*

*In the course of our two-and-a-half-hour conversation,
Rita Michaels told nearly a dozen stories about the disappoint-
ments, disagreements, and disputes that characterize daily life.
Through her accounts of consumer problems, neighborhood
parking problems, and health-care billing difficulties, Rita
described her view of how one manages such "private" matters. At times during these stories, she conveyed a sense of resignation. More often, she portrayed herself as a competent,
pragmatic manager of such problems. She complains when
warranties are not honored. She negotiates with workmen
who she thinks have overcharged her. She challenged her insurance company when, she said, they mistakenly converted a policy from whole life to term without her permission or knowledge. In several instances, she described herself as having*

accepted the costs of what she thought were unfair and "aggra-
vating" business practices because she did not think she could
do anything further. For example, she had purchased a new
refrigerator for which the salesman had successfully pressured
her to buy a special warranty for an additional $150. Within a
year, the compressor on the refrigerator broke but she still
had to pay over $100 for repairs. "I was a little aggravated,"
she said.

> *I mean I think there should really be something done with those*
> *people. I don't think that should be, that they should be able to*
> *do that, you know . . . I was going to the Better Business Bureau*
> *but I just got tired of arguing with the store and I just forgot*
> *about it.*

In another instance, however, she described how she
joined with some people in her neighborhood to complain to
the town about workers from a nearby factory crowding the
residential street with parked cars. Sometimes the cars blocked
driveways and at other times the cars made it difficult to
observe and supervise children. Although the town never sys-
tematically ticketed people who ought not to have parked
there, Rita and some of her neighbors succeeded in having the
town paint yellow lines marking driveways and no-parking
zones. "It kind of worked," she said.

In talking about neighborhood noise, children's squabbles,
and the like, Rita Michaels was explicit about her ways of deal-
ing with life's common problems. She believes that you accept
what cannot be otherwise, negotiate and make peace where
you can. She attributes this perspective and her skillfulness in
negotiating to her experience as a parent, a role in which you
learn to be tolerant and empathetic. Responding to our inquir-
ies about possible noise and other neighborhood disturbances,
she commented, "I have children myself and I think I kind of
understand that it [noise] wouldn't happen often and if it hap-
pens you just put up with it." Sometimes, Rita noted, minor
disputes among children or neighbors became exaggerated to
the point that her peacemaking efforts, borne of her pragmatic
mothering skills, were particularly useful.

> *When the children were growing up you know we had a lot of*
> *problems like that . . . I did get involved . . . I tried to be a peace-*

*maker, to be honest, because I have a couple of neighbors that
are kind of high-strung. They get very upset, can't deal with it . . .
I would try to straighten the situation out between the kids and
the neighbors . . . I think it was the parents' fault truthfully . . .
You know the kids started the fight and maybe if they let things
just go, the kids kind of work it out themselves. But I think when
parents get involved and say, "Oh, it couldn't be my son that did
this." They get very defensive. I think the parents put more pres-
sure on these kids and they caused more trouble than the kids
themselves because the kids get over it tomorrow. But the parents
don't forget too easily. Oh, it's sad.*

Despite the conventional features of her biography, Rita
Michaels experiences herself as deviant, believing that defining
events in her life discredit and mark her with observable
stigma. At the outset of the interview, she commented that she
is different from her neighbors because she is divorced, and
because she works long hours. "I guess that puts me in a different category, socially," she noted.

After having been married for seventeen years, during
which time her husband had been chronically unemployed,
eventually refusing to work at all, Rita Michaels decided to
end the marriage. Her decision, she said, was difficult and
painful. Her family did not support her action, and her
friends and neighbors, Rita thought, did not understand her
situation.

*The neighborhood was a very nice neighborhood, people knew
me from when my kids were little, knew my husband, but no one
really, no one knows what goes on inside someone's house. So,
when I was divorced, or when I was in the process of doing this,
a couple of my neighbors really were very upset. And my husband went and told these people that I was this terrible person
and that I was throwing him out.*

Later in the interview, Rita Michaels said,

*The neighbors, their acceptance of the fact that I was going to do
this terrible thing, that I was this terrible person, um . . . And I
don't know, I think that maybe was the most painful.*

Her failed marriage undermined her sense of competency
in her role as mother, as well as neighbor. Discussing child
rearing and discipline, Rita Michaels alluded to the fact that

the problems of her adolescent sons were connected to her divorce. In one incident, her eighth-grade son was caught drinking in the back of the school; in another her son had his ear pierced. In recalling each of these events, Rita Michaels reiterated the stigma she felt as a consequence of being divorced. In response to these minor delinquencies, her stepfather, she told us,

> *really hit the ceiling. Thought I was this terrible mother. Yes. To get this earring . . . He kind of assumes that because I don't have a husband, that maybe I can't handle. He hasn't done it too much anymore . . . It's not always easy sometimes being a single parent.*

Remarkably, in light of these recurring expressions of pain and inadequacy associated with the divorce, Rita Michaels described the legal transaction ending the marriage as gratifying. She told us that "the divorce was a rather pleasant experience, believe it or not."

> *The court experience, what it felt like to go to the courtroom and face the judge or whomever. I don't mean that it was pleasant, I just think that I was pleasantly surprised because the judge had evidently read all the whatever they have, before time, . . . it was evident that he had done his homework . . . I don't think I was in that court more than, I would say maybe forty-five minutes and he awarded me the divorce. He said that there was no reason for me to have to live under these conditions . . . It left me with a good feeling. That I did do the right thing, and that he thought it was right also. Funny, I remember his exact words because it left a lasting impression.*

In contrast to family and neighbors, the judge affirmed her experience and her decision to seek a divorce. Rita Michaels did not easily choose a divorce but turned to the law because she believed she had no alternatives and sought the only help she thought it could provide—release from her obligations to a husband who himself had failed in his marital obligations. In doing so she found, in addition to formal termination of her marriage, a validation that she had not expected. Rejected and stigmatized by her family and friends and feeling outside the moral universe they guarded, Rita found that the law offered a desired refuge.

There existed, she found, a broader set of values, rights, and expectations, something less particular and partial than the world of her family and friends. Her husband had not fulfilled his obligations under this larger, more general set of norms. She took comfort in the fact that she could point to these norms as grounding and legitimacy for her action. Here, Rita Michaels articulated a very traditional conception and function of legal ordering: protection of the individual against local group norms, a protection that derives from the fact that legality resides outside these local norms.

Rita Michaels welcomed the court's affirmation at the same time as she experienced its distance from the world she regularly inhabited. The court's remove from her world made it possible, however, for the law to supply the moral sanction her family and friends had denied her. That distance between the public space of the court and her private world of friends and family represented, to Rita, the court's authority for the service it provided. Nonetheless, by going to court and getting divorced, she had crossed a barrier that excluded her from the networks that had up until the divorce defined her social position and identity. Although she has forged a new conception of herself in opposition to her family and friends, that newly expressed identity includes prominent marks of the struggle out of which it developed. In this sense, Rita Michaels's invocation of the public realm of law upon her private life constitutes her deviance.

Rita Michaels repeatedly traces this boundary between public and private; it often determines the interpretations she offers for her own and others' actions. Thus, the divorce had been difficult, not only because she was Catholic, but because she had gone outside her network of family and friends for what she believed was a private matter. Normally, Rita Michaels avoids such action. She believes that private matters should be handled privately. Counseling and therapy sometimes help people "when you can't iron it out yourself and you can't sort it out. You need some help sometimes to put it back together again, you know." But you do that privately; and you don't turn to law except as a last resort.

As one example of law avoidance, Rita explained that she never collected child support although the court ordered her

husband to pay. "His lawyer said he really wasn't earning
enough money. I would wind up paying for it. So to be per-
fectly honest with you, I never took him to court."

　　Rita Michaels expressed her view of the law as transcendent, impartial, and powerful in another story. She told us
that she accompanied her son to traffic court after he had
been in an accident. She claimed that in the traffic court a
police officer changed his story, contradicting her son's claim
to have been hit by another driver.

> My son was sideswiped on the way home and the lady that hit
> him kept going. He took her license plate number and went to
> the police to tell them . . . When he got to the police department
> he talked to the policeman who told him that he was going to
> investigate that number to find out who the person was and so
> on. So he did, and my son went to see this person on his own
> before he made any formal complaints about it, and the lady said
> no, she did not [hit his car]. She was a very motherly type person
> and she said . . . that he hit a tree in her yard and that she was
> not involved in the accident.
>
> 　　Well, there was quite a lot of damage done to my son's truck
> so we pursued it further and went to court. We spent the whole
> night in court. We were there for an entire evening and maybe
> they called us at twelve o'clock at night. The police officer got up
> and denied knowing anything about my son, could not see where
> this lady would have ever had this problem, and it turned out
> that he's a policeman right on the corner of where this lady lives.
> And so he went against everything he had said . . . we lost the
> case . . . It makes you lose faith in human nature, police people.

Later in the interview, referring to this experience, Rita
Michaels remarked,

> I came away feeling kind of disappointed in the system that this
> man could change his story . . . You know, you kind of put police
> officers and the courts on a higher level and you would never
> expect them to go to this level.

　　Rita Michaels's disappointment in the police officer's testimony was premised on her expectations, forged in part during
her previous "pleasant" experience in divorce court. Her deeply
felt disappointment nonetheless displayed her belief in the

*essential fairness and integrity of legal actors and the legal sys-
tem. Her experience in the traffic court revealed to her the
human or fallible side of law.*

*Rita Michaels also served as a juror, an experience she
characterized as "interesting." The system "worked," she said,
"although it could be improved upon." According to Rita, the
major area for improvement would be in making the process
less drawn out.*

> I do think that it's hard to be a juror, it's hard from the fact that
> you're taken away from your job and you have to go down to be
> at this courtroom and it seems like they have a million people
> there and you waste a lot of time. You go and you wait and you
> wait and you wait and you wait. It seems like a lot of wasted
> time.

*Serving on a jury, getting divorced, and her son's traffic
case were the only formal interactions Rita Michaels had with
courts or legal agents. In fact, during the interview, the law
was conspicuously absent from her narratives of work, neighborhood, and family. Yet her life was clearly not unproblematic. Rita experienced and characterized her difficulties with
medical care, consumer issues, schools, and town services as
part of everyday life, to weather or endure as best she could. In
a world firmly divided between the personal and the public,
Rita Michaels believes that the law belongs in a realm that is
unsullied by everyday life.*

*When asked whether she would call the police in response
to a neighborhood conflict, she readily rejected the idea, claiming, "I don't use my police that way." At one level the statement seems enigmatic and even contradictory. It expresses
both ownership and identification ("my police"), as well as dis-
enfranchisement and distance (her reluctance to call the police
for personal problems). Yet, when we unpack her meaning,
putting it in the context of her other experiences, it becomes
clear that the two meanings expressed in her utterance are less
oppositional than interdependent. In point of fact, Rita
Michaels identifies with the police (claiming them as her
police) precisely because they do not attend to the messiness
of everyday conflicts.*

Dwayne Franklin

Dwayne Franklin lives on the edge. "This is the borderline," he says, between one city and the next, between safety and danger, respect and uncaring. Keeping an eye on his neighbors' properties, as they in turn watch over his, Dwayne Franklin and his neighbors "police the neighborhood . . . observe any criminal activity," building a barrier to keep Newark's problems from spilling across the divide that marks Irvington as a separate, cleaner, and safer place to live. "Its like you're living in a fort . . . you are behind this wall . . . It's safe around here, but yet it is not." The boundary between Dwayne Franklin's fortress and the world beyond is both spatial and metaphorical.

Dwayne moved to this detached two-family row house shortly after it was built a dozen years ago, having lived in Newark for the first twenty-seven years of his life. He lives in one apartment with his parents; his sister and her children live in the other.

An exact replica of all the other houses on the block, the Franklins' house sits on a small yard separated from its neighbors by narrow alleyways that punctuate the rhythm of the high white brick stairs and ground floor garages running the full length of Exeter Street. There are many tidy gardens, but Dwayne's is outstanding: a precisely ordered plot of begonias and Daisy Millers in a succession of alternating rows. The carefully maintained gardens and newly paved driveways stand in contrast to the street itself, littered with broken glass and crowded with cars.

Exeter Street appears to be an island of respectability in a rough and menacing surround. Bounded by a highway on one end and Newark's city limits on the other, the transition from homeowner pride to urban decay is marked by tall apartment buildings on the corners. Once inside Newark, the street is a procession of shabby retail shops, empty lots, and abandoned cars. It is an effort, Dwayne Franklin suggests, holding on to middle-class propriety and security with the city lapping at your door.

When asked, "What do you like most about this neighborhood?" Dwayne said, "The cleanliness, okay, because right

across the street is Newark . . . And, I guess not just the cleanli-
ness, but the cooperation since we are on a borderline street
. . . People pretty much know each other." He disliked the cars
that go racing up and down the street. "We do have a tendency
to get people who come by at four o'clock in the morning
doing spinouts at the intersection" where Irvington meets New-
ark. "Those noisy cars are stolen cars . . . Nobody would burn
that much rubber off their own tires and expect to drive to
work the next day." The problem, of course, is that "by the
time the Irvington police arrive, and they do things very rap-
idly, the guy has spun out and gone across the border. And the
police have to get permission to go across the border."

Crime and fear figure prominently in Dwayne Franklin's
stories. He told us about an incident of vandalism and theft
from his sister's apartment that was thwarted by a formidable
series of locks and dead bolts.

> The police were called. The perpetrator left a wine bottle . . . I
> don't know how this person could have done it, but, well, my sis-
> ter had a roommate at the time so it was probably someone [the
> roommate] knew or someone that had something against him.
> And it was the roommate's stuff that was taken. [Interviewer:
> Nothing else was taken?] He couldn't go any further than that
> room because he had a lock on the side door, a shackle lock, so
> the vandal had no access to any other parts of the house.

He seems matter of fact about crime and calls the police fre-
quently. Dwayne

> asked the police if they were going to take the wine bottle left by
> the intruder and check it for prints. Of course, they said no. I
> mean it is a possibility that this person has a prior record. They
> ended up taking the bottle with them, but I think they threw it in
> the garbage because when I looked out front I saw them do that.

Many years earlier, Dwayne was

> downtown with a friend. We ran into these guys at the market,
> and went down about a block with them. The guy pulled a gun. I
> looked down the barrel of a gun. I fought one of them and he ran
> . . . I went to the police department and reported it but they
> didn't believe me . . . They just didn't take a report . . . Back then
> I was a little younger. Because of the guy I had with me, I think
> they didn't believe me . . . Had they checked our job IDs, they

might have acted a little differently. He worked for AT&T, but he didn't look like it.

More recently, Dwayne Franklin faced a gun again. He was accompanying his niece back from a Halloween costume party around the corner.

> We passed this group of guys. They spoke, so my niece spoke back. We got to the corner downhill, she looked back, she said run, here they come, and I said, well, go ahead. And so she ran to a neighbor's house and starting knocking on the door and ring-ing the bell. I didn't know where she went because down that way at night, it used to be dark before they cut the trees so the lights could show through. There was three of them, two of us. Two were chasing me, one was chasing her. I managed to get over to where she was, just to the neighbor's house, which was close to the corner down there. Before I did, though, I had to pass someone holding a gun. I had a knife. He fired the gun, and he missed me at close range, so I think it was a starter pistol. I went up on the porch and finally the neighbor stuck her head out the window and said what is going on here? And they left.

This time he didn't report the incident to the police. He could offer them nothing to go on and thought they wouldn't believe him.

> We didn't call the police on that one because we couldn't identify those people. And it was dark. It happened so quickly. It would have been no way that I could have even given them a descrip-tion of what the people had on . . . Plus, I had had a few drinks, so, you know, while I wasn't intoxicated, when you talk to a policeman and you've had a drink, they think you're drunk.

Despite his experiences, Dwayne believes "the police gener-ally do a good job in the community." During the last five years, he estimated that he has called the police four or five times, complaining to the taxicab commission, reporting a tree fallen across the street during a storm, reporting an acci-dent on the corner. He is unwilling, he said, to ignore crime or corruption.

Calling the police is simply good sense, and like not burn-ing good rubber off new tires, "it is the proper thing to do." You pay a price, he said, for not following through with legal matters. When we asked Dwayne a question about a hypotheti-

cal accident in which one of the children in the family was hit
by an automobile, but not injured, he replied,

> I would tell the driver that things relating to the accident are
> being handled by my attorney and if he wanted to know informa-
> tion pertaining to the child's condition, he should contact the
> lawyer. You know, if you tell the driver that the child is all right,
> you don't know who is sitting in there with him. You know, if
> anything goes wrong you have a problem . . . I've seen people in
> that predicament where they were the friends of drivers and expe-
> rienced very serious injuries, and they didn't do anything about
> it. And they are paying a price today.

According to Dwayne Franklin, the law and courts are
there to protect. Although they, like the police, don't always
succeed, they are worth the cost, Dwayne Franklin said. He
was emphatic that courts can "handle the problems of ordinary people" fairly well and that minorities didn't necessarily
have a harder time. Courts are fairly predictable, he added,
and "judges are generally honest in dealing with each case."
Courts are expensive, Dwayne commented, but not so much
that you would not use them if you really needed to. "You see,"
he explained to us, "I was afraid at one point when I first
started going into court. I was very nervous about it . . . It
was a new experience, you know, so I was a little nervous.
Court is always looked upon as this force." But with experience you discover, he said, that "It's a place you go to get justice. It is for you to get justice." Emphasizing the role of initiative and the sense of a layered organization, Dwayne added, at
least "it is a good place to start."

Dwayne Franklin has always worked at several jobs simultaneously. As a consequence, at thirty-nine years old, he has
had many and varied positions. When we interviewed him,
Dwayne was leaving a five-year stint as a welfare investigator
for the city. Prior to that he had worked as a ward clerk keeping medical records in the county hospital and as a paralegal
for the Rutgers University legal services bureau. When he was
younger, Dwayne worked for a trucking company and for a
chemical company, but for the past ten years or so he has
settled into his public service work. "You know, it's always
helping people who can't help themselves."

During this period, Dwayne also worked part-time as a private detective for local attorneys, and when we spoke he was completing the paperwork to obtain his private investigator's license. Unwilling to rely on the income from just one job, however, he is also about to begin another position, "moving across the desk," he told us, to represent the client rather than the government. Dwayne is joining a new program housed in the hospitals to help patients manage their medical payments and the associated paperwork. In addition, Dwayne Franklin is in the Air Force Reserve. The current four-year tour of duty follows eight years in the naval reserve and two years of active duty in the Navy. He also volunteers as a tutor and counselor at the local junior high school.

It is clear that the rules and regulations of formal organizations, such as welfare offices, hospitals, schools, courts, and the military, are Dwayne Franklin's métier. His familiarity with law and courts matured with his various jobs, and from those employment-related experiences Dwayne developed personal relationships with many of the people working in the courthouse. Nonetheless, Dwayne does not present nor seem to regard himself as an insider. He is a user of the system, he suggests, but his use, as was evident in his decisions about when to call the police, is careful, measured, and varied.

Rules and regulations define situations, and according to Dwayne Franklin, the prudent actor works within those constraints. Dwayne described several situations in which he defined his options and rights in terms of a formal rule or law. In the past, he explained, his easy deference was a matter of inexperience. For example, when he was much younger, working for the chemical company, he "had gotten some chemicals on my skin, and also my fingers smashed." He went to the doctor but,

> It wasn't a situation where workman's compensation would apply . . . A lot of the chemical smell had actually gotten into my body so that when I left work, I took the smell with me. It also got into my system internally, you could tell from when you go to the bathroom, the color. So, I quit . . . Had I been thinking I would have called OSHA because it was an occupational hazard to work there. And the company did blow up. Yeah, right after I left . . . I quit because I felt like it was endangering my life. I

*knew enough to quit and find a better job. I wish I had been a lit-
tle smarter back then.*

At other times, Dwayne treats the existing rules as intractable facts—not because he still lacks experience, but because
there seem to be no sensible alternatives. Thus, as he was leaving his position as a welfare investigator with the city, he was
owed sixteen days' vacation pay that he had not collected either
as days off or as compensation. "They have in our contract
that they prorate our vacation days. When I left, I had sixteen,
they prorated it to ten days, so they took six days away. But it
is in the contract. There is nothing I can do about it."

Although experience and rules may limit possible and practical action, Dwayne Franklin acknowledges that the rules can
be changed. Dwayne told us about a time that TRW provided
a mistaken credit report about him. When he inquired, he discovered that the company had a rather long delay between
receiving and posting new information. He wrote to the
company.

> But there was not much you could do, you know . . . They said
> that that was their recording procedures. They also said that the
> companies submit their information to them. They try and say it
> is the companies' problems and not theirs.

Now, Dwayne said, the situation is different.

> Since then, people have taken them to court . . . I read in the
> newspaper yesterday, in the business section, that New Jersey
> is not one of the states involved in the action against TRW
> although I believe the attorney general is looking into it now.
> But at this point, it has something to do with the Fair Credit
> [Reporting] Act. They are saying that TRW is not complying with
> the Fair Credit [Reporting] Act.

Accepting the boundaries drawn by law, Dwayne recognizes that there are alternatives within the law when things do
not work out satisfactorily the first time. Thus, he was ordered
to pay child support for his ex-wife's child by a previous husband. He appealed the decision and although he did not get
all the money back, and it seemed that "too much time had
lapsed between the time they told me I didn't have to pay and
when the light went off in my head telling me to go back and

get my money," the court order was eventually withdrawn. Another time, when his veteran's disability benefits were stopped because he and the doctor had failed to connect on two different appointments, he appealed the decision to the Veterans Administration. "I was seen by the local hearing board. They denied it, so I appealed to Washington . . . The local decision was reversed. I was reinstated."

Dwayne Franklin acknowledges that he may be more willing than others to work through legal channels. When we asked if he had ever been discriminated against or treated unfairly because of his age, sex, race, religion, or nationality, Dwayne Franklin said that he thought that he had been unable to rent an apartment once because he was African American. Despite his desire to take legal action, however, he deferred to his girlfriend's reluctance to formally complain.

> *I went to the apartment complex in Irvington and I noticed that no other black people live there. The super on the premises was very nosy. I was going to move in with my girlfriend and he asked if my girlfriend was going to work or to be home all day. The kind of questions the guy was asking was like, you know, why do you need to know that? The people that lived on the premises were coming out of their apartments to see if he was going to rent an apartment to us . . . We wanted to rent it, but then a lady came and said that it had been promised to someone else.*
>
> *I wanted to look into it a little further . . . I did contact the tax [bureau] and tried to find out who the actual property owner was, but because it was my girlfriend, we just didn't pursue it. A lot of people do not have faith in the judicial system for some reason. She may have faith in it now but she didn't back then.*

Dwayne explained that his girlfriend had been raised, as he had, as a Muslim but more strictly.

> *She was raised in that religion by her father. They told her, they taught me at one point, and they teach their followers, to distrust Caucasian people, and the court system seemed to them to be run by Caucasian people. So, they thought they would not be treated justly . . . I think she is still being pulled that way, but she is . . . now a Sunni Muslim, so they think differently. It is not as strict as it was.*

Dwayne Franklin's ex-girlfriend is currently appealing a ruling of the welfare department. He has been helping her with an administrative hearing because now "she realizes that you can't get what you want unless you go for help . . . especially the problem with welfare. You've got to request a hearing."

Despite Dwayne's advice to seek legal counsel, his father like his ex-girlfriend also refused to appeal what he thought was a costly error from the water department. Even though the elder Mr. Franklin owns several shops around the corner as well as the house the family lives in, the water bill of several thousand dollars was ridiculously excessive. When the Franklins complained, the city installed a new meter and reduced the bill because there clearly had been something wrong. In the end, however, the elder Mr. Franklin paid the adjusted bill, although Dwayne thought that they should appeal and get a further reduction. He went so far as to consult a lawyer, a friend at Seton Hall Law School, but his father declined the help and advice.

> My parents, they are like this: they would rather not pursue the legal route. I think they don't feel like being tied up in court. If it were me I would have done it. I really believe they were in the wrong. Unless you take them to court, you are almost telling them that they are right. If you're going to challenge them, you have to challenge them on a legal level. You can't just walk into the office and say, "We don't owe you money." Because even if you talk to that person, the best way to resolve it is in front of a judge. Let the jury decide whether we owe them money or not. There is a possibility that the company is negligent.

Dwayne Franklin's confidence in "pursuing the legal route," as he calls it, is not, as we have already seen, a rigid insistence that it is the only way to do things. He is not unaware of the downside. "We were going to go the legal route with it, but . . . time and cost."

> You know, the Irvington court system, you spend a day over there before the case is called. Chances are for one case you might have to go back two or three times. It's a big waste of time. Time is money.

Moreover, he recognizes the need to work around as well as through the rules, explicitly confessing ambivalence about *people who always "go by the book." Describing the way he handled some welfare fraud cases, he explained how you can sometimes do better and achieve your goals by working more informally.*

> *I chose not to take the people to court because they get put on probation, they pay the money to probation, the money that probation collects takes ten years for the welfare department to get it, and chances are if the person doesn't pay the complete restitution, the money goes to the county. So already you have lost control of the money. The department did pretty good with collecting the money outright.*

As a welfare officer, Dwayne is rather proud of the various efficiencies he was able to achieve. Yet his efforts have been hampered by his superior's tendency to "always goes by 'it's the guideline' . . . [even though] his interpretation of the guidelines have oftentimes been incorrect." His boss

> *likes to run [the department] like you are helping them, but you're not . . . wants the kind of investigator that is going to take somebody to court. If you ask him to write a letter, he'll give you a letter of rhetoric. I'll give you a letter spelling out exactly what you need to know . . . There were situations where we'd get calls from hospitals' collection agencies wanting to know when they were going to get paid. I'd be told, "Tell them to call back" or "Tell them to send a bill." Why get them to send a bill if you are not going to do anything with it? When we got the computer system, I set up certain programs on the word processor so that if a bill came in you could find out if we were responsible for it.*

In contrast to what Dwayne sees as mindless rule-following, he explained his approach.

> *I grew up and I was told that you had to have initiative in doing things. You had to improvise if other things didn't work. When you go to work, you go to work to get a job done. You don't go to work to shuffle paper around on a desk from one side to the other. You go to work to complete a project and move on to something else. And for the five years that I was there I would say that three of the years was spent shuffling paper around on the desk. It doesn't make sense to have stacks of paper if you can't go to it and get what you want. It's a paper chase.*

In the end, Dwayne felt useless. "I had to present a program that is not working for them and you can't really say anything to the people." The government needs to

> do something more about what they are giving people for welfare
> assistance . . . There is no way you can take care of purchasing
> your personal needs and the needs of a child, pay rent, and be
> able to live. They wind up getting evicted or put in a shelter.
> That's why there are so many people in shelters.

After having worked in a bureaucracy that values guidelines and rules over substance, Dwayne is moving to the hospital, as he said, to the other side of the desk, to represent the
needy against the system. It is also why, he said, he works on
Saturday mornings at the junior high school tutoring and
counseling kids.

Working in the welfare office, he felt that he was too often
hurting the people who needed him.

> Every time I was working on what I could to help the person,
> they suffered. If my director found out that I was helping this per-
> son, say, get their vacation approved or whatever, he would make
> it difficult for me and the client. I thought that was wrong.

The damage was exacerbated, Dwayne said, because
no one thought about these people as like themselves.
They lacked empathy. Some of the "people that work in the
office have received assistance. And the way they treat some of
the people, you wonder to yourself, why do they do that? You
were going through the same thing" at one time. "I've had a lot
of arguments with people at the office about how to treat
people but it got nowhere fast. All it did was make matters
worse for me."

Dwayne Franklin believes, however, that it was not only
rigid rule-following and lack of empathy that aggravated the
situation in the office. He thinks that he may have made
matters worse for himself, and for those he wanted to help,
because he crossed the boundary between public and private,
between personal and professional roles. He could not leave
things alone. He was not only writing computer programs and
developing systems to make the process more efficient and the
office more accountable, he was not only trying to secure bene-

*fits for needy people, which he thought was his job, but he
took the office's problems home and to the political arena.
And, he said, "when you go over authority, you really rock the
boat."*

*When the director said, "This is how it stands," I wouldn't hesi-
tate to call his boss and see what her opinion is, or call the may-
or's office or whatever it involves. Because I don't think the law
had stopped right there where I was standing.*

Standing before the Law

Before the Law stands a doorkeeper on guard. To this doorkeeper there comes a man from the country who begs for
admittance to the Law. But the doorkeeper says that he cannot admit the man at the moment. The man, on reflection,
asks if he will be allowed, then, to enter later. "It is possible," answers the doorkeeper, "but not at this moment."

FRANZ KAFKA, *The Trial*

"The law" . . . accumulates, but it never passes; at any in-
stant, it represents a totality. It is by definition complete,
yet its completeness does not preclude change. It is a human achievement, yet, by its reversible and lateral excur-
sions, and by its collective voice, it is not identifiably the
product of any particular individual or group.

CAROL J. GREENHOUSE, "Just in Time:
Temporality and the Cultural Legitimation of Law"

In the last chapter of *The Trial*, Joseph K is instructed by his manager
at the Bank to escort an Italian visitor on a tour of the local cathedral.
There he encounters a strange and solemn priest who describes himself as the prison chaplain and who immediately attempts to expose
K's delusions about his trial and the courts by telling a parable often
referred to, and separately published, as "Before the Law."

In this story, a man comes from the country to the city begging
admittance to the Law. A doorkeeper before the entrance tells the
man that he cannot enter just now and that he must wait. The doorkeeper dares the man to "try to get in without my permission," but
cautions him that were he do to so he would encounter a series of

increasingly powerful doorkeepers. Despite his belief that "the law should be accessible to every man and at all times," the man from the country decides that he must wait for permission to enter. He waits for years and at the end of his life when all else is becoming dim, he perceives "a radiance that streams inextinguishably from the door of the law." As he is dying, all of the man's experiences before the law condense into a single question: "why," he asks the doorkeeper, "if everyone strives to attain the Law . . . no one has come seeking admittance but me?" "No one but you could gain admittance through this door," the doorkeeper answers, "since this door was intended for you. I am now going to shut it."

Kafka's story is intentionally enigmatic as it provides K and the priest an opportunity to explore competing interpretations regarding the law and power on one hand and subjectivity and delusion on the other. Offered as a parable, the story emplots the relationship between the man and the law, disclosing and typifying their respective moral positions. The law is depicted as remote, removed from the man and his life in the country not only by the distance he traveled to seek admittance but by the ever-increasing relays of power represented by the hierarchy of doorkeepers. The parable places the man perpetually outside of the law's space, unable to receive permission to enter.

But at the end of the parable, the autonomy of law's authority is shown to have been somewhat illusory, sustained all along by the man's cooperation and deference. Rather than being separate and remote, there is a vital and direct connection between the man and the law. This connection is expressed as a physical linkage: as the years pass, as if by some transference of energy, the man shrinks while the doorkeeper grows ever larger. In the end, the man's eyes "grow dim" while a radiant light streams from the law. The doorkeeper finally discloses this vital connection and shuts the door.

Kafka's parable serves as a powerful description of a form of legal consciousness we, following Kafka, call "before the law." Apprehending the law as having an ontology and authority that is severed from the multiple concrete social practices and relationships that enact it, the law confronts us as existing outside of everyday life. Despite its constitution and enactment in particular social exchanges, legality confronts people as external, unified, and objective. In this interpretation of law, as in Kafka's story, the law is rendered inert rather than dynamic, a place rather than a system of ideas or persons. Perceived as independent of human action, desire, or interest, the law is depicted as impartial. It achieves its impartiality and objectivity through a deliberate indifference to the particularities of biography or personality. Thus it is understood that as they stand before the law, all persons appear and are treated the same.

Although legality is perceived as a general, objective, and impartial power, it is not seen as omnipotent. The technical procedures and rules of law are understood to define the boundaries of legal agents' legitimate action. These procedures and rules not only constrain legality, they are also responsible for its capacity for impartiality and objectivity. Because rules instruct and constrain legal actors, the powers of those actors, and their possibilities for partiality, are confined.

Those same rules that limit the play of discretion and personal preference also create a division of labor and relay of authority that enables action without that action being reducible to any single actor. People experience themselves before the law whenever they apprehend the consequences produced by this organization without identifying the mechanisms that accomplish those effects. They describe a powerful, apparently autonomous place of ordered rationality whose capacity transcends particular human actions.

People often experience the law as a space outside of everyday life. Law and everyday life are seen in juxtaposition and possibly opposition, rather than connected and entwined. The distance between law and everyday life is a chasm through which mundane and personal matters pass and become transfigured in awesome but also costly ways. One pays with time, as the man from the country did with his life, seeking access to the timelessness of law.

Thus, in certain situations and interactions—for reasons we will identify—people find themselves before the law, struck by its externality and coherence; they act from and reproduce this interpretation. Positioning themselves outside of the law, people express in words the reified character of the law; they enact it in their behaviors. But *how* is the effect of externality, unity, and distinctiveness achieved? How do innumerable discrete, often disjointed and sometimes contradictory, transactions cumulate to produce the experience of singularity and coherence? In other words, through what social practices and discursive forms is the law apprehended as an object: thinglike and inert, powerful and permanent, fixed and remote?

We suggest that legality's appearance of externality, coherence, majesty, and timelessness is achieved by greater degrees of formal organization. Confronting the organized features of law, people abstract and reify legality so that what is partial becomes general, what is transitory is made timeless, and what is historical and contingent is treated as permanent. Before the law, the human social production of legality is eclipsed. Its everyday presence is erased. In this view, the formal institutional apparatus of law is synonymous with legality.

Finally, much like Kafka's supplicant standing before the law, the attribution of legality's power derives in large part from the apprehension of it as external and unified. Imagining that entering the law's space required some special permission, the man from the country actively disqualified himself from entering the law. Similarly, people make decisions and interpretations that defer to the law's status as distinctive and elsewhere.

Reification of Legality

"Objects in mirror are closer than they appear."

In the experiences and incidents Rita Michaels recounted, she acted upon an understanding of the law and her life as representing different orders of existence. To Rita, her affairs were immediate, subjective, and trivial in contrast to what she described as the permanent, remote, and solemn public realm of law and legality. Furthermore, to Rita Michaels the differences between law and her life are not just a matter of degree. Rather, to her the law seems transcendent, literally incomparable to the mundane affairs of her personal life. The law, existing on a different plane, occasionally descends into the everyday, but only when the fabric of ordinary interactions is ruptured. Once order is restored, the law disappears from view. Legality thus seems to exist outside of any particular time and place. It seems to enframe daily social life, determining its course without being present in it.

The lack of connection between law and ordinary life was articulated by many people. For these persons, encountering the law in the course of their lives—whether it involved being stopped by a police officer, being audited by the IRS, or serving on a jury—represented a disruption. Moreover, in deciding whether to mobilize the law, people often thought about it as "breaking frame," that is, rupturing normal relationships, practices, and identities. When asked what action he had taken in response to what he described as the deterioration of his neighborhood, Don Lowe disavowed the possibility of doing anything out of the ordinary.

> *I'm not a person who goes down and pickets or creates a distur-*
> *bance like that. I'm a normal taxpaying person. I work, come*
> *home, pay my bills, pay my taxes, and, you know, try to keep a*
> *low profile.*

For this man, being "normal," a word he used frequently, clearly entailed "keeping a low profile." Although he was upset by the fact that his neighborhood was "being ground up," he refused to break frame. He believed he had to accept the neighborhood decay in order to sustain his identity as normal.

Rita Michaels's, Dwayne Franklin's, and Don Lowe's views of legality are starkly different from the theoretical description of legality we offered in the preceding chapters. Rather than perceiving law and legality as a constellation of related actors and actions, objectified in particular material forms and enacted by historical subjects, for these and many other persons legality has an ontological status apart from its concrete manifestations. Theirs is a dehumanized vision of legality. While legality might find expression in human action and intention, such as the judge's pronouncement, the police officer's testimony, or the jury's deliberation, to people like Rita, Dwayne, and Don, legality is only incidentally related to such enactments. As Dwayne Franklin said, "I don't think the law stopped right there where I was standing." The observable, discrete, and particular world of social interaction is a vessel for the legal, which exists independently of these forms.

Rita Michaels, and many others with whom we spoke, expressed such a reified view of the law. By that term we refer to the tendency to impart to historically specific processes and behaviors a thinglike quality. According to Berger and Pullberg, reification is a process that "converts the concrete into the abstract, then in turn concretizes the abstract."[1] In the context of Rita Michaels's stories, the specific pronouncements, testimony, and deliberations are abstracted into something apprehended or labeled as law. The process is completed when this abstraction is itself concretized, endowed with the ontological independence of a thing that exists separately from these empirical manifestations.

In part, reification is achieved through language. The linguistic formulations we use to refer to certain forms of social action mask the specific practices that constitute those actions. Previously we alluded to the term "the law" in precisely this way (and have been awkwardly trying to avoid such unreflective formulations in this text). The ubiquitous but unnamed *they* (as in "they say that . . .") similarly accomplishes reification insofar as it abstracts from the beliefs and utterances of many persons a singular view that it then attributes to an anonymous *they*.

The process, however, is not only linguistic. Rita Michaels's view of police and courts as existing on "a higher level" (despite empirical evidence to the contrary), her reluctance to call "her" police to manage neighborhood conflicts, her deference to her former husband's lawyer's advice all enacted, without explicitly referring to, a reified legality. In each of these instances, Rita Michaels acted in relation to something she understood to be operating outside of ordinary human relations in the everyday, empirical world. Her decisions and actions acknowledged legality's existence as she deferred to its capacity to shape and constrain her, and others', behavior.

As these examples illustrate, the reification of legality, in particular the final concretization of legality into a thinglike entity, entails more than a description claiming in effect "this is the way the world is." Endowing legality (or any institution or social phenomenon for that matter) with the ontological independence of a thing involves more than passive reflection upon an object. It involves the active construction of the object and, at the same time, a disavowal of that construction.

Reification always entails a transference of power. When the law is reified, the internal connection between legality and particular social action is severed. Evidence of this severing was often expressed in people's assessment of legal institutions. In many instances, after strongly condemning particular actors or practices of a particular court, police department, or government agency, people would conclude by observing that "the system" or "the courts" or "the police" were in general "just," "effective," or "honest."

Don Lowe, the middle-aged business manager who refused to take any action to save his neighborhood from a deteriorating infra-

structure, declining property values, and infrequent municipal services, still believed that "the system" worked. Later in the interview,
he expressed dissatisfaction with another aspect of the law. Having
had two experiences serving on juries, Don Lowe said that the general practice of jury selection was "manipulated" and "stacked
against the prosecution." According to Don Lowe, jurors are selected
for their demographic characteristics and the predispositions these
characteristics are likely to represent.

> They try to get people near the defendant's age. They try to get
> minorities if it is a minority case, this is a fact, this is not just
> being . . . I'm just telling you the way it is. If you are unemployed
> or you are on welfare it's even better. They also try to look for sin-
> gle young girls. Whether they are black, white, or Spanish, they
> are preferred also. They seem to be more in their own world, not
> in the reality of what is going on around them. Like they don't
> read the paper or watch the news and so forth. They are not too
> attached to the problems of the world. Older people they don't
> want. And they don't want people who have authority because
> they are not sympathetic to a lot of these people.

Paradoxically, Don Lowe concluded his discussion by observing
that the "system is decent" and "justice prevails." The apparent contradiction between his indictment of the system of jury selection (as
"manipulated" by "unscrupulous lawyers") and his final pronouncement that the system is both legitimate and effective illustrates how
a reified law is isolated from the observable world of particular actors
or practices. For Don Lowe, because law is only partially or incom-
pletely represented in the observable and material world, the law
cannot be assessed on the basis of that reality.

The most significant consequence of this severing of law from
particular social action is a reversal in the moral and causal relationship that is understood to exist between conduct and its reified form.
Rather than perceiving legality as a product of human interactions
expressing the intentions, desires, needs, and values of specific persons and groups at specific times, people endow the law with the
capacity to construct those persons and groups. Rather than seeing
persons as the authors of the law, people understand the law as the
author of individuals, their behaviors and needs, desires and values.
In short, failing to perceive the emergent and reciprocal relationship

between their experiences and behaviors and legality, people like Rita Michaels disqualify or subordinate their own experiences and perceptions before the law. The thing becomes the standard of objective reality against which the subjective, concrete, and immediate is assessed and interpreted.

Reification is not an inevitable feature of consciousness, however. The social world is not uniformly or constantly externalized and objectified in this way. While we heard abundant references to a reified law in the accounts of many of our respondents, there were many accounts of legality that acknowledged it as a human and contingent enterprise. Moreover, sectors of social life that are reified at certain times and places are understood very differently at other times and places. This historical and situational variability that characterize processes of reification thus provoke questions regarding when, why, and with what consequences legality is reified.

To pursue these questions, we read our respondents' interviews to identify those moments when legality appears to them to be most "lawlike" or "thinglike." In particular, we looked for expressions, instances, anecdotes, and allusions in which identifiable human actors and human qualities were absent or denied. By identifying these moments we hoped to specify the conditions under which such reification is likely to occur.

Based on our reading, described in some detail in the pages that follow, we suggest that there are certain features of social organization that facilitate the process of reification. In other words, the behaviors, roles, and relationships, and cultural norms that come to be reified as "the law" are those that have been rationalized (to use Weber's term) or disciplined (a slightly, but not entirely, different process described by Foucault). These rationalized and disciplined practices produce different experiences and outcomes from the social practices we generally refer to, and experience, as everyday.

Historically, of course, reification was achieved through the invocation of supernatural beings as causal agents determining the affairs of the world. In the premodern world where individual lives were wholly contained within the communities in which people were born, lived, and died and where social conduct was marked by its similarity rather than its variability, the world should have appeared transparent. Action never extended very far beyond the reach of the actor or cumulated to produce consequences and effects that could not be traced back to their enactment. In fact, the very concreteness and transparency of social action may have shaped the form reification historically assumed: the suprahuman actor, eternal and elsewhere, often acting through nature.[2]

In a more secular but equally reified world, dehumanization is achieved by locating power within social institutions, such as the law, the state, the economy, or other disciplinary apparatuses. The characteristic experience people point to when they express the reified form of legality, for example, appears to be achieved through a specific type of social organization. The multitudinous, discrete, often disjointed, and sometimes contradictory transactions that some of us describe in lawmaking, litigation, enforcement, and judgment cumulate to produce "the law" to the extent that they are characterized by the following: the specialization and coordination of tasks, hierarchy of authority, role-based relationships, and reliance on inscription or the use of written rules and records. To put this somewhat differently, legality appears most "thinglike" in its most bureaucratized qualities: those that are suprahuman, impartial, rational, objective.

Dimensions of Legal Consciousness

In the following pages, we describe this reified view of legality as it was expressed to us by our respondents. We interpret these stories of law in terms of four dimensions of legal consciousness. We refer to these analytically distinguishable aspects of social action as normativity, constraint, capacity, and, finally, the time and space of law. These dimensions of legal consciousness should be understood as axes of interpretation that provide alternative vantage points from which to view legality. As we describe the dimensions of legal consciousness, we want to emphasize that our theorizing about legality and analysis of the transcripts proceeded interactively so that these are empirically generated as well as logically deduced categories. Having worked with these categories to identify references in our respondents' interviews that might fall within and would appropriately be described by these dimensions, and having returned to the theoretical literature on the structure of social action, we imagine that these dimensions may constitute the most basic and significant variables for describing not only legality, but any instance of social action.[3]

In the schema we call "before the law," the dimensions effectively reify legality, simultaneously ridding social action of human agency, while constructing the thinglike nature of "the law." This conception of legality as a distinctive, coherent, and autonomous entity enframing daily life enacts many of the same qualities that liberal legal institutions claim for themselves. This then is the law's own story as well as our respondents' stories. We will talk of the significance of this correspondence in the conclusion to this chapter.

Normativity: The Impartiality of Law

> A consistent system of abstract rules . . . [and] the application of these rules to particular cases.
> MAX WEBER, *On Law in Economy and Society*

> An essential characteristic of law is its generality . . . a body of general principles, not a collection of special commands . . . Law being a general principle applying indifferently to all cases which in the future can arise under it.
> JOSEPH BEALE, *A Treatise on the Conflict of Laws*

Any account of social action or phenomena, including legality, is not just a description but also a statement of the normative grounds "whereby it may be justified."[4] What we refer to as the dimension of normativity describes people's beliefs about the ways in which parties to legal interactions, both professional and lay, should act. It also specifies why law should or should not be invoked, obeyed, or resisted. In short, references to normativity describe the moral bases of legality. As such, the normative understandings of law both inform and are revealed by individuals' decisions to mobilize the law, their evaluations of legal processes and actors, and finally their own invocations and uses of law outside of formal legal settings.

When people describe what we are calling reified legality, they repeatedly refer to the law as impartial and objective. Impartiality corresponds to the absence of a historical, biographical, and socially located, and thus "interested," self. Legality is disassociated from persons who have particular needs and relationships. According to this conception, individual actors—that is neighbors, bosses, spouses—have only partial views of situations, views that express and reflect among other things their interests. By contrast, legality, not being embodied in any individual, is experienced as existing outside of particular interests or positions. It is this unsituated externality that endows legality (and particular legal decision makers) with the impartiality that constitutes its authority for many people.

Rita Michaels's reified view of legality was expressed in the validation she received from the judge. Whereas her neighbors lacked information ("one never knows what goes on inside someone else's house") and could be swayed by the misrepresentations of her husband that she was "a terrible person," Rita Michaels perceived the judge as informed (having "read all" and "done his homework") and impartial.

This same view of legality was later challenged in her experience with the police in the trial involving her son's car accident. She expected an objective report, an account of what had happened at the accident. Instead, the performance of the police officer's role as legal agent was contaminated, Rita Michaels believed, by his relationship to a neighbor, a relationship that was particularistic and thus partial. Her perception that the policeman misrepresented the facts—when he claimed that he knew nothing about the accident and that the old woman could not have been involved—humanized legality and as a consequence disappointed Rita Michaels. She was perplexed and disturbed precisely because the lawlike nature of the law broke down.

The impartiality imputed to legality is not just a claim for the objectivity of the law's agents; the objectivity inheres in what the law itself will or should cover. In other words, the conception of an objective law defines an arena of action that is appropriate for public attention. Respondents, including Rita Michaels, often police this boundary separating the law from the private worlds of self-interest and individual actions. Individuals' decisions to mobilize the law thus often involved the crucial interpretive move of framing a situation in terms of some public, or at least general, set of interests.

In Rita Michaels's statement that she doesn't "use her police that way," the referent to "that way" was a situation of individual interest. Other respondents articulated a similar standard for mobilizing the law, a standard that disqualified the personal from legal significance or legitimacy. Claudia Greer, a minister and licensed practical nurse living in Camden, complained to us about the conditions in her neighborhood: "the loitering, the noise, the graffiti, the crime, and the boarded-up buildings." When we asked her whether she had ever called the police about these or any other neighborhood problems,

Claudia Greer proudly responded, "I haven't bothered the police . . . I don't bother the police." She then went on to specify the conditions under which she would "bother" the police.

> *I might go to the police, but then again I might not. If they were*
> *destructive, or fighting, or, you know, then I might. I'd call the*
> *police . . . if there are gunshots or something like that, then,*
> *because everybody's threatened then. (emphasis ours)*

Notably, in the above statement it was not entirely the severity of the action (the firing of a gun) that Claudia Greer gave as the reason for calling the police; it was the potential for collective harm that was invoked.

In another interview, a respondent similarly disqualified mundane problems as legal matters, in this case for being petty, and even infantile.

> *I think that . . . if it's a neighbor, you should try and resolve dis-*
> *putes yourself. I don't think the police are there for that purpose,*
> *to be honest with you . . . We have a police force to solve, you*
> *know, to take care of crimes. Not to be our daddies and mom-*
> *mies, because we can't handle something ourselves. (Gretchen*
> *Zinn)*

Many persons rejected self-interest not only as a grounds for calling the police, but even more commonly as a motive for using the courts. Many persons condemned what they saw as excessive litigiousness, characterizing it as greedy and self-serving.

> *My husband and I feel that people are too sue-happy today. (Amy*
> *Shull)*

> *I think the United States is too litigation conscious . . . I just can-*
> *not believe that there is virtually nothing you can do without*
> *someone challenging you on it, you know. And I think if we all,*
> *if we tried less to make money off of medical accidents or what-*
> *ever, we'd all be a lot happier. (Ann Shields)*

For some people, refusing to use the law, even if it requires accepting injury or harm, is an indication of moral strength and independence. Sophia Silva criticized a friend of hers, Joanne, for suing a neighbor after that neighbor had run over Joanne's child. Sophia Silva's criticism of Joanne's action is drawn implicitly as Sophia describes her parents' response to a similar situation many years before.

> *I hope you don't have to interview Joanne, but my friend*
> *Joanne's daughter was on a bicycle, and a neighbor was coming*
> *out of her driveway and the child was knocked down, and they*
> *sued [the driver] . . . And I myself would not . . . I remember as a*
> *child sitting on the pavement, and I was run over by the car of*
> *the people next door. Now you have to remember that my parents*
> *had no money, this was Depression time, and my father was*
> *bringing home five dollars a week . . . And the car backed over*
> *my leg, and my parents refused any medical help. To this day I*
> *have a limp.*

Carolyn Robinson told a story with a similar message. First, to endure injury without complaining is a morally superior way of behaving. And second, such restraint was more characteristic of an earlier time, before the United States became "sue-happy."

> *When I was twenty-one years old the ceiling in my office fell on*
> *my head. And that's how I got engaged. [My husband] thought I*
> *was going to die. A nail this big missed going through the center*
> *of my head. There I was lying there with this concussion and . . .*
> *the next day he put the ring on my finger . . . I did not sue the*
> *company. We didn't do things like that in those days.*

When the law was mobilized by persons expressing a reified sense of legality, the situation was often described as posing some real or potential collective harm. The possibilities of others' being hurt or suffering some loss justified, where narrow self-interest did not, the mobilization of law. Thus, when Dwayne Franklin called the police, it was for fallen trees and automobile accidents, as well as burglars. In these instances, he said, "It was the proper thing to do."

In another example, Carol Dealy was concerned about what she saw as a mounting trash problem developing in a neighbor's garage. The garbage collection trucks had not picked up the accumulating refuse and the place thus became a magnet for more trash. It was the proverbial attractive nuisance, a concept whose technical terms were unfamiliar to Carol Dealy but whose meaning and legal status she seemed to comprehend. Unable to get the city to address the situation, she began to think of other ways to get a response and believed that if it were a threat to neighborhood children, the police might come.

I'm afraid because you know children are very inquisitive . . .
And if they see something like that it's like, well, let's go inside
and check it out. So, I'm beginning to think that maybe . . . some-
one could really go in there and get seriously hurt.

Sophia Silva, after having been critical of her friend Joanne for being litigious, revealed that she had, after all, been a plaintiff in a lawsuit. Having slipped on a piece of fruit in a supermarket, Sophia sued the store and collected thousands of dollars in damages. In explaining her reasons for bringing the suit, she observed, "I did sue, because it would be hard to think of some senior citizen slipping on that." Thus, the injury or harm that she presumably suffered was not offered as the grounds for her lawsuit. Sophia Silva conjured up the possibility of others' being harmed, in particular older and more vulnerable others, and implied that her suit was, in fact, on their behalf.

A thirty-four-year-old personnel officer expressed a remarkably similar sentiment in telling us about a lawsuit he had considered initiating against his physician. Ralph Jeffers believed he had unnecessary cataract surgery and had suffered permanent damage to his eyes as a result. After consulting with an attorney, Ralph Jeffers decided not to sue the physician, but stated that one of the principal reasons he had seriously considered going through with the suit was to protect others.

I would have liked to have gotten a little bit of money, that
wouldn't have hurt. And I would have liked to have gotten at-
tention to the fact that this guy was not practicing real well.
Because the majority of his patients were very elderly people com-
ing in and out. They may not be aware that this guy might be
doing cataract surgery on them when he didn't need to.

The importance of a collective purpose in using the law was most explicitly stated by Jules Magnon. "I don't have to be afraid to pursue justice. As long as I am doing something for everyone's benefit." Nor, Jules Magnon continued, should the pursuit of justice be impeded by self-interested or affective relationships. "Friendship should not interfere," he told us.

The sincerity of Sophia Silva's, Jules Magnon's, or Ralph Jeffers's altruistic motives is not, of course, the issue. What is important is the perception that such a casting is necessary. Through such a vocabulary of motive,[5] the law is constructed and apprehended as impartial.

Constraint

> Bureaucracy . . . evokes the slowness, the ponderousness, the routine, the complication of procedures . . . Impersonal rules delimit, in great detail, all the functions of every individual within the organization. They prescribe the behavior to be followed in all possible events.
>
> MICHEL CROZIER, *The Bureaucratic Phenomenon*

> Institutional arrangements constrain individual behavior by rendering some choices unviable, precluding particular courses of action, and restraining certain patterns of resource allocation.
>
> PAUL DIMAGGIO AND WALTER POWELL, *The New Institutionalism in Organizational Analysis*

In referring to legality, respondents would often allude to the determinacy of rationalized and structured action. Coming before the law, individuals encounter, of course, human actors: embodied, uttering their own words, and making particular decisions. Nonetheless, in face of this corporeal, particular, and undeniably human action, people construct a transcendent and reified law by focusing on the ways in which the observed behavior is seemingly constrained. While recognizing that there are things that the law should do (i.e., operate impartially), respondents also recognize that there are things that the law cannot do.

In a reified law, people locate constraints in rules and regulations. These rules seem to produce effects independently of human action and afford legal decision makers little choice in interpreting or acting upon matters before them. In the face of such constraint, respondents suggest that legal actors and subjects, including themselves, are, to paraphrase Durkheim, "acted upon, but they know not by whom." Legal actors are understood to be, to a large extent, programmed by instructions that eliminate the possibility of human intervention. Respondents construct a reified law by ignoring discretion and commenting upon the relative absence of intentionality and will.

As in Kafka's story "Before the Law," this sense of intractability of law is often expressed by the image of hierarchy, the relay of increasingly powerful doorkeepers that dwarf, and in some sense render unnecessary, the authority of any particular doorkeeper. This sense of controlled sequence is at the heart of modern bureaucracy and legally regulated action. The specialization of tasks is coordinated through a circuitry of rules and regulations that appear to take the place of human action or decision making.

In the view of most citizens, judges occupy the pinnacle of this hierarchy of decision making. Yet even their discretion and authority are notably constrained by the facts, by precedent, or by what numerous respondents simply referred to as "the paper." Thus, Millie Simpson told us that because the judge "just had to read the papers," she did not repeat the story of how her car was taken and involved in an accident. She believed that the judge's action was determined by the previous court exchanges and the papers he had before him. He had, she thought, no degrees of freedom within which to act. Rita Michaels also observed that the judge who had awarded her divorce was constrained by the paper and the facts reported there. "He did his homework," she had commented.

The authority of the paper and the facts committed to paper are thus understood by many to preempt, or render irrelevant, the discretionary power of official legal actors, including judges. Nell Pearson, a thirty-five-year-old white author, told us about having once gone to small-claims court to recover money from her ex-roommates for some unpaid bills:

> I could not believe this judge. We sat in this little room with this man, I had my receipts in my hand, . . . and he spent a half an hour haranguing us about why can't women live together, and . . . why don't [we] live in dormitories, and we explained we weren't students and he would just go on into this tirade about how women can't get along with each other. In the end, he awarded me the money, because I had the receipts in my hand.

Nell Pearson described the judge as sexist (asking "why women can't live together") and out of control ("haranguing" them for half an hour, in a "tirade"). Yet, despite this perception of him as frenzied, at the end of her story in an almost offhand and perfunctory way, she depicted him as being tamed by the text. Confronting the receipts, even the most unpredictable, irrational, or emotional decision maker must defer.

Because of the constraints that are perceived to be operating to shape human action, the law is also understood to be predictable. This quality allows citizens to anticipate and define matters before them in terms of their supposed legal character. In other words, they often defer to the constraint of the law.

Voicing this understanding of legality, Ben Thompson, an African American man, explained his failure to take any action in a situation in which he believed he had been discriminated against. Having worked for a food service management company for many years, Ben Thompson claimed that he was not paid the same as others who had preceded him in the position. Yet, he claimed,

> [there] was not a lot I could do. I spoke to them about it, and
> you know, they said, they [came] up with a grading system or
> grade unit or operation, . . . and [said] the most you could get in
> an increase is a certain amount.

Speaking hesitantly and somewhat unsure of the technical details on which his claim was rejected, Ben Thompson expressed the futility of challenging his superior in the face of the "grading system," a mythical doorkeeper that constrained his boss and seemingly justified what Ben Thompson believed was an injustice.

Increasingly, social reality is reified in the abstract space of statistical graphs, actuarial tables, and systems of classification. Such representations come to preempt the particular persons, relationships, and behaviors from which they are constructed. These ways of representing the world extract people from their historical and social contexts and construct them as cases, data points, or simply as bearers of some social characteristic, such as gender or race. These actuarial practices locate authority and responsibility within impersonal representations. In doing so, they immobilize the traditional bases of resistance and challenge.[6] In failing to express his dissatisfaction with his pay and position, Ben Thompson deferred to the authority of these actuarial representations.

Capacity

> Law makes long spokes of the short stakes of men.
>
> WILLIAM EMPSON, "Legal Fiction"

> A government of laws and not of men.
>
> JOHN ADAMS, "Novanglus"

> A judge articulates her understanding of a text, and as a
> result, somebody loses her freedom, his property, his chil-
> dren, even his life . . . Thus, what may be described as a
> problem of will with respect to the individual becomes, in
> an institutional context, primarily a problem in social or-
> ganization.
>
> ROBERT COVER, "Violence and the Word"

All of our respondents recognized that, despite constraints, the law
acted and produced powerful effects. These effects are varied: property is created and rights validated at the same time as claims are
ignored and standing denied. By legal effects, we mean both action
and inaction. We use the term *capacity* to refer to our respondents'
understandings of this productive side of legality. From whom or
from what are legal effects generated? In a reified law, people recognized that the same features of social organization that limit and
constrain human action also make action possible. Recognizing
those diverse effects of law, respondents locate legal efficacy and capacity in institutions and organizations as opposed to individual
actors. For instance, the same hierarchical organization that constrains legal action is also capable of instigating action. Socially
structured behavior enables individuals to operate by proxy and produce results that, in terms of their scope and durability, extend beyond the capacity of any individual. Thus, outcomes exceed the immediate and observable and imply, but do not necessarily reveal, the
invisible threads of organization that authorize and enable action.
The surplus between what is understood to be individual capacity
and the reverberating outcomes is frequently attributed to "the law."

This capacity associated with bureaucratic structure is well understood in the context of modern criminal justice, where the organizational capacity links the judge's word with the violent acts of the
jailer or the executioner. "The context of judicial utterance," Robert
Cover writes,

is institutional behavior in which others, occupying pre-existing roles, can be expected to act, to implement, or otherwise to respond in a specified way to the judge's interpretation. Thus, the institutional context ties the language act of practical understanding to the physical acts of others in a predictable, though not logically necessary, way.[7]

Thus, the rational organization of an array of agencies (police, the bar, the courts, prisons) involving thousands of actors and decision makers (doctors, judges, attorneys, juries, janitors, and executioners) imparts to mere words the capacity to inflict pain and death.

Respondents provide evidence of apprehending the effects of this organizational capacity when they describe something happening in law, but cannot account for how it was produced or by whom it was produced. For example, in the case we presented at the beginning of this book, Millie Simpson was first found guilty of having an uninsured vehicle and leaving the scene of an accident and several weeks later, on appeal, found not guilty. She was unable to describe the process that produced this final outcome. Millie described her sense of mystification.

> They called me and we went up, you know, to the table. And I don't even know what the judge said, I couldn't even understand what he was saying. And the lawyer told me, he said, "Okay," he said, "that's it, it's all over." I was right there and I don't even know . . . I didn't even know what he was talking about.

Bess Sherman (whose stories we present in chapter 6) described an ongoing series of difficulties she had securing disability payments under SSI. Over sixty-five and recently having undergone surgery for cancer, she was unable to complete all the paperwork necessary to have her disabled status officially certified. After visiting numerous doctors and welfare and Social Security offices, a doctor she was consulting acted on her behalf. Bess told us she didn't know how exactly he did it, or why, only that he said he would take care of it. Very soon after, she received documentation of her disability.

> He was talking through something. He had this tape thing, and then he wrote it in writing, on paper . . . I'm not knowing what they're going to put on the paper. I'm telling them the case, but still I'm not knowing what they're going to put on the paper and turn back to the Social Security, and that's the way it works.

Gretchen Zinn, after characterizing her experience serving on a jury as "interesting, very interesting," alluded to this enhanced capacity of organized action. The deliberation and collective judgment of the jury was something different from the opinion of an individual juror.

> *[Interviewer: What made it interesting?] The presentation of the case and then the way the jury sort of comes together to make a verdict, . . . I found it interesting, you know, . . . it just, . . . the whole process. Not any part of it.*

Respondents are not always mystified by the capacity of institutional action; nor do they always interpret or experience this capacity positively. In fact, the most frequent references to the institutional capacity of this sort are to the ways in which it obstructs, denies, confuses, and complicates.

Speaking about her difficulty getting reimbursed by Blue Cross, Gretchen speculated:

> *I remember getting list upon list upon list of all the prescriptions for the whole year from the pharmacy and the reasons and the diagnoses from the doctor, I mean it took a long time to do, send it in, and [I] never got a penny from them, never heard from them . . . What they said is that they never got it, and I, I just really questioned that they didn't get it . . . [T]hey sometimes make it so difficult . . . the whole process is so difficult that it's almost geared up so that some people will, particularly an elderly person, will just simply give up on it.*

· What is significant about Gretchen Zinn's account of her experience is her sense that this is not a failure of organizational action, or an unanticipated cost of bureaucratic function. Her assertion that the organization is "geared up *so that*" clients will "give up" describes a structure designed intentionally to produce that outcome.

Raymond Johnson suggested that the economy creates pressures so that companies and government agencies are unable to provide services or to respond to complaints. Businesses and government agencies have ways of putting you off, he said:

> *In other words, they drag their feet. Or, they say no, with the hopes that you wouldn't pursue it any further . . . maybe with a stern voice . . . making you call back . . . talk to a supervisor. A lot of time, and I imagine that is more prevalent today, with the*

economy the way it is, if they can get you to give up after the ini-
tial request, that's what they want.

Here, Raymond Johnson articulates what every bureaucrat knows: whatever the product or service, they cannot provide for all who deserve or request it. Welfare offices, police, social workers, consumer protection agencies, prosecutors—all agencies servicing the public—must ration their resources devoting limited time and energy to the never-ending flow of requests for service.[8] Because the demand is greater than the resources, part of the organizational capacity is to "convince" the citizen that it is not worth the effort.

Well, sometimes they'll say that it's one thing and then they'll say,
"Oh, we didn't know, this here needs to be done also." I guess
they'll kind of try to convince you. (Jane Elliot)

Trying to obtain reimbursements from Medicare, Allen Horner commented on what he referred to as the institutional culture that frustrates even those who are adept at navigating bureaucratic structures.

Now, I think I'm pretty together, okay? And I know how to do
these things. And I send them stuff, I keep an exact copy of every-
thing I send them and they'll come back and say, "You didn't
send this, you didn't send that, you didn't establish this, you
didn't . . . And what they put you through. I mean, there were
times when you complain, I mean you wrote letters, I explained
in elaborate detail. I resubmitted. Months, and months, and
months and months. I mean, you just, after a while, want to
scream to high heaven.

Time and Space

> The law constantly writes itself on bodies. It engraves it-
> self on parchments made from the skin of its subjects. It
> articulates them in juridical corpus. It makes book out of
> them.
>
> MICHEL DE CERTEAU, *The Practice of Everyday Life*

> I wasted time, and now doth time waste me.
>
> SHAKESPEARE, *King Richard II*, 5.5.49

In addition to its normativity, constraint, and capacity, legality is described by the way it organizes time and occupies space. This time-space dimension of legal consciousness is perhaps the most salient feature of a reified law. Here, respondents depict legality as timeless and transcendent, quite different from the here and now of everyday life. While commonplace social interactions are experienced as momentary, recurrent, and ever changing, legality is described as constant and immutable.[9] In short, when the law is reified it appears to stand outside of time.

Of course, people understand that law changes and develops. People know that new laws are passed and old laws amended and revoked. They acknowledge that contracts are revised and wills rescinded. But when people imagine themselves standing before the law, they conceive of legality—if not any particular law or legal instrument—as timeless. Legality anchors and limits the speed and range of change and thus the compass of human will (or whim). For instance, what marks a commitment as legal is the perception that there are higher costs and more significant limitations to changing existing arrangements and expectations. In this sense, legality is understood to bind the effects of passing time.

Legality seems to extend the linear, finite, and irreversible lifetime of any individual. It accomplishes this largely through its emphasis on precedent and continuity. For the law, relevant time exists long before and beyond the present. Thus, the law symbolizes "all-times" in which "the endpoint of the law in time is neither fixed nor envisioned."[10] Because it is timeless, legality is not only cumulative and expansive but reversible. The past can meet and control the present, but the present can reverse the past as well. "The reversible aspect of the law . . . underscores its claims to transcend any particular era or individual's life."[11]

Ironically, legality's timeless, transcendent status as something distant and removed from everyday life is achieved not by representing it as intangible, but by associating it with material phenomena: buildings, courtrooms, benches, pews, tables, files, codes, and prison cells. By identifying legality with concrete things that occupy space, our respondents explain how legality is able to overcome fleeting time and become timeless.

Our respondents' accounts expressed a spatialized and thinglike conception of time in two ways. First, they identified legality with specific places and times that were at a distance, removed from the affairs and spaces of everyday life. Second, in this schema of a reified law, our respondents' stories associated law with inscription and textualization. They attributed its transcendent status, in large measure, to its physical embodiment in texts, as well as places.

Another Time, Another Place

Modern time is marked by a tendency to condense time relations into space relations. This transformation of time into space began in the late eighteenth century when the emerging rationalization of social life demanded and produced new spatiotemporal arrangements of human interaction. Industrial production, public education, and the creation of permanent standing militias brought together workers, students, and soldiers, respectively, at centrally located places. The factories, schools, and barracks constructed as part of this historical process were both a condition for and a material manifestation of attempts to organize human action through interconnected grids that marry time to space.

The construction of such places required a radical transformation in the meaning and experience of time in the lives of individuals. To enter these spaces, as workers, students, or legal supplicants, necessitated partitioning one's week into days, one's day into hours, and so forth. As E. P. Thompson noted, this partitioning had the affect of producing a distinction in the mind of workers disciplined by industrial capitalism between "their employer's time and their 'own' time."[12] Moreover, it accomplished a redefinition of time from something lived into something spent and potentially wasted.

Scientific management, the dominant managerial ideology in the early twentieth century, further rationalized time and space relations by converting labor and time into space and motion. These new institutional forms, epitomized in the assembly line, categorized people and tasks, and then arranged and distributed those categories across space. In effect, the desks, rows, columns, and queues of modern organizations transformed complex ongoing activities and interactions into variable units that can be sorted, rearranged, monitored, and in this way disciplined.

Our respondents described law's time as part of a rationalized and spatialized system when they talked about the time they took going to the places of law. Because the formal institution of law is physically located in designated places, people often have to enter literally the space of the law: taking time from work and family and traveling to a specific location. At the same time that legality is located in specific places, these places are dispersed over broad geographic distances, linked by organizational structure and jurisdiction. A bureau located in Washington will have branches in Englewood or Cherry Hill; a hearing in one city will require documents housed in another; a dispute occurring in one's backyard will be adjudicated in a city, building, and room that are remote in both miles and culture from the local neighborhood. These themes of law's distance and dispersion are common in respondents' accounts. And both of these features of legality—located in physical spaces and geographically dispersed—contribute to the experience of remove from daily life and support the conception of reified and transcendent law.

As respondents interact with legal institutions and organizations, they literally move across hundreds, sometimes thousands, of miles. Nikos Stavros told us about trying to settle both an unpaid wage dispute and a tax matter that had occurred while he lived in New Jersey and worked in New York.

> *I then happened to move to upstate New York. So it was awfully hard to do this thing from Rochester and to talk with people in Trenton, where the state has the offices and everything . . . I was talking with the IRS office in Boston, not Boston, where is the northeast center? . . . The adjudication office? I think it's in Massachusetts?*

People's experiences before the law also invoke a sense of time spent away, time spent waiting for something to happen, to be called for jury duty, to have a case heard, or to receive a benefit or service. In an account of an automobile accident Susan Kligfield told us about her experience after the other driver took legal action.

> *[They] went to the town, or to the police station—I don't know where you do this kind of thing—and swore out a complaint against me. [Interviewer: What happened?] Let's see. The first date was canceled. I went to the court and it was canceled. This happened in December. So four months later, in March, finally, the court date comes up . . . I had to go down there and sit there for a couple of hours while they went through . . . a lot of other people's problems.*

The sheer number of offhand and casual allusions to waiting defies reproduction here. Several typical accounts, however, serve to illustrate the relationship between time, space, and reification.

> *The problem I see with motor vehicle is the line is just so excessively long, no matter when you go. I mean, you wait in line a good—a minimum of two hours."* (Diana Taylor)

When I was going to traffic court, one time I went there the lines were just horrendous . . . It's a pain. (Jay Oren)

Nobody can afford the time it takes to go to court. It's such a waste of time. (Stanley Warshawsky)

You sit down in the hall and just wait around all day, and maybe you'll get called to hear a case, and maybe you won't. You're just sitting there waiting, waiting, waiting, waiting, waiting. (Ray Civian)

We went to the police station and waited the whole night. After that I went to court six times. (Jules Magnon)

Well, it was long and drawn out. (Joan Walsh)

[Interviewer: What was it like at court?] Long, arduous, costly. (Ann Shields)

Go to the police department, and go to the auto theft department, and it's just a hassle . . . Have to take time off from the job, and I had no way of getting there. (John Collier)

Slow, the traffic court is inconvenient. You got to go at night, you got the police officer who doesn't always show up, so you have to return. The usual stuff. (Paul Dyson)

It's physically confining, it's hot, noisy, going to Newark is a pain . . . So there we were, we would wait and wait for hours. (Susan Kligfield)

I literally had to drive to Parsippany, which is about an hour away, and stand on line . . . So it was a pain in the ass . . . the time and the effort. Terrible organization. (Gretchen Zinn)

Hopefully you might get compensated for all the time and inconvenience that you're caused. (Raymond Johnson)

The point is that the time spent is, to paraphrase E. P. Thompson, "the law's time": time spent away from work, or family, or neighbors, or leisure. The law's time is experienced as a disruption of the repetitive cycles of everyday life. It is not part of normal routines but, as Kafka's man from the country experienced it, some place apart from the everyday. Rita Michaels also expressed this sense of law's time when she told us of her experience as a juror, which she thought was an interesting and valuable adventure despite the time it took.

Textualization and Inscription

Much of the transformation of time into space has also been achieved through textualization. Here we refer to writing, inscription, and other modes of encoding communication that permits its extraction, preservation, and retrieval separated from ongoing interactions. Law extracts time from everyday relations and further extracts those interactions by embodying them in physical phenomena. Writing and textualization involve spatialization in the obvious sense that through writing ideas are converted to physical symbols that occupy space; that space can be paper, microfilm, a computer file, a videotape, or a screen. The spatialization of legal relationships through textualization contributes to the experience of a reified—thinglike—legality. Legality is not only a place (office building, police station, or courtroom) that one must travel to (away from the routines and places of one's life) but, at a microlevel, the law is materially in the texts it produces.

The sense of writing as spatialization is revealed in the way that texts are linguistically coupled with spatially orienting prepositions: people talk about going "on" the record; putting an agreement "in" writing; writing "out" or writing "up" a complaint, or getting "wrapped up" in paperwork. As Lakoff and Johnson contend, these idioms and metaphors are not simply rhetorical flourishes that give nuance and variety to language.[13] They find their source in our experience of the world and in turn organize that world. In this sense, writing or, more accurately, textualization locates us in a particular place. It marks that location, holds it, making it resistant to the erosion of time, change, and memory. As such, writing, and spatialization more generally, are integral to modern forms of power, particularly legal-rational power.

Textuality confers authority to the judge's printed opinion through the system of precedents. To bind current decisions by prior decisions, and to distinguish later precedents from earlier precedents, requires a record and valorization of the record that are a hallmark of a postprinting world. "Lawyers are trained not even to think of the reality of the case and therefore, to pay attention to only the printed version of what occurred. As a result, over time, it has been forgotten that the printed opinion is only a representation of reality."[14]

Textuality also defines the grounds of participation in the modern trial. The textuality of law demands that "the trial's result must endure the way a written text endures," James Clifford observes in his account of the Mashpee Indian land claim trial. Plaintiffs have "to represent themselves through scripted exchanges with attorney, by statements for the record, in proceedings witnessed, passively and objectively, by jury members with no right to enter, to ask, or to venture an opinion."[15] The judge may write, but the jury may not; depositions become the grounds for interrogating and perhaps discrediting persons. The law itself has come to reflect the "logic of literacy, of the historical archive rather than of changing collective memory."[16] Most important, by locating legal authority in written texts, professionals and laymen remove human agency from legality and locate social authorship in nonhuman artifacts.

People's interpretations of textuality and its role in organizing social interactions are complex. Yet almost without exception, the people with whom we spoke recognize the ways in which textualization—writing, documentation on paper, film, or tape—operates as a central organizing principle of modern legal-rational society. They generally acknowledged and deferred to the authority of the textual over the oral. The greater authority of the written word derives from the fact that texts, as opposed to spoken words, can be preserved, retrieved, inspected, and interrogated. In this way, texts convert momentary utterances and events into permanent, timeless artifacts. Indeed, the record or the papers were often referred to as if they were a third party in people's disputes with neighbors, businesses, and the government. Recognizing that space—embodied in paper—can subdue and control the effects of time, when respondents depicted a reified law, they described how they could enter its space by various processes of inscription. Unbiased, reliable, and undeniable, the record could be used to validate or discredit, to bear witness to the disputed events of the past or the contested claims of the day.

People expressed their understanding of the role of textualization in offhand but revealing ways, often counterpoising the authority of that which is written against that which is merely spoken. "I had no proof," Jamie Leeson told us, "nothing in writing," he quickly added, "they could just deny everything I said." Like a refrain, people acknowledged the inherent weakness and assailability of their claims when they were "just verbal" or "only verbal." Explaining why she paid a significantly higher than quoted price for some home repairs without protest or complaint, Rita Michaels shrugged and simply said that she had "nothing in writing, just a verbal agreement."

Another respondent described a dispute he had with a former employer who withheld a month's salary:

> It wasn't a big amount of money, but I knew I had been cheated, and unfortunately I lost this case because I didn't have a way to prove my claim, because all the employment records were kept by the company, so that company didn't want to present the employment records, the only thing I had was the offer of employment by the consulting company, that was the only thing that I had with me, so it was my word against his and I lost. (Nikos Stavros)

Almost everyone with whom we spoke claimed to have written letters of complaint or inquiry. In their efforts to manage daily conflicts and disputes, letter writing is a nearly universal, and for many a routine, tactic. Putting it in writing or filing a complaint is seen as a necessary step in engaging or mobilizing the institutional machinery. In a world of anonymous bureaucracies, writing is a modern mythical practice[17] that has the capacity to transform immediate, ephemeral, and idiosyncratic experiences into a stable and legible form. Even as writing abstracts events and experiences from one context—that of immediate social action—it endows them with the characteristics necessary to exist in a more formal, timeless, institutional context. Writing embodies the often desired capacity for transcendence.

Emphasizing the textual permanence that transcends lived experiences, Rita Michaels compared the fragility of memory and the erosive quality of time when she described the criminal trial for which she was a juror.

> The caseload in Essex County is very heavy. The trial was a year and a half after the incident occurred. Who remembers? Even the people that were called up to be witnesses. They didn't even have their facts straight. So it was difficult to convict this person because there was not enough proof. Too much time elapsed.

Had the testimony been written down, time could not have eroded memory. Thus, to write it down is to impart to an account, a request, or a complaint an ontological independence. Once something becomes textualized it exists independently, not only of time and space but also of author and audience. Writing a letter—whether to the electric company, to the mayor, or to the IRS—allows people access to that institutional field where there is no visible, known, or recognizable audience, where there is no assurance that there is anyone available to listen, remember, or act upon a verbal request or complaint. The writing connects the living, acting person to the transcendent, timeless law. People understand that a letter makes them intelligible in a highly spatialized society. As de Certeau has observed,

> The act of suffering oneself to be written by the group's law is oddly accompanied by a pleasure, that of being recognized (but one does not know by whom), of becoming an identifiable and legible word in a social language, of being changed into a fragment within an anonymous text, of being inscribed in a symbolic order that has neither owner nor author.[18]

Moreover, inscription and textuality do not simply register discontent or validate accounts of past actions or agreements. They are also seen as the basis for validating identity claims. Papers, documents, identity cards, and permits represent material evidence of social existence. Often to receive one's papers, whether a green card or a handicapped-parking permit, is to become someone different, to be officially recognized, and thus to enter the social script. As one man, a soon-to-be-naturalized citizen, remarked,

> Until you get your green card you're a visitor, you know, you have a visa, you know. But I guess it's all right, I mean after a while, after you know you're going to get your papers, and you're okay. (Nikos Stavros)

In another interview, Aida Marks, a woman in her late fifties, described herself as "legally blind," attaching great significance to the legal status of her condition. In relating to us an argument she had had with a neighbor over the handicapped parking sign in front of her home, Aida Marks asked,

> Do you think that the city would give me the permission of the blind . . . and give me a permit and everything if I wasn't disabled? . . . You're not gonna get that sign unless you have papers showing that you're entitled to that.

Later in her interview, Aida recalled receiving an identification card from the State Commission for the Blind seven years earlier. The card did more than simply attest to her lack of sight; it provided her with evidence of an identity and even an existence, something she claimed to have lacked up to that point.

> *I really had no identification until I got in touch with the commission of the blind and then they gave me my, what do you call that transportation card for the busses and the trains? They gave me an ID card, . . . I never had really no identification, there's a lot of women that don't have identification if you're a housewife or something, you don't have anything that says Aida Marks that says that, I didn't have anything.*

Because texts can achieve an independence from ongoing, ephemeral behavior, they can provide moral validation. To put it in writing, to enter it into the record, designates it as serious and sincere. Nonetheless, the pleasure that de Certeau referred to of becoming a word and thus becoming recognizable in a textualized world is, as he also noted, accompanied by "an act of suffering." One must pay a price to enter legality's textual time and space. Although having one's words in writing or going on the record allows one to enter the realm of strategic power, it also requires relinquishing some control over the social interactions and identities that are to be embodied in the paper. The processes of inscription concretize conditions, actions, and identities, abstracting them from the flow of ongoing interaction, freezing them in time, making them visible but silent, seen but mute. Inscription creates a material impediment to reinterpretation and thus limits the influence we might exert over the interpretations others might make. Because inscription permits—indeed encourages—interpretation dissociated in time and space from one's own participation, the ability to actively intervene in future interpretations is reduced. Thus even while inscription allows one to enter the institutional script, it does so only by opening up the possibility of being erased.

In speaking with our respondents, we found two forms of disempowerment that were associated with textuality and inscription. The first form of disempowerment was simply erasure. This cost was acknowledged by many of our respondents who understood the risk of having their identities and relationships textualized and rendered independent of ongoing construction. People made references to the possibilities of "being written off" or of having their cases "filed away." These metaphorical allusions describe the experience of being expunged by the very processes of inscription that were to ensure their being heard or seen in the first place.

Nell Pearson recounted a dispute she had with some members of a collective of feminist writers in which she worked. In the course of describing the deterioration of relationships with her collaborators, the developing lawsuits, and her various legal and extralegal efforts to settle the dispute, Nell Pearson mentioned one judge in particular.

> We happened to end up with a judge who basically was notori-
> ous for being incredibly lazy. Wouldn't hear when we tried to
> argue . . . to indicate that it could be settled, wouldn't hear the
> argument and never bothered to read the papers. (emphasis
> hers)

In another interview, a woman told us about a disability claim she had made. After filling out what she described as "lots and lots of forms," which included instructions from her doctor indicating that she could not sit for extended periods of time, she was assigned to a job involving eight hours of sitting. "It's like they don't even read what all the doctors" wrote on the papers (Shirley Joslin). In a claim for reimbursement of extensive medical and dental bills, Jamie Lee-son described his erasure by his employer's failure to file employment and insurance records. "I had fifteen hundred dollars of dental work done when I worked for [the employer]. They never mailed in any of my paperwork. So when we sent the bill into the insurance company, they'd never heard of me." Similarly, Millie Simpson came to under-stand through her experience the limits of paper and inscription to empower legal subjects. "Some of them [judges]," she acknowledged, "probably don't even read the paper."

Our respondents reported a second form of disempowerment as-sociated with textuality, that of being up against it, confined to the paper, unable to effect the social exchanges purportedly represented rather than instantiated in the paper. In talking about their interac-tions with legal agencies and other bureaucracies, respondents re-peatedly referred to the intractability of the text. In fact, the qualities of durability and stability that create textual authority and make the text a compelling witness at the same time render it difficult or im-possible to revise or contest. A textualized account can be used to verify, test, or discredit a verbal account in the present. Many people report that they have spent months, and in some cases even years, trying to amend or correct what they claim to be errors or misrepresentations once they are recorded. These experiences, reported by almost every one of our respondents, often involve mundane problems such as incorrect bills; but they sometimes implicate the most damning assaults on character, identity, or life itself.

One respondent described her continuing dispute with an insurance company that had used the paid-up value of a policy to convert her insurance to a larger term policy and then began charging her premiums for the new policy, which she could not afford to pay. For several years, Laura Flanagan had been trying, she said, to correct the record and return to the insurance policy she had originally. Another respondent described a dispute with the telephone company about a ninety-dollar charge for service that was never performed. The telephone company billed him for the additional ninety dollars for several years; not until he was ready to move and order new service was the dispute resolved. Rita Michaels described a similarly ongoing dispute with a large department store that continually billed her for a returned item for which she had the receipts: "They charged me for an item that I returned and it took a long time to resolve . . . because for some reason they have no record of it. I did have the receipts."

Writing, by resisting change and amendment, can also eclipse the emerging present. In disputes where there is some portion of the transaction in writing, pieces of the dispute that are written are privileged over the oral. Depositions or statements made and recorded at one point in time are routinely used in litigation to undermine the testimony offered at another time. Changes of heart or mind are interpreted against the standard of truth and fact set by the documented record. The presumption is that any discrepancy between the recorded account of the past and the oral account invalidates the veracity of the witness. The possibility of someone amending or upgrading their memory, changing their mind as they try to remember what happened, is discounted. In her research on a gang rape trial, Kristin Bumiller provides an example of this strategy as it was used by the defense attorney in an attempt to discredit the victim. "The major challenge to her credibility," Bumiller writes,

> rested on the record of her "exaggerations" in the police report written the night of the attack. In subsequent police reports she retracted the claim that there were fifteen men involved . . . [During the trial she] was continually harassed for days about these inconsistencies.[19]

By associating legality with distinct places and spaces, with public buildings and certified documents, respondents mark its remove from the interactions that constitute common everyday life. By thus concretizing and spatializing legality, respondents locate it in a timeless realm of paper, concrete, and rational discipline.

Conclusion

Our respondents' conceptions of the law as a distinctive institutional phenomenon embody the same characteristics that liberal law claims for itself. American legal ideology describes the law as neutral (justice is blind) and fair (the scales are balanced). It also claims for law an enormous transcendent capacity: "to form a more perfect Union, establish Justice, insure domestic Tranquility, provide for the common defence, promote the general Welfare, and secure the Blessings of Liberty to ourselves and our Posterity." Liberal legal ideology claims for legality a timelessness, as the past (in the form of precedent) is preserved and continually enacted in the present. Beyond the actions and lifetimes of particular persons, legality transcends the here and now, the specific who and what, to instruct and guide through the generations. Aspiring toward grandeur and permanence, law houses itself in monumental buildings of marble and granite and arranges its agents behind desks, counters, and benches. It expresses itself in a language that is arcane and indecipherable to most citizens. The theatrical scripting and costuming of trials creates an unbridgeable distance from the interactions of everyday life. The reified law is, then, the law's own story as well as our respondents' stories.

Kafka represents this image of law when the doorkeeper explains to the man from the country that "[n]o one else could ever be admitted here, since this gate was made only for you. I am now going to shut it." Here Kafka reveals that what appeared to be general and universal was, all along, particular and concrete. In doing so he suggests that there is no law without embodying it in human action, that the structure of doors and doorkeepers relies on, even while it denies, human agency. Much like the legal supplicant from the country, the expressions of a reified law we have reported here describe the law as general, remote, and powerful.

Although these may be incomplete accounts of legality, they are frequently heard and widely shared. Legal elites, as well as ordinary citizens, articulate and enact this story of law. And in their neat dra-

matizations of legal contests where evil is avenged and justice se-
cured, the media often represent this conception of a powerful and
exalted legality. We urge caution, however, in too quickly dismissing
these reified views of law as illusion or delusion. For in the very process of articulating and enacting this view of legality, by "getting it in
writing" and "not bothering the police," people actually do construct
something that is very different from everyday life.

CHAPTER FIVE

With the Law

Charles Reed

I have a reputation in town for getting involved with things, and people know who I am. When I go to see somebody, they generally know that they're dealing with me, and that they have to deal with me.

Sun streaming through the French doors leading from the large, carefully decorated living room to the patio beyond, Charles Reed explained his strategies for success. Most people, he said "beat around the bush"; he goes to the heart of the matter. Most people "don't have the courage of their convictions," but "I know where I stand all the time." Being prepared, presenting himself as better informed, better dressed, and more powerful, "I always get my way." Being in control is important to Charles Reed. "I want them to know that not everybody is stupid."

"The strength of my success . . . is my presentation." Indeed, Charles Reed presents himself, his home, and his family with unconcealed pride. He invited us to tour his gardens and his neighborhood. He is conscious of its opulence and its physical beauty. He makes no apologies for it, nor does he camouflage his pleasure at having arrived at this happy state. Like others in this town, where "there is a tendency of people . . . to migrate up," Charles has traveled some economic and geographic distance from where he began in upstate New York. "A lot of people get to a certain spot where they think they belong in this town and they don't like to go back to where they were . . . There are some very snobby people around this neighborhood . . . I don't like that . . . There is an expression the Irish use: 'I knew him when he had nuttin'.'" Unlike the snobs among his neighbors, Charles Reed likes to remember

*that he once had, if not nothing, much less than he has now,
"remember, remember absolutely." Remembering seems to be a
way of experiencing the present as different and of appreciat-
ing the difference.*

*Still, Charles Reed is not entirely different from what he
once was. Nor does he want to be. "Friends are friends. They
shouldn't be left behind because of changes in your own personal inventory." Mrs. Reed grew up on Long Island, "where
people don't use each other's driveways to turn around." That
is "a different part of the world" from what Charles was used
to in upstate New York and different from what he has tried to
re-create during the nine years the family has lived in this
affluent New Jersey suburb.*

*Charles Reed spends a great deal of time getting around,
making connections, and generally "keeping an eye on things"
in his town. When some undeveloped land in his neighborhood was to be subdivided and sold, he organized his neighbors to stop the sale. Although the zoning ordinances permitted division of the property, Charles and some of his neighbors
did not want what they thought would be new, tasteless
homes set among their more stately Tudor, colonial, and Victo-
rian houses. Because they could not get the minimal acreage
increased (some of the neighbors occupied less land than the
proposed building), they sought to prevent any future development by getting the area certified as a historic district.*

*Charles organized the neighbors who supported the
change, arranged for the legal representation, attended all
the relevant meetings, and was generally applauded and
admired by his neighbors—even those who did not support
the campaign—for his "effective leadership," "extraordinary
energy," and "generous efforts" on behalf of the neighborhood.*

*Charles Reed recognizes the importance of mobilizing oth-
ers as he pursues his own interests. When we asked Charles if
he had ever been the victim of "bait and switch" sales techniques, he launched into a long account of how this happens
routinely but that he is not suckered.*

> *Happens all the time around here . . . Well, actually, what hap-
> pens generally is that I wind up with a real good deal on some-*

thing better. I don't take it from them. I always bring my newspaper with me, and bring my information with me. I've been in the sales business, and I'm an analyst, have market abilities. I train salespeople, too.

When an interesting sale comes up, I go out and make sure everybody's doing the right thing, and I use my skills in the right spot . . . If I go out, if I finally decide to go somewhere and buy it, I almost always call first. I'll ask for the person's name. When I get there, then I've got them already because they've been singled out by name.

And, it's not unlike me to call other customers over and tell them what [the store is] attempting to do. [Other customers] are getting ready to buy a good TV or something like that and I'll even ask the salesman if he'd like me to explain to those five people over there right now what, what he's not willing to do for me. They get disorganized and say, what can I do to get rid of this guy? That's what they have to do . . . I always get my way.

Unconcerned with the stares and opinions of other people, Charles Reed says, "I don't pay attention." Besides, "most of them will come up to me and ask me what I think they should pay for something else. I always go looking confident . . . I always go looking, not that that's hard to do, I always go looking better than the salesman."

Charles is white, forty-five years old, and well educated. His medium brown straight hair, parted in the middle 1920s style, is beginning to gray ever so slightly, adding a hint of distinction to what otherwise might be an ordinary-looking gentleman.

Charles Reed began his successful career in sales, marketing, and financial advising while still in college, spending summers and holidays working for a construction company. From summer jobs as a managerial assistant, he went into the insurance business and quickly into reinsurance. He sometimes describes himself as a salesman: "That's my business, presentation of self."

Over the years, Charles made a great deal of money selling reinsurance, moving up, he says, to this town and to this house. He has multiple sources of income from diverse investments (e.g., real estate in Florida and Texas, a restaurant in

New Jersey) and his new reinsurance firm. He spends two or three days a week in Philadelphia and the rest of the time working at home. The sale of his business a few years before, plus some capital ventures that went bad, have involved Charles Reed in extensive litigations, including more than one class-action suit, each involving millions of dollars.

In 1981 Charles Reed and his partner sold their reinsurance company to another firm in Philadelphia. As part of this transaction, he signed a rather conventional agreement in which he promised not to go into business in competition with the buyer for at least two years. As another "part of the agreement of sale," Charles explained, he would work for the company, and "they would institute, set up an executive compensation program which would pay me for my efforts." He would receive some sales commissions "up front" the first year, and the rest of the commissions distributed over the next three years.

"A year and a half or so into the plan, it was changed, to my detriment. I protested it but I was not asked to accept it. It was just put into effect." Apparently the new plan stipulated that should the insurance renewals decline in value, the decrease would be taken out of the original commission.

Charles claimed that he was owed about $400,000 but considered taking the $112,000 or thereabouts offered as a settlement. He believed that if he didn't accept it and went to court, he would have to pay the lawyer between 30 and 40 percent, receiving little more than the settlement offer. In addition, it might have taken years and might not have been accumulating interest. "You're better discounting all of this. I would take the money and run." So, for that advice Charles Reed paid his lawyer about eight hundred dollars and decided to settle.

But when the papers for the settlement arrived, the firm he was suing insisted that Charles re-sign and thus extend all of his original contracts, including the promise not to compete. By then he was working for a new firm, also in reinsurance, and the new employer would not sanction any agreement in which he would not be able to sell insurance.

> *So I had to reject the offer . . . So I wrote them a letter and I said "I am entitled to this money, and I appreciate the fact that you*

don't want me to compete with you. However, I cannot sign this, my current employer does not want me to sign it, and I feel obligated to them. They are paying my salary. I will keep you posted of my activities and remind you from time to time that I am not competing with you and ask you to check into that, to be sure. And at the end of the two-year period, I expect you to pay me the full amount, please do. So, I sent them a letter every six months.

At the end of two years, I marched into my lawyer's office in Philadelphia . . . We filed a complaint in Philadelphia City Court to which the parent company had fifteen days to respond. They responded. They showed up for a meeting.

By the time the negotiations on the complaint began, Charles Reed believed that the actual figure was more like $456,000. Charles reported that at the meeting his attorney informed the others that Charles had never signed and accepted any change in his original compensation package.

There's a term the lawyer used which I can't recall but he said something like they took back compensation without compensating him which as you know is a violation of this or that . . . It's there, it's covered by the law.

Charles explained to us, "as a matter of fact, I did not know that when a compensation is granted that if it is changed, the person subjected to change is entitled to compensation. I did not know that, but it was a point of law." Even though he had not known that he had the law on his side, he had pressed his claim and filed suit. He believed himself justified in principle if not in law. The case was not resolved when we spoke, but Charles Reed was quite optimistic about the probable outcome and effusive about how well he and his lawyer performed at the negotiations. He believed that he was going to win and that the other side was on the verge of collapse.

Now, the guy knows, and I know, that my lawyer is getting paid by the hour to sit with me, and my lawyer's a good guy. He works for the largest law firm in Philadelphia . . . So [the defending firm's officer] knows he's in a real live law firm. This is no small-time shyster . . . It's in [a prestigious office building] in Philadelphia. They own the building and it's twelve floors of lawyers. This is one of the biggest firms in the country . . . He knows he's in a major-league ballpark, and he knows that his guy next to him is in trouble. So he turns to my lawyer, and he says, "We all know that we have figures in these cases, what's yours?"

Charles described the case as "just routine," a business negotiation. His participation was crucial, nonetheless.

I was asked . . . to synopsize my case. I wired him. He had nowhere to go when I was done. There was so much that the [defendant] hadn't told [his lawyer] that when they heard the whole story, he was just ready to give up. They may choose to fight it, and the offer to settle was off the record, but what we know is that I will take ninety, ninety-five, or a hundred [thousand dollars]. Whatever the 25 percent was plus a little . . . We went a little high so that they figured that they'd come back somewhere between the two. They know.

Charles didn't press for the full amount "because the lawyer advised me how these things are done. He said I've done a number of these, and this is how you do it." Charles Reed often follows his lawyer's advice, not only about litigation strategies but about possibly lucrative investments. In one instance, a lawyer he no longer hires colluded with others in an investment in which there were all sorts of paybacks and conflicts of interest. That went quite bad: "It went bankrupt . . . I lost a lot of money."

In addition to being a party in the compensation litigation and a class-action with other investors in the Florida insurance company bankrupted by its board of directors, Charles Reed was also a victim-witness in the prosecutions of a real estate fraud in Texas. He described this one as a "big one . . . the most notoriety . . . the largest real estate fraud in the history of the state of Texas." Despite the significance of the case, both financially and for the legal community, Charles treated it as a routine part of doing business. "You put deals together and if things do not work out, you sue because there is usually a way to get some return." His assessment that the case was a big one referred to its notoriety, rather than to any inconvenience or special moral status among his affairs.

Some years back Charles had invested in a new concept he referred to as "homesharing." One group of investors would buy homes, usually condominiums, and then lease them—

*through the development agent—to others. The purchasers
would write off the acquisition costs at an accelerated rate,
while the lessees' rent would pay off the mortgage. "It was like
a dealership owning a car and then leasing it. That same kind
of business."*

*Unfortunately, in this instance the imaginative business-
man who put the deal together sold the same one hundred condominiums to eleven different groups of owners.*

> What he got us to do is to pay in eleven times as much money as
> he needed to do the deal. And then falsified the tax numbers . . .
> It was fraud from the beginning and we proved that . . . He is in
> jail and will be for a very long time.

*Charles Reed and most of the other investors were able to
get their money back—it was being released, he claimed,
within the week—because the company providing malpractice
insurance for the law firm that falsified the documents was
paying the claims (about $15 million). The general partner,
whom Charles claims helped execute the fraud, was awarded a
judgment against the firm, as were the investors and other lawyers involved. Charles described how the lawyer, whose collusion was revealed in the federal criminal suit, was nonetheless
able to have that testimony excluded from the civil suit. "A
judge in the other case awarded complete damages to him
under the policies that covered him. There was, we believe
strongly, there was collusion between the . . . judge and the
law firm, the Texas law firm." There were malpractice claims
and all sorts of charges and countercharges and much media
coverage.*

*Charles Reed presented the information about these busi-
ness suits in a matter-of-fact manner. In contrast, he was visi-
bly angry about the petty corruption he claims to observe
around town. With some energy he declared,*

> The thing I dislike about this town the most, it's the politicians.
> People who would use the town and the people in it to their
> advantage . . . I believe there is corruption on a personal level
> where the politicians are corrupt for their own personal
> advancement.

*And some are corrupt, he claimed, for financial advantage.
"The worst kind," however, "is the person who takes or enables*

another to have an unfair advantage, from a monetary economic standpoint . . . to allow somebody to have something
that they should have to work for."

Although securing economic advantage is the nature of
business and the goal of a good investor, Charles Reed is clear
that it is unacceptable elsewhere, especially in the running of
local government. The networks through which he invested
and made profitable business deals are, to Charles Reed, legitimate and appropriate instruments of self-interest. He expects
there to be smarter and less able players and thus winners and
losers. But when it comes to schools and police, libraries and
parks, courts and judges, he has different expectations. Public
officials are "supposed to be managing . . . supposed to be exe-
cuting the mandate of the people." Thus, Reed explicitly recognizes two distinct normative orders, one for business and one
for community life. The law is a device that can be mobilized
in either of these arenas but ironically with much less success
in the public political realm. The rezoning of his neighborhood
to a historic district was an exception among the stories
Charles Reed told about community matters. For most community issues, Reed generally relied on local organizations
and a certain amount of personal authority rather than legal
resources. Invoking law was pointless where legal authority
was already corrupt.

For example, Charles Reed told several stories about his
interactions with the local school board as well as the principal and teachers in his children's school. In one instance he
joined with other parents in the neighborhood to protest the
transfer of a teacher. It was the first day of the school year
when one of the third-grade teachers was moved to a first-
grade class on the other side of town. "A real nasty political
payoff situation. They waited until the school year started and
called it a transfer because they knew they couldn't do it otherwise."

The teacher had two years to go before retirement, and
somehow Reed believed that rather than seniority conveying
advantage, the proximity of retirement seemed to limit the
teacher's ability to refuse the transfer. The parents collected
"750 signatures in two days."

The superintendent justified the move to the angry parents

by explaining that there were financial constraints, insufficient teachers, and some crowding in the elementary schools. He decided to reduce crowding in the first grade and suffer with larger classes in the third. Although this seemed like a reasonable explanation, Charles Reed and his compatriots did not buy it. More to the point, he claimed,

> *It was a setup. Nobody will convince me otherwise, and I know the people involved . . . The minute I walked into that room, and the newspaper, editor of the newspaper was sitting there next to me . . . And I turned to him and I said, "What do you think the chances are that one of the board members has a first-grader in that school?" And they do. They do.*

Although he could get little satisfaction in this and several other school matters, Charles Reed nonetheless claims that when he complains and makes a forceful presentation, "I usually walk away better off." Often, "being better off" is symbolic rather than material. It means having demonstrated control, having hobbled someone who had not recognized whom they were dealing with, that "they have to deal with me."

Some years back, his oldest daughter had been sent home from school early as a punishment for filling a "Mad Libs" booklet with profanities. It was her pad and had her name on it, but the child, whom he described as "very proper," had not done the writing. Another child found the book and turned it in to the teacher. The teacher did not report it because apparently he recognized that this was not Emily Reed's handwriting. The pad was taken out of the trash, Charles claims, by a second teacher and reported to the principal. Although there were several styles of handwriting in the booklet, Emily was sent home early from school as a punishment for using profanity.

> *I went back the next day . . . I walked back to school with her, and our middle girl was in the kindergarten at the time, and our youngest was still small, so I had them in tow. And we went down to the principal. I asked to see the principal. I was let in. I had the book that she was sent home with . . . I went in and I said, you know, this is a very sensitive girl. You've known her, you know who she is. You're very active, you know all of the kids*

and all of the teachers and so on . . . I can't believe that you didn't believe her, number one, but that's your choice. You have the option to believe or not believe. But it's quite evident that this writing is not hers. I don't care about that so much. But I have a real problem with you . . . having this child's idea of her education and her school shattered by being sent home for something she obviously didn't do. Of course, I overlaid the deal by saying it that way, but I had the three kids with me and she was really in a tough spot . . . We were right, no question about it. I made her apologize. The principal, apologize.

Although Charles believes in community organization, "keeping an eye on things," and having people know that he is a person "with whom they have to deal," he is a "vocal and active opponent" of the favoritism he sees in the town and schools.

I'll go down and check, and my point to them [is] that the reason there's no room in the honors class for my daughter is because you have too many people that you're paying off with their children in there . . . They roll their eyes . . . They can't deny it . . . When your child is in class with the same boy or girl for two or three years running, they tell each other their scores and their grades . . . So, I say, look, I just want you to know that I know what you're up to and a lot of other parents do too. And it's not a good idea.

Letting people know that he knows, and getting them to apologize for their actions, is one of Charles Reed's common tactics. "I'm careful to make these kinds of allegations when it's past the time" for the decision maker to hurt him or his. Often, Reed does not expect to change the immediate situation; rather, he is positioning himself, displaying his knowledge, and waiting for another time when he might use his knowledge to better advantage.

In both serious and relatively insignificant matters, Charles Reed insists on letting people know that he is on to them, even when he cannot stop it. He is willing, nonetheless, to tolerate a certain amount of corruption. "The thing that I dislike about it is that it happens . . . I don't really care if somebody pays somebody off . . . because they have to suffer the consequences. Generally when you pay somebody off to overlook something," in housing inspections, for example, "espe-

*cially for a code violation, you're exposing yourself to danger
. . . But if the electrician is supposed to put in twenty-gauge
wire and puts in something else, I have a problem with that
because he's cheating you. He is stealing from you."*

*In particular, Charles is incensed by what he sees as the
collusion between service and construction companies, real
estate brokers, and public officials, who he believes work
together to get homeowners to spend money unnecessarily. He
says that they scare people about asbestos and radon in their
homes. "The names are scary . . . My God, radon. I'm not
going to buy this house. I'd be crazy to buy this house," the
person says.*

> *There's an assistant in the duping process, and that is that inter-
> mediary that stands to gain . . . the guy that stands there and
> says, My God, look at this, there's asbestos. And then he takes a
> device like a screwdriver or something and he pokes it through
> and it comes out and he goes, Oh look out. And they say, you're
> right, I mean look at that, it is asbestos. He says, "Well, I would
> put in there as a condition of the sale that this, whatever . . ."
> And they wind up splitting it with the seller and buyer, thirteen
> hundred bucks when you're buying a house for seven hundred
> thousand dollars is nothing, thirteen hundred bucks when you're
> paying that is nothing. And these characters take the twenty-six
> hundred bucks, he probably gets six hundred of it just for poking
> his pencil through there, and the other guy gets two thousand dol-
> lars for about a hundred and fifty dollars worth of work . . . And
> it's a scam, and scams, especially when you put a small scam
> inside of a big price . . . it's nothing.*

*Some of these scams are just products of greed, like the
driveway-sealing companies that frighten elderly people into
thinking that someone is likely to fall on the cracks in their
driveways. Other scams, Charles Reed explains, are generated
by government regulation. For example, because environmen-
tal laws insist on separating glass and other forms of trash, it
fosters corruption, he says.*

> *It goes on all over the place. All over the place. We have a garbage
> stall behind our restaurant. It's fenced in, has boards, has a
> Dumpster in it. And the Dumpster is taken away by, what do you
> call it, a trash collector, refuse removal, no, disposal company.*

They don't take glass. Okay, but . . . if you pay the driver, he will overlook the fact that there are bottles in your garbage. He's taking it where there's not supposed to be glass, and he must be paying off somebody when he dumps it with the glass . . . It's all connected.

The big problem, Charles Reed believes, is that "people are victimized by people who seem to have the ability to make recommendations that sound like requirements," as in the house inspections. "People . . . come in and take advantage and use an authority figure to supplement the belief mechanism . . . Oh, I . . . really don't like that at all." At some level, it is also a matter of incompetence: the incompetence of the consumer-citizen, and the incompetence of the public official. Reed has little tolerance for either. Part of his sense of mastery—even when he cannot control situations—derives directly from this sense of others as less competent. It also derives, we suspect, from a heightened sensitivity to class differences and to that distance Charles Reed has traveled to reach his present comfortable—but also quite self-conscious—position.

When he was called away from a pool party several summers back to answer a police call that a bomb had been found on his lawn, Charles Reed "never stopped trying to get to the bottom of things." The police had disarmed and removed the device, but resisted explaining themselves, or the situation, to Charles. He pressed his case with the patrolman, then with the lieutenant, and finally met with the captain. As Reed moved up the police hierarchy, he increased his threats and demands for information. It took a month or more but he eventually collected several eyewitness stories—about how the police and fire department had first moved the bomb and then realized that they should not have and then returned it to its position on the Reeds' lawn before taking it away in the trunk of a police car.

Charles Reed was angry about the waste of money in the number of police and firemen called out in shorts and swimsuits on a holiday, collecting overtime, he said; he was angry about the incompetence in handling the bomb, which posed a serious danger to people and property. "This really frosted me," he said. But what really angered him, "the thing I cared about

*was the jerk who tried to dismiss me," the lieutenant who
would not provide information when Charles inquired. He
explains it by pointing to incompetence, corruption, arro-
gance, and class resentment.*

> *Arrogance on the part of the police department. They think, you
> know, they know that this is a very wealthy neighborhood. A lot
> of policeman on the police department grew up here and it's the
> best job they could get. And they don't mind every now and then
> exercising a little authority over people that have money.*

Nikos Stavros

*Nikos Stavros immigrated to the United States from Greece
when he was in his early twenties. He completed college and
two years of postgraduate education and now, thirty-two years
old and separated from his wife, is a systems analyst and programmer. Except for a brief period in Rochester, New York, he
has been working in Manhattan and living in Weehawken,
New Jersey, a crowded commuter town directly across the
Hudson River from New York City. At the time of the interview, Nikos Stavros told us that he was about to complete the
naturalization process and was studying U.S. history and the
Constitution in anticipation of his citizenship exam.*

*Nikos Stavros is a consummate storyteller. With little prob-
ing, he colorfully recounted dozens of incidents and events—
stories of his relationships with friends, failures and successes
at work and at school, disputes with landlords, and experiences in various legal settings. Speaking with a slight accent,
he would punctuate his stories with emphatic hand motions,
occasionally rising from his seat to draw illustrations in the
air. Although Greek is his first language, and the language he
speaks at home, his searching and thoughtful responses do
not reflect linguistic difficulties; his English is excellent. The
numerous accounts he shared with us formed an overarching
narrative of personal change and development that was characterized by a strong sense of legal and organizational efficacy.
Believing in the intelligibility of the law and in his own ability
to eventually master its ways, Nikos presented himself as an*

able technician of bureaucratic procedure and an effective
legal player.

In his accounts of his early experiences in the United
States, Nikos described himself as compliant and naive in his
relationship with others, often accepting or "lumping" what he
saw as legitimate grievances. As a graduate student, for
instance, he simply found another place to live rather than
challenge his landlord's right to evict him.

> I didn't have the time to bother with that, plus I was very new to
> this country and I didn't know how to go about these things.

Later in the interview, Nikos described another incident in
which he lost a legal dispute with a former employer over a
month's unpaid wages. He had been hired by a consulting firm
and had been instructed, he claimed, to be available for con-
tracting out. During the two months, he was never given any
work and was never contracted out. When he did not receive
compensation for the second month, he first complained to
the New Jersey Department of Labor, which initiated an investigation. After a year, the case ended up in court; Nikos lost. In
this case, as with the landlord, he interpreted his failure as a
result of his lack of knowledge and experience, of not knowing
"how to go about these things." Having taken this case to
court, Nikos attributed his defeat to his failure to document
his claim and to act expeditiously.

> I lost the case because I didn't have a way to prove my claim
> because all the employment records were kept by the company
> . . . The only thing I had was the offer of employment by the con-
> sulting company, you know, that was the only thing that I
> had, . . . so it was my word against his and I lost.

> I think my mistake was that I waited too long, and I, when they
> were telling me that your check is in the mail. I should have been
> more adamant, and up front and I should have requested imme-
> diately my salary.

In contrast to his future expertise and success, Nikos
Stavros summed up this particular story by observing, "No, I
was not ready, I mean I didn't have a good chance, I think
that's why I lost."

In contrast to these stories of early failure, Nikos

recounted a series of successes that illustrated his acquired skill in engaging the law to manage his relationships with others. Underwriting this skill was an emerging understanding of bureaucracy, an understanding that would instruct him in how to behave in relation to the world of American institutions. Describing the frustrations of the naturalization process, he says

> I guess it's bureaucracy again, you know, that's the way they do it, that's the way they're going to do it. And I'm not going to even try to change it, you know.

To Nikos Stavros, bureaucracy—epitomized for him by the excessive rules and regulations of large organizations—is a pervasive and inevitable part of modern life. Recognizing the futility of changing it, he accepts the necessity of learning how to survive while working with it. Nikos came to understand that people who work in bureaucracies have very limited interests. Their principal concern is to follow the rules and avoid trouble. Nikos learned to use these operating concerns to achieve his own ends.

> Well, what I'm trying to tell you is, you see what the requirements are, and you try to find out what they're looking for, and then you try to go about these requirements and see how you can satisfy them. Because that's what a bureaucrat really does, you know. He looks at the requirement, or whatever the law specifies, and then if you meet these requirements, you have a good chance.

From his early experiences he learned that paramount among the skills necessary to deal successfully with this world of bureaucrats is maintaining documents.

> When you deal with bureaucrats, I think my understanding is when you present them with documents that one way or another fulfill the law, whatever the law might be, they are going to be happy, you know. If you give them enough documents to apply any law, you make their life easier. They're going to go get home at five o'clock, you know it's going to be over.

In fact, according to Nikos the labyrinthine rules and regulations that define modern organizations are not obstacles to, but rather opportunities for, getting what one wants. He describes the rules as open (creating "loopholes") and facilitating, as opposed to closed and constraining.

> So that's another way of looking at the system, you know, identifying the right loopholes, . . . It's amazing what things can be done and cannot be done with . . . within the law.

As he searches for the appropriate preposition, "with" or "within" the law, Nikos depicts the law as both a space "within" which to operate and something "with" which to work.

Like any skillful and experienced gamesman, Nikos Stavros is acutely aware of the importance of his opponent's abilities and material advantages. While he acknowledges the truth or moral rectitude of a position or claim, he sees these qualities as being only contingently related to the outcome of any legal case. People might be "right" and still lose if outpositioned by their opponents. The law may be predictable, allowing one to calculate odds or probability of success, but it is not determinant. Chance and the variable skill and resources of opponents will always introduce uncertainty into legal contests. For these reasons, Nikos chooses his opponents and tactics warily, always trying to maximize his chances.

> If it is worthwhile, and if I feel that I have a fair chance, if I feel that I'm not going up against any, uh, I don't know, major institutions or organizations . . .

In light of his perception of the law as a contest whose outcome is contingent upon the skill, experience, and determination of the parties, it is not surprising that he is extremely cautious in dealing with organizations. Nikos Stavros recognizes organizations as advantaged opponents, having greater resources, experience, and access to legal knowledge and advice.

> You know, you have these special-interest groups and lobbies, a lot of money, a lot of vested interests, you know. Organizations that have invested money in a product or service or some project or operation . . . So you know you can't do much as an individual unless you join forces with other people, or you try to see if there are any loopholes you can capitalize on . . . Because you know, major institutions use these loopholes. You know, they

*don't do tax evasion, they do tax avoidance. You know what I
mean?*

In the context of this perception, he told us of a dispute he
pursued with the IRS. Nikos maintained that scholarship
money he received years before was not taxable, while the IRS
claimed it was. Accessing the records of his college, Nikos
Stavros constructed documentary evidence regarding the scholarship income, evidence that he believed would provide crucially important leverage with which to rebut the IRS. The
faith Nikos placed in the documentary evidence and the confidence he had in his ability to construct his case (such as
accessing the archives of his former college) was eventually
affirmed by the IRS's admission that the income was not, after
all, taxable.

The various experiences that constituted Nikos's narrative
culminated in his description of a lawsuit he filed against
Isuzu. After repeatedly and unsuccessfully attempting to get a
water leak in his Trooper repaired, Nikos concluded that he
had been sold a "lemon" and requested that Isuzu refund the
purchase price. When they refused, Nikos, without a lawyer
and arguing on his own behalf, sued the corporation. Whereas
years before "he wasn't ready" or willing to dispute his eviction—not knowing much about "how things work"—at this
point, six years later and with the tax case "under his belt," he
believed that he was ready. His account of his decision to sue,
the tactics he employed, and his interpretation of how and
why he succeeded clearly express his sense of the law as a
game.

Nikos Stavros began this story by alluding to what he
understood to be the statutory definition of a "lemon,"

> [A]ccording to the law, a car, a new car is a lemon if you take it
> three times to the dealer to fix it, it's a genetic defect, and if by the
> third time it's still defective . . . then you are entitled to a refund
> or a new car.

Although this formal definition informed his decision to
pursue his legal claim, Nikos also acknowledged the contingent nature of his case. He understood that it was more than a
matter of applying a rule or formula to the situation. The out-

come would result from a contest, a process of argument and decision making.

> But, you go to the judge and, he hears both parties, and, it's bet-
> ter if you try to settle out of court.

Because he believed the outcome of any legal claim to be problematic and affected by one's ability to persuade others, Nikos left little to chance. The tactics that he had learned ear-lier—the importance of documents and reliance on the resources made available by other organizations—were skill-fully employed in constructing his case.

According to Nikos, after unsuccessfully attempting to get his car repaired or a refund of the price of the car, he wrote to the state consumer affairs division for information regarding the lemon law in New Jersey and the procedures for pursuing redress under it. He received, he told us, a "package of informa-tion [that had] all the steps outlined very clearly."

Based on these recommendations, as well as his own expe-rience, Nikos assembled meticulous records regarding his attempts to repair the car and his efforts to negotiate a solu-tion with the company.

> My experience is that if you have a case like that documented
> in a very precise way, then the law can, you can use that law
> in your favor.

Nikos's care and inventiveness in "using the law" far exceeded the recommendations of the consumer affairs divi-sion. Recognizing the fragility of memory and the vulnerability of verbal recollections, Nikos took steps to establish the "facts" against what he anticipated to be an alternative set of facts likely to be presented by the defendants. First, he took state-ments from friends of his who had been passengers in the car and who could testify that the car still leaked after each of the attempted repairs.

> I had two short statements from friends of mine who had driven
> with me and had experienced the problem. So, I used their state-
> ments as testimony. Because every, every time I would bring the
> car to the dealer, and they would try to fix it, I had documented
> the repair, and then next week or when two weeks later when I
> was driving in the rain and the problem was recurring . . . water

*leaking, water coming in the car . . . rain water . . . Well, my feet
[were getting wet] because it was underneath the dashboard.*

Second, in order to confirm the testimony of his friends,
Nikos Stavros obtained meteorological information regarding
the dates and times of rain in the area. In this way his own
and his friends' memories of riding with water on the floor of
the car were supported by the Department of Commerce.

*I [also] went to the Department of Commerce in New York, they
have the weather bureau . . . So I got, monthly listings of exactly
when it rained in the tri-state area. What dates, what time, what
precipitation we had, so when I talked to the judge, I told him,
"Listen, that day I traveled from Town A to Town B with this
friend of mine and that is the proof that it was raining."*

Against his picture of personal competence and sophistication, Nikos belittled his opponents for making what he clearly
interpreted as a naive and costly gaffe. When asked by the
judge whether a car would lose value because of a defect such
as the one under dispute,

*the customer service representative said, "Well no, you don't
reveal that to the potential buyer." And he said that in, in the
court! [laughter] . . . and that was the customer service representative not just in New Jersey, you know, he had a few states.*

The customer service representative's candid answer in
court about his willingness to deceive potential customers
was, according to Nikos, "awful to say." Awful, he explained,
not because it was immoral, but because it was a stupid move
in this strategic legal game. Notably, Nikos did not express
shock or disapproval that Isuzu committed the deceit, rather
he was shocked that the company representative would voluntarily and naively admit the deception in court. The admission
cost Isuzu the game according to Nikos. The moment of laughter punctuating his story indicates his pleasure in recollecting
this critical moment. The judge also reacted strongly to the
Isuzu representative's statement.

*Well, the judge was shocked and actually he put it down in the
six-page decision, you know, that he found that statement appall-
ing, very bad.*

Summing up the experience, Stavros once again explained,

> I had to document this case as well as possible and as good as
> possible so I did . . . Because first of all I didn't have a lawyer
> and I needed to present the case in a good way, and I thought,
> "What the hell?" [Laughter]. That was a pretty good experience,
> actually, yeah.

Laughter and pride suffuse Nikos's telling of this and
many of his other experiences. He clearly takes pleasure, if
only retrospectively, in his victories and the chance to display
his skill and acumen. The pleasure he expresses indicates a
ludic quality to outwitting his opponents ("What the hell?"). It
is not simply getting a refund for his car that satisfies him,
although that is clearly important. It is playing the game well
that pleases him. It was, he recalled, "a pretty good expe-
rience."

Like many of the people with whom we spoke, Nikos told
us that he was currently having a little trouble because his
landlord does not live in the building or nearby. "It is diffi-
cult," he said, "when the owner is not part of the community.
The trash does not get taken out regularly" and nobody tends
to the everyday issues of the building. However, Nikos does
not regard these problems as very serious. Nor does he regard
frequent consumer problems as anything out of the ordinary.
Life is filled with all sorts of little inconveniences. He is rather
matter of fact about his troubles, whether they are big or little,
and the actions he employs to solve them. He is not always
turning grievances into disputes and notes that often he tries
to solve problems through informal, friendly channels. In fact,
Nikos Stavros is now renting without a lease; he has an oral
agreement with the landlord. "He trusts me, I trust him, in
other words, we don't really bother . . . I mean he's a nice guy."

Two years ago, Nikos encountered what he experienced as
the capricious power of the law. But even in the face of what
seemed to be harassment, Stavros calculated the odds of
resisting successfully and chose resignation.

> Two years ago, I was at a beach resort. There was a small village.
> Some friends and I started walking down the street. It was a
> quaint New England village, no traffic, the waterfront, you know,
> houses and everything. A policeman was ticketing a car and

when he saw me walking down the street he told all of us to walk on the sidewalk. They went up on the sidewalk but I continued to walk on the street. Because I didn't want to walk on the sidewalk. There was no traffic and you're just in to relax. And you just happen to walk, not in the middle of the street.

When Nikos returned to his car, a police officer was waiting for him, and said, "So, you don't want to walk on the sidewalk?" Nikos replied, "Sir, if I need to protect myself, I will protect myself. I don't need you to tell me what to do."

Now the bastards, what they do, what they did, they radioed each other and two minutes later as I was driving, fifteen miles an hour very slowly through the village street, I saw two police cars and a motorbike. I said, "What's going on, officer?" He said, "License, registration," "What's the charge? What's wrong?" And the guy goes to me, "You were driving on the wrong side of the street." It was a lie! There were four cops! It was a lie. Because I was on the right side, going very slowly you know . . . It was outrageous.

Despite his outrage, Nikos paid the ticket he received that day. Had the incident occurred in New York or New Jersey, he said he would have contested it. But "I would have had to take the day off and go back to Connecticut, to that small village. Because if you don't pay the ticket, you have to go to court."

Throughout the long and varied litany of minor disputes and disagreements, claims, and counterclaims recounted in his interview, Nikos's understanding of the law and how it operates in social life remained remarkably unchanged. From the first incident involving the landlord and his eviction, Nikos Stavros expressed an understanding of the law as a game: a highly circumscribed and rule-bound arena of contest in which the players' relative skill strongly determine the outcome. At that point, he opted not to play rather than risk what he saw as certain defeat. As he acquired experience and skill, his willingness to engage the law increased. Nikos's interview offered a tale of personal development in which he changed in relation to the law, moving from a novice to a master, but in which the game remained more or less the same.

Playing with the Law

> To the pig keepers . . . the law was a domain of conflict in whose construction they participated.
>
> HENDRIK HARTOG, "Pigs and Positivism"

> If, however, the Usa Trial is not a game, it is not not a game either.
>
> ARTHUR LEFF, "Law and"

> That's another way of looking at the system, you know, identifying the right loopholes . . . It's amazing what things can be done and cannot be done with . . . within the law.
>
> NIKOS STAVROS

We began the analysis and interpretation of chapter 4 with a description of Kafka's parable "Before the Law." In that story, legality is depicted as a remote, seemingly autonomous institution whose authority derives from its perceived location outside of everyday life. This representation of legality often found expression in our respondents' accounts, although it was not the only story of legality they told. In this chapter we turn to a different interpretive schema and begin with another cultural representation, one that differs from Kafka's parable in terms of its form and content as well as its location in social space. We turn from the moral instruction canonized in Kafka's masterpiece to the vernacular humor of a picture postcard.

The picture on the front of this postcard is a drawing of an apple about to fall on the top of a man's head. The trajectory of the apple is indicated with a series of meticulously drawn and convincing angles. The caption at the bottom of the picture reads: "Gravity. It isn't just a good idea. It's the law."

Where Kafka's parable serves as a description of dehumanized legality or reified law, this postcard depicts legality as a socially constructed phenomenon. The postcard's joke turns on the recognition and simultaneous rejection of the law's claim to be like gravity, a natural, inevitable, and determinant phenomenon. The postcard mocks, as it displays, the pretensions of law. Typically, the reminder "It's the law" is tacked on to the end of some injunction (for example,

Gravity.
It isn't just a good idea.
It's the law.
Sponsored By The Physical Universe In Cooperation With The National Safety Council.

"to buckle up," "don't smoke," "register for the draft") and is meant to preempt argument or resistance in circumstances where noncompliance is likely. Thus, by reminding us that gravity is not just a good idea but that "it's the law," the postcard juxtaposes the human to the natural, the variable to the eternal, the particularity of public policies to the universality of the physical world. By playfully invoking the law of gravity, the postcard challenges the gravity of law.

This card was purchased in a national bookstore chain in a typical suburban mall. As a piece of popular culture—mass produced and familiar—the postcard reminds us that if we are to understand legal culture and consciousness we must track these commonplace readings and, as important, their constitutive relationship to the law.

In addition to understanding legality as a set of transcendent ordering principles before which people live, our respondents also experienced the law as an ensemble of legal actors, organizations, rules, and procedures with which they managed their daily lives. In this view, legality appears as an arena in which actors struggle to achieve a variety of purposes. Understanding legality as available and multipurpose, people often see the possibility of putting the law to their own ends. In contrast to the reified view of legality, here self-interest is understood to operate legitimately. Furthermore, acknowledging the possibility of using the law for one's own interests encompasses an understanding of legality as available to others as well, others who can be counted on to use the law for their own purposes. Varied and sometimes conflicting interests define the purposes to which law might be put and are thus a central part of legal institutions. Since interests are attached to persons and positions, legality reflects the multifaceted, often conflicting and shifting objectives of both official and lay participants. This is a vision of legality as engagement and conflict, resource and process.

Seeing legality as an arena of contest, potentially available to self and others, is not to say that the perceived uses are thought to be infinite. People recognize the constraints that operate on law. They understand that there are rules governing what law can do, rules that stipulate when, where, for what, and by whom the law might be invoked. They also understand that the law is compelled to settle matters, to provide closure by deciding cases. Moreover, those outcomes cannot be known beforehand but must be open ended and dependent upon the particularities of each case.

When expressing a vision of legality as an arena of engagement, people also know that it is not constantly or equally available to everyone. They understand that there are costs associated with using the law, or with using it in a certain way (e.g., threatening to call the police rather than actually calling them, or settling with an insurance company rather than hiring a lawyer to defend your claims). In addition to costs, however, our respondents also acknowledged the significant consequences of players' different levels of skill and experience. In other words, legality comes with costs that are differentially burdensome, and thus legality is differentially available.

Recognizing these constraints on legality and the different capacities of litigants, citizens often decide to turn to the law, or challenge the law, only after a rough calculation of the probability of realizing the ends sought. Citizens, in short, often act strategically in relation to identifiable legal actors, organizations, and rules.

If bureaucracy is the schematic representation of a reified law, the schema underwriting this form of legal consciousness is the game. Many respondents allude to the law as a game; many report playing it, or refraining from playing it, as one might speak of a game. Often, our respondents judged legal experiences in relation to their ludic features: for instance, whether it was fun or pleasant or played fairly. By suggesting the schema of the game to describe this form of consciousness of law as contest and struggle, we are not asserting that law is a game, or merely a game. We are claiming, however, that one can distinguish this expression of the role of law in society from other ways of participating in legality by considering the ways in which legality is understood and played like a game.

Law as Instrument v. Law as Game

The understandings of legality expressed by Nikos Stavros and Charles Reed could be characterized as instrumental. As it is typically understood from an instrumental perspective, law makes available tools, resources, symbols, and vocabularies useful in the construction of social life. This view emphasizes the accessibility of law as an open-ended device that self-conscious agents deploy, along with a variety of other instruments, for all sorts of purposes. From this perspective, legality is often described as an amoral or apolitical medium that may nonetheless, because it is overlaid on a structure of social inequality, produce systematically biased outcomes.

Although each of these features of legality—its availability, utility, and partiality—was expressed by Nikos and Charles, as well as by others with whom we spoke, we are not using the familiar schema of law as instrument to describe this understanding of legality. As a way of capturing the meaning of legality expressed by our respondents, the metaphor of law as instrument or tool simply assumes too much and conjures too little.

First, a crucial shortcoming of the image of law as an instrument is that it begs the question of rationality. Although respondents often described themselves as rational actors calculating utility and weighing costs in pursuit of defined objectives, the law plays a variety of roles in their management of social relationships. In some cases, legality was described as a token, a trump, or a gimmick deployed to best an opponent. In other instances, respondents described themselves and others as wielding law as a weapon to harm others, rather than to just defeat them.

Although many citizens and legal agents frequently calculate the ways in which one or another legal technique may be deployed to achieve desired ends, the rationality expressed is not limited to a simple means-ends calculation. For instance, people often use the law for expressive or communicative purposes. Consciously positioning oneself in relation to the law provides a culturally interpretable way of expressing something about oneself or one's relationship to others. Thus, tolerating the noise of a neighbor is used as a way of enacting the role of good neighbor or showing that one is a nice guy (i.e., tolerant and understanding). Or assuming the costs of a legal contest, even in the face of likely defeat, might be used to show that you are not to be pushed around or that you are the type of person who, as one of our respondents claimed, "must have justice." People often made explicit statements that tied identity claims to legal actions taken or forgone.

At other times people make decisions about how to act in a particular case on the basis of what they consider to be morally appropriate, regardless of their self-defined interests or their perception of the probability of satisfying them. People turn to legality to assert values, rights (their own or others), or even some conception of justice.[1]

Finally, many actors use the law for the pleasures or challenges it provides, rather than, or in addition to, its utility in achieving desired ends. These persons see legal encounters as opportunities for plying their skill in besting an opponent. They experience legal interactions as thrilling or amusing or satisfying. When Nikos Stavros characterized his encounter with Isuzu as a "pretty good experience," it is clear that the satisfaction he derived was radically different from the "pleasant experience" reported by Rita Michaels. Rita found pleasure in the moral affirmation bestowed upon her by the judge. Nikos's is a satisfaction that derived from his own meticulously orchestrated legal contest. Similarly, Charles Reed took enormous pleasure describing the quality of legal talent he could hire and his negotiation strategies.

In short, legality functions as both a means and an end for those we interviewed.[2] It sometimes provides tools for achieving some purpose and at other times it becomes a purpose in itself. In order to denote the variety of roles assigned to the law by our respondents, the word *instrument* would need to be construed so broadly as to render it meaningless for purposes of interpreting or recognizing distinctions in social action.

A second problem with the conventional image of law as a tool or instrument is that it fails to fully capture the interactive and social aspects of legality. When people spoke of using the law, it was always in relation to others; there was always an opponent, another person or organization, imagined or real, whose interests and actions defined the content and limits of their opposition. In this construction, legality is inextricably embedded in the web of social relationships, out of which interests and disputes emerge. Legal regulations and statutes may specify the obligations and privileges of persons occupying various roles and statuses, for example, car owner, tenant, landlord, parent, or employer. Legality emerges out of and continually shapes those roles and relationships. In short, the law is not simply a tool used to adjudicate disputes between persons with opposing interests; legality actually operates to constitute the interests (as well as the obligations and privileges) sought by citizens.

The law is also understood as defining objects or things, in addition to persons and relationships. Stavros invoked the statutory definition of "lemon" to characterize his car. Within the context of his legal dispute with Isuzu he understood the status of lemon to be a result not only of some "genetic" defect, that is, some state or condition that described the car. Lemon is a categorization that the law stipulated would apply only after certain efforts to repair the car were made. As a status to be conferred, lemonhood made available, but did not ensure, legal redress.

Finally, the instrumental conception of law fails to reflect the strong sense of contingency expressed by respondents. When used correctly a tool works in determinant ways. A hammer squarely striking a nail drives it in; a key when turned opens the lock. But people we interviewed understood that the law, even when used appropriately (by its own internally defined rules) has no determined result. For them the law is designed to provide closure in any given case—a verdict, a finding, or an award—but not to determine what that outcome will be prior to the particular engagement. Nikos Stavros understood that both the uses and the outcomes of law are always contingent—dependent on the particular circumstances, relations, resources, and interactions that define a given case. Indeed, for Nikos Stavros and others this sort of indeterminacy is believed to be essential to its legitimate operation, rather than a basis for critique.[3]

The qualities of legality that are lost in the instrumental image—its expressive and nonrational qualities, the relational and social contexts in which it is enacted, and the sense of it as contingent and open ended—were expressed in the accounts and interpretations of our respondents. Our objective in displacing the law-as-instrument metaphor was to find an alternative way of capturing an interpretation of legality that understood it to be a socially constructed and socially organized means for seeking a variety of ends or expressing a variety of meanings in relation to, and typically in opposition to, others.

A metaphor that expresses this engagement with the law was that of a game. Games are distinctive types of social encounters. Despite the fact that few of us could easily define the generic social-organizational features of gaming (i.e., those features that Monopoly, football, chess, poker, and Mah Jongg have in common), we all more or less know what to expect when we commit ourselves to watching or playing a game. Our familiarity with games is not surprising. Learning to play games is an early and critical part of our socialization. And, many have argued, games are a central part of our cultural cosmology.[4] At any rate, because of the numerous explicit and implicit references to law as a game, it is instructive to explore precisely what is entailed in that metaphor by examining the relationships between the cultural meanings of law and games.

Legality and the Social Organization of Games

> What sacred games shall we have to invent?
> FRIEDRICH NIETZSCHE, *The Gay Science*

As they are defined in American culture, games are clearly demarcated encounters, bounded in space and time, with formal beginnings, turn taking, and endings. As a set of constraints specifying permissible roles, transactions, and purposes, a game contains within its rules all that is necessary to realize its aim. Within the gaming encounter, the rules provide the only legitimate normative framework. It is, in other words, only within the rules of the game that action makes sense. According to Leff, "The means of play are not open to question in any non-game terms—justness, for instance, or legitimacy or efficiency—for [the rules of the game] do not so much regulate the activity as constitute it."[5]

The fact that games have clearly defined endings means that, unlike most other social encounters or experiences, games provide closure and resolution. Games offer closure by defining the conditions under which the game will end and a winner be declared. It may be the passage of time, the taking of a specified number of turns, the decision of a judge, or the achievement of some particular or designated state of affairs. Yet even as they provide closure, games are never designed to stipulate ahead of the play just who the winner will be. In this way, games provide the promise of both closure and contingency. In order to achieve this contingency, games must be defined and organized to reflect the relative skill, determination, preparedness, and attitude of the players. In other words, games are deliberately designed with degrees of freedom around which outcomes are produced but not predetermined.

The rules of any game specify what does and does not matter in the game. These rules of irrelevancy may cover material, social, or psychological phenomena.[6] For example, one can play the game of checkers with marble divots or with bottle caps; it does not matter. The game is not defined by the material of the checkers but by the design of the board, the movements allowed, and some means of des-

ignating the opposing checkers. Similarly, social status is irrelevant
to the rules and playing of most games, and it would violate the spirit
of the game to invoke attributes that derive from outside the game.
More to the point, the phrase and concept "playing fair" mean that
participants are expected to adhere to the rules of irrelevancy, that
is, to ignore things that are not part of the structure of the game. For
this reason, players are treated (for purposes of the game) as formally
identical. When they are placed in competitive positions, each player
is given the same resources and opportunities to play. If resources
(such as turns, points, or time) are forfeited it is only under clearly
stipulated conditions. The pleasure of games derives, Goffman argues, from exactly this structure of irrelevancies.

Operating in concert, these features of games function to bracket
the gaming experience from what we understand to be the real world.
The roles, relationships, rules, and expectations that might operate
in the real world are suspended during the game. Unless expressed
in the rules of the game, ethical principles and normative commit-
ments or laws are meaningless. We take it for granted that antitrust
law or charitable impulses toward our opponents have no place
within the game of Monopoly. One might act upon them, but in doing
so one would be doing something other than playing Monopoly (being a parent of a novice player, for instance). Because of this bracketing, games represent a suspension of "real" life. Consequently, we
often dismiss games as trivial or childish diversions. Yet it is precisely
because of their capacity to suspend reality that games are considered to be "world-building activities."[7] The very same rules that exclude aspects of everyday life and render them irrelevant produce an
alternative world of meaning and relevance within the boundaries of
the gaming encounter.

Given these properties of games, it is not surprising that the law
has frequently been described as a game (or in gamelike terms) by
legal and socio-legal scholars. Arthur Leff[8] describes the American
trial (using the transparent pseudonym Usa to refer to American society) as an agonistic game. Played against an opponent within rules
that attempt to ensure some formal equality (the proverbial "level
playing field") and providing closure to the contest (a winner and a
loser, a decision and a disposition), the trial reflects, Leff argues, the
cultural significance the Usas attach to gaming.

In many instances the game metaphor was explicitly invoked by
our respondents who referred at various times—with disgust, resig-

nation, or pleasure—to the legal game. The following observation by Michelle Stewart, a single, white woman in her early thirties, illustrates this view of law.

> *[Interviewer: What was the experience of going to court like?] Difficult because I was naive. I really didn't think people would lie in court. I don't know why, but I just thought like justice would be done and . . . they just lie . . . I feel like the truth has very little to do with it, that it is just really a chess game.*

Others echoed this sentiment, expressing disillusionment.

> *[Interviewer: Why do you think people use lawyers so much when they're dealing with these agencies?] I really don't know but I . . . feel like it's a gimmick and it's sure, however you do it, the lawyers get some, the welfare gets some, all of them get some.* (Bess Sherman)

Still others described the gamelike features of legality without necessarily expressing a sense of illegitimacy or rejection. For them the fact that legality is a game represents an invitation to play or to enjoy the sport. In one interview a man described his experience as a witness in court and the skill of lawyers to shape his testimony,

> *You know lawyers can pick and choose what they want the court to hear and I found that there was a great deal of mental stimulation in situations where they were playing games.* (Arthur Williams)

In other interviews, respondents described their experiences in terms of the social organization of games, but without explicitly referring to the law as a game. Both Charles Reed and Nikos Stavros, for instance, described their encounters with police, government agencies, employers, and businesses in terms of strategic engagements in which they considered their options and goals and then decided on actions that would get them where they wanted to be. Both Reed and Stavros often enjoyed these contests and, even when they lost, claimed that they had nonetheless gained by accumulating knowledge and experience.

To clarify this type of legal consciousness and to unpack the schema of the game, we now locate it along the four dimensions we used earlier to describe the reified vision of law: normativity, constraint, capacity, and time and space.

Normativity: Partiality

In chapter 4, we stated that the norm of impartiality is a critical constituent of a reified and remote law. Attributing an impartial position to the law and to official legal actors creates the distance that separates the mundane world of colliding self-interests from the dispassionate and transcendent world of legality. The distance is constructed daily when citizens invalidate claims or reject lines of action on the grounds that they reveal only personal interests. At other times, however, the expectations of impartiality, and the actions it warrants, were absent in the stories people told.

Partiality as Normative License

Describing the characteristics of a game, people often referred to the law as an arena for articulating and pursuing self-interest. Consider the comments of Raymond Johnson, an African American resident of Camden, New Jersey. After completing a bachelor's degree at one of the state colleges, Raymond Johnson worked as a purchasing agent and as a data processor. Because his employment had been sporadic, he was supplementing his unreliable income, less than ten thousand dollars in 1991, by helping with maintenance and management responsibilities in the building in which he lives. He has not, however, always gotten along well with some of the other managers and tenants. Some years back, Raymond Johnson had an argument with the landlord. His lease

> was coming to the end that month. [The landlord] was really
> upset about it, all right? So, I said, "Don't war and argue with an
> angry person." You get nowhere, all you do is just perpetuate the
> conflict. So I turned around, walked out. Waited half hour, called
> him on the telephone . . . And said that according to the lease
> here, you cannot cancel the lease . . . You have to give me an
> option to renew. Says so right here! You don't have the option
> not to let me renew. You have to renew it if I choose to renew it.

Raymond Johnson described his landlord as a skilled, powerful, and experienced player in this game of rights, entitlements, and interests. Yet despite the landlord's skill and reputation, Raymond Johnson was prepared for the engagement,

> [T]his guy was a leading man in the community, and he had ties
> in City Hall, he used to get people evicted out of here in a week.

> *They didn't know any better. He'd intimidate them. He'd do what-*
> *ever he did with City Hall, and they'd get the paperwork pushed*
> *through, and they'd be gone. So he went into his little spiel about*
> *what he was going to do and so on and so forth. And I said,*
> *"Yeah, well, no matter how you look at it, if you want me to per-*
> *suade you that I have a right to this apartment, yeah, we can*
> *have that discussion." And we did! Over about two weeks, two-*
> *week period . . . We talked about it. Well, I had no fear that it*
> *wasn't [going to work out]. He couldn't evict me!*

The right to the apartment to which Raymond Johnson alluded was not a right he saw as grounded in legal principle or natural law. It was a right that he deduced from the rules of the game. Later in the interview Raymond Johnson declared, somewhat defiantly, that "there is no justice. You either win, or you lose. As long as you can accomplish your objectives, you win. I'm not concerned about justice."

In another case that illustrated the usefulness of law for realizing or defending personal interests, Joan Kinsler, a thirty-three-year-old white dental hygienist, told us about an incident that occurred seven years earlier when her landlord tried to have her evicted. Although Joan was not aware of it at the time, her landlord was very ill and needed to sell the house in order to pay for medical care. All she knew, she told us, was that she was being thrown out on the street because the new owner wanted her out. She contacted the Housing Department and used the information it provided regarding her rights to delay her eviction. Daring her landlord to "take me to court," Joan deployed her knowledge of the housing laws to protect her interests against those of her landlord or the new owners.

> *I finally understood, [that the landlord was ill] . . . maybe I*
> *could've been a little bit more sympathetic to her. I said, "Well,*
> *you can take me to court." I was real cocky, because [the Hous-*
> *ing Department official] told me ninety days more, you know . . .*
> *I said, "No, you can take me to court, because the judge is only*
> *going to give me an additional ninety days because I called the*
> *Board of Health. I mean the Housing Department." She knew,*
> *you know, that she wasn't playing with somebody that she could*
> *push and push and push and say, "Okay, all right. I'll just get out*
> *and live with somebody until I find something."*

In both of these stories, the law defines and offers a normative space within which to pursue one's interests. Although there are rules constraining the pursuit, such as the terms of the lease, the tenant-landlord laws, and the procedures of the housing court, these rules do not neatly correspond to the rules and norms that operate elsewhere. Identifiable rules of irrelevancy distinguish the law's moral space from everyday spheres of action where the pursuit of self-interest may be modulated by ethical considerations, such as sympathy for a dying landlord, or even generalized norms of honesty. In other words, legality and legal forms produce for these respondents a kind of mutually realized, but authentic, bracketing of the everyday world, and with that the suspension of rules that operate in and define the everyday as elsewhere.

In fact, in stark contrast to the image of a trial as a mechanism for determining the truth, people often referred to court as a place in which deceit and manipulation prevail, where opponents can be expected to lie, bluff, or manufacture a story that will present their interests in the best light. One respondent stated simply,

> I learned you need proper representation because people tend to
> tell lies when they go there [to court]. (Ambrose Grant)

Notably, this respondent was not making a general assessment about human nature and the propensity to lie. The pointed reference to lying "when they go there" expresses the view that the tendency to lie is linked to a particular place and time where it is expected and permitted.

Another respondent made a similar distinction between moral and legal definitions of honesty in describing the way lawyers produce testimony in court through the strategic use of examination and cross-examination,

> I mean morally it's dishonest, legally it's not dishonest . . . the
> legal system allows these adversarial games to be played . . . To
> me withholding information is dishonest. I mean, morally it's dis-
> honest, legally it's not dishonest. (Arthur Williams)

Thus, respondents perceived legality as providing a sort of normative license that permits and even sanctions some level of misrepresentation and manipulation. This license seems to suspend or render irrelevant many of the everyday constraints on unmitigated self-interestedness, such as ethical or practical considerations dictating some degree of empathy or reciprocity.

The normative license offered by legality seems to do more, however, than simply grant permission to pursue some preexisting set of interests. As respondents acquired information and experience regarding what is legally available or permissible in the pursuit of their interests, the legal definitions, rules, and protections would often come to define those interests. When Joan Kinsler learned that the judge was "going to give [her] an additional ninety days" before she could be evicted, those ninety days came to define what Joan Kinsler sought. Those ninety days came to represent, moreover, the price Joan would have to pay if she acted upon the sympathy she felt upon learning of her landlord's illness. Thus, even though people do not always, or even frequently, pursue what they understand to be their legal entitlements or protections—often lumping their grievances— the legal definitions are nonetheless significant insofar as they come to constitute the interests forgone.

Law as Commodity

Perhaps the clearest expression of the perception of legality as being deliberately designed for self-interested uses was captured in numerous references to law as a commodity, something to be bought and sold. According to this view, once people pay the price, typically understood to be exacted in the form of taxes, they own the law and have a proprietary right to the services it provides. Nikos Stavros expressed this view in response to a question as to what he would do were a police officer to treat him unfairly,

> I would, I think I would complain, because from the simple point of I'm paying for the service, you know, as a consumer.

George Kofie stated similar expectations.

> Okay, people play—pay the police a salary for protection. And I think that protection should guarantee that when you go to sleep at night, you will wake up tomorrow morning without having someone standing over your bed with a gun or somebody having broken into your house over the night or someone having stolen your car.

Alan Fox, an upper-middle-class professional living in Essex County in northern New Jersey, implied that the state tax structure served as a means of distributing access to public institutions and power.

If you lived in Trenton [in southern New Jersey], let's say, and
you were driving through to go skiing or something like that and
you got into an altercation, you'd come to use the Essex County
court system . . . And I'd be paying for it, but you wouldn't be a
resident of my county.

These statements express a sense of legality as one of the active,
interested parties to a market transaction rather than the disinterested
arbiter. Indeed, rather than understanding themselves to be citizens
standing before the law, they see themselves as consumers engaging in
transactions with the law: paying police officers for protection and respect, or purchasing, through one's property taxes, the right to use the
courts. To the extent that the law is understood to be a party to a contract, providing a variety of services in exchange for taxes, it also represents a set of (potentially opposing) interests in its own right.

Another of the self-conscious allusions to law as a commodity—
something one can purchase, use, distribute at will—was also provided by Alan Fox, one of the few lawyers in our random sample of
respondents. Alan Fox grew up in the upper-middle-class community
in northern New Jersey in which he still lived at the time of the interview. Alan made numerous references throughout the interview to
his friends, some of whom he has known since childhood, and to his
neighborhood and community. Among his many ties to the community was a group of male friends who regularly meet to play poker.
In the context of telling us of this network of friends, and as a way
of conveying his feelings toward these men, Alan Fox mentioned that
if any of his friends might benefit by an easy litigation, he initiates it
for them for no fee. In one particular instance, Alan Fox mentioned
the property reassessments about to be undertaken by the town.

So I thought what I would do, in a magnanimous gesture, is I
would file an appeal for everybody in my poker game. Just do
them all at the same time.

Thus, central to Alan Fox's idea of friendship and caring is his
ability to offer his friends his legal skills and experience. For him,
legality is a gift he can bestow upon others. Deploying the law in this
way provides opportunities to achieve personal objectives, not least
of which is displaying his attachment to his friends. In fact, Alan Fox
plays law as he plays poker. "Because people who are really my
friends, I couldn't do enough for them." And, Alan Fox told us, "it's
fun."

For these respondents, self-interest is as central and legitimate in their legal relations as it is in the transactions they enact daily with shopkeepers, plumbers, and others they encounter in the market of goods and services. Thus, the law is a commodity that can be acquired for whatever purposes are desired, like toothpaste or automobiles, as long as one pays the price.[9]

Limits to Self-Interest: Corruption

The fact that these respondents believe that law and legal forms function on the basis of self-interest does not mean, however, that they understand the pursuit of interest to be unregulated. People recognize limits to what ends might be sought or what means might be employed legitimately. For persons who enact this type of legal consciousness, corruption, immorality, and malfeasance are not simply violations of generalized norms regarding honesty. They are transgressions of the highly circumscribed ground rules of the law-game. Since many of these rules operate to ensure the contingency of the game (an aspect of legality we will discuss in greater detail below), corruption is frequently defined as that which predetermines the outcome of legal processes such that only one set of interests can prevail.

For some, like Charles Reed, corruption is exemplified by officials taking bribes or legal opponents using particularistic connections to their advantage. Yet for other respondents, even this form of official malfeasance is accepted as simply part of the game. Michael Chapin, a marginally employed carpenter, described the deterioration of his working-class community and the existence of local corruption. His complaint, he assured us, was not with the corruption per se but with the way it interfered with the delivery of town services.

> I don't really care if they are corrupt, if they want to keep a couple thousand for themselves, I just want the town to be nice. It's just dirty. They could clean it up and make it look nicer.

For Michael Chapin, his interests in a clean community and the interests of public officials in making "a couple thousand" dollars are not necessarily opposed and could, he concedes, coexist. The situation becomes intolerable for him only when the interests of officials preempt his interests in a well-run town.

Another critical factor that seems to affect where the line is drawn between tolerable and intolerable partiality, permissible and impermissible corruption, is the position of the corrupted official within the legal hierarchy. Compared to other legal actors, local town or city officials were most likely to be described as corrupt. While respondents did not always accept or endorse this corruption, they often expressed a resigned tolerance of it. A sixty-seven-year-old white school secretary, Laura Flanagan, described the long history of municipal patronage in her town.

> *The mayor, he became mayor right after the Second World War.*
> *And at that time we didn't have civil service in [town]. Our*
> *police and fire department were appointed by politicians. Okay?*
> *And that's how the town was. [Lowers voice to a whisper.] And*
> *that's how the town is now.*

After describing a current controversy regarding the hiring of a second assistant superintendent in the school system within the patronage system, Laura Flanagan summed up her response.

> *You just walk around and smile. I decided, I'm not a brownie, I*
> *can't be, it's not my makeup, but I mind my own business.*

As one moves up the legal hierarchy, from police to lawyers to judges, or from trash collectors to council members to mayors, the expressed tolerance for corruption declines noticeably. What seems to account for this lack of tolerance for corruption among those legal agents with greater power is the understanding that these higher officials acting upon personal interests, by virtue of their power, substantially increase the likelihood of skewing the outcome and fixing the game. The delicately maintained balance between local officials getting a little extra income and the interests of people like Michael Chapin is likely to be destroyed under these circumstances. Jaded by experience, Charles Reed recognized and rejected the legitimacy of the school committee member's shaping teaching assignments to enhance the quality of her own daughter's classroom. People understand the vulnerability of their interests in the face of the dishonesty of those with power and authority.

Aside from these violations of the rules, an important point to emphasize regarding the normative space defined by a gamelike legality is that, while respondents recognize it to be different from the norms of everyday life, they do not necessarily see it as illegitimate. The legitimacy attributed to it derives from its utility in resolving

conflicts and adjudicating interests fairly. In other words, legality offers a highly circumscribed world of rules, rights, roles, and responsibilities that apply to all who play and, like the rules of a game, have
an internal logic and legitimacy.

Constraint

Turning to the second dimension of our interpretive schemas, we see
that our respondents noted how rules constrain what can be done
legally. When people work with the law, many of the rules, procedures, ordinances, and even constitutional amendments are perceived as historically and socially constructed. As human inventions,
they are understood to be open to challenge, vulnerable to change,
and available for self-interested manipulation. Whereas a reified view
of law understands substantive guidelines, such as an actuarial table
or a statute, as limiting and at times preempting human action, the
gamelike view of legality interprets rules as creating spaces, the proverbial loophole, within which action can occur and advantage be
taken. Nikos Stavros recognized the intractable bureaucratic character of contemporary life, with its labyrinthine procedures, but he also
believed that energy, experience, skill, and strategy can make a difference in what happens. Much can be done, Nikos Stavros said, "with"
and "within the law." Jokingly, he said that he was marshaling his
skills so that

> next time, I'll be in the Supreme Court. Nikos Stavros is chang-
> ing the law, you know, the Stavros amendment.

Within the openness of the law, however, respondents alluded to
two other qualities that they understood to be defining and constraining elements of legality. Within an arena of play, such as legality, what makes the game worth playing is that it ensures both contingency and closure. These aspects were perceived as constraints on
the action of ordinary people and legal agents.

Contingent Outcomes

As we discussed earlier, at one level, legality-as-game evokes and relies on a construction of legality as contingent and uncertain. This
is true in the sense that the outcome of any play, or any particular
game, is not ordained by the rules in any a priori sense. That uncertainty is the basis of the decisions people make regarding how and

when to invoke or turn to the law. Just as we generally refrain from playing, or even watching, games or contests where we know the winner ahead of time, we refrain from using the law under such circumstances. So central is contingency to the meaning of a game that in a situation where the outcome is predetermined, by the rules or their enactment, we often deny such an event the status of a game, declaring it to be "no contest."

In short, the law is actively engaged only when its effect is uncertain. Consider, in this vein, the practice of plea bargaining, a contest used to avoid another, more formal contest. Plea bargaining is common when an outcome seems foregone and undesirable. In other words, defendants engage in plea bargaining when it is futile to play the trial game because it is clear that there will be a finding of guilty. Thus, the plea bargain is premised on the certainty of outcome, a guilty verdict, but the substantive indeterminacy—the length of sentence—is maintained by substituting a negotiation for a trial.

When mobilizing law, people often engage in a type of anticipatory decision making, basing their decision to act—their willingness to play—on a faith in the openness of the legal process. What ensures this openness and thus defines legality for these respondents is not substantive law but rules of procedure. The rules of due process provided by the American Constitution and elaborated through statutes and court decisions provide the means of keeping the substance of decisions uncertain while simultaneously ensuring that some outcome will be produced. These rules—for example, the right to be represented by a professional legal advocate, to hear the evidence, to have probable cause before incurring the social and economic costs of a trial, to confront witnesses, and to refrain from testifying against oneself—are designed to create a reasonable balance of power between the parties so as to ensure against unfair advantage.[10]

Furthermore, American law's attempt to ensure the uncertainty of outcomes by eliminating unfair advantage is also evident in the institutional structure of the legal system itself. For example, small-claims courts were created as an arena for hearing the kinds of claims and interests that would not be adequately considered in the general-jurisdiction courts. The point here is that the rules of the system are designed to ensure that the outcomes of legal contests will not be able to be determined in advance of the play because of some irrelevant characteristics of the players, such as the material circumstances, or the emotional affect generated among the parties.[11]

As we just noted, the perception that legality assures contingency is often the basis for mobilizing the law. People turn voluntarily to the law because their cause, so to speak, is not lost beforehand. The contingency associated with legal forms and procedures is more than a description of how people expect it to operate, however. It is also understood and invoked normatively, as a quality that the law should, but does not necessarily, embody.

The objections people voice to corruption and cheating are not simply that the legitimate partiality of law has become excessive or that the represented interests are improper ones. The objection to cheating and corruption is also an expression of this insistence that the result of a legal game be a product of the play itself, rather than of those supposedly bracketed irrelevancies. Cheaters are abhorrent because by fixing the game, through bribes for example, they determine the outcome. By bringing into the game what is specifically excluded as irrelevant, cheaters destroy the reality-generating power of the game and therefore its claim to legitimacy.

Promising Closure

At the same time that legality is defined as that which ensures contingency, it is also defined in terms of its ability to provide closure. This closure is achieved by a decision or verdict. In fact, the dispositiveness of the law—the fact that it trumps all other authority—is seen as a defining characteristic and a principal attraction of legal process. The promise of a game is that the process ensures a means for producing an end to itself. Many people turn to law not so much for the playing as for the end of play, for providing, as one man observed, "the final solution" to conflicts and disputes.

The closure that the law provides can even be valued independently of the substantive disposition, "Even . . . losing," Leff writes, "may, at least some of the time, be a pleasant alternative to a lifetime of never knowing."[12] After two years of disputing with her health maintenance organization over whether it would pay the costs of health care received out of state, Maryann Sayer told us that she finally said to the HMO, "Take me to court and get it over with."

Echoing this sentiment, Michael Chapin described his reaction to a court case in which a judgment was made against him for breach of contract. Although he lost the case and had to forfeit a five-hundred-dollar deposit he had made, Michael welcomed the final decision.

> *I wasn't happy and I wasn't displeased. It was just over. I was happy it was over. Get it out of the way. It's like having something taken off your back, you know. It's a weight you carry around.*

Individuals turn to law to attain closure when alternative methods of dispute resolution such as argument or negotiation have failed to settle the matter. Moreover, some alternative methods of resolution are themselves conditioned on the imagined possibility of law's judgment. Not using the law, for instance relying on informal agreements or negotiation, is often premised on and conducted in the shadow of legal decisions.[13] People often resolve disputes informally in order to avoid the law. Such an implicit but mutual awareness of legal alternatives is crucial in sustaining the so-called nonlegal relationships and transactions that overwhelm social life. Thus, even when it appears absent, legality imparts meaning to behavior by framing interpretations of alternative courses of action. It offers the possibility of coercion and closure not legitimately available elsewhere.

This observation—that closure through law frames nonlegal behavior—invites a somewhat different interpretation than has been conventionally offered to explain the findings that legality seems relatively unimportant in everyday life. For instance, Stewart Macaulay concluded that formal contract law was rarely used to resolve differences about the purchase, delivery, or distribution of cars and parts by the automobile manufacturers and dealers he studied.[14] More recently, Robert Ellickson found that among cattle ranchers in northern California, the law was also infrequently invoked to settle cattle trespass disputes, concluding that law's relevance to large segments of everyday life is minimal.[15] Both Macaulay and Ellickson suggest that expectations of continued relationships and the norms of reciprocity are more powerful inducements to informally mediate differences and resolve disputes than is the possibility of legal recourse and sanction. Even in light of this empirical evidence of nonuse where legal recourse is possible, such a conclusion regarding the irrelevance of legality may not be warranted. Persons engaged in continuing relations may be hesitant to invoke legal processes to handle competing claims and disputes lest those relationships be disturbed by the threat (or fact) of legal coercion, as Macaulay and Ellickson demonstrate. Nonetheless, those same relationships, and the circumstances out of which the disputes emerged, are already shaped and conditioned by legal forms and obligations, e.g., the right and thus ability to sell a particular manufacturer's automobiles, or the title to a specific piece of land or herd of cattle. Not only are disputes infused with law, but the immediate inducements to settle are interpreted against the alternative not sought: legal action and litigation. As Sarat and Kearns point out, "[O]ne is apt to catch more than a fleeting glimpse of law's presence in the putatively alegal responses."[16]

Capacity

> There is a common sense view that games are fun to play when the outcome or payoff has a good chance of remaining unsettled until the end of play . . . To speak of the outcome as problematic, however, is, in effect, to say that one must look to the play itself in order to discover how things will turn out.
>
> ERVING GOFFMAN, "Fun and Games"

> But the law is still, in certain inevitable cases, the pre-engaged servant of the long purse.
>
> WILKIE COLLINS, *The Woman in White*

If the outcomes of play must remain uncertain, what legitimately determines the outcome? Here we see another marked distinction between the consciousness of law as a reified, transcendent order and the consciousness of legality as a game. Whereas the reified model reflects the capacity located in the hierarchy of roles and responsibilities to create relays of effect beyond any individual decision maker, the consciousness of law as game locates agency squarely within the legal players.

Experience and Learning

Where the division of labor was the productive agent in the schema "before the law," the skill of actors in deploying their knowledge and experience is seen as the crucial factor in the legal game played with the law. In this interpretive schema, the particular facts and legal rules that can be brought to bear upon an event are themselves subject to interpretation, selection, and strategic presentation. Material facts, statutes, court decisions, and formal legal procedures do not dictate in any simple way what is to be done legally, or how things will turn out. Indeed, playing the law game often entails not just playing by the rules but playing with the rules. It may even involve attempting to create new rules if doing so would advantage the player. Depending on the situation, individuals view legal and material factors as resources or, alternatively, obstacles, but they still believe that ultimately the players' skills and resources will shape the outcome. Perhaps most revealing of this understanding of legality are the abundant references to learning and the significance that people attached to their legal education and experience.

I was naive. (Claire Delorey)

I didn't know any better. (Leroy Tanner)

I wasn't ready. (Nikos Stavros)

We were stupid, we didn't know about taking him to court or whatever. (Jamie Leeson)

These references express belief in the importance of acquiring a stock of knowledge and experience. Although they are presented as characterizations of the self, and are often embedded in narratives of personal development, they reveal critical, albeit unstated, assumptions regarding legal processes and legality. They describe a process in which individual experience and knowledge matter, a system in which outcomes reflect individual acumen and know-how. In other words, these references, and the stories of which they are a part, do not depict law as a machine that evaluates raw facts in terms of some disembodied rules and renders decisions. Instead, they are founded on an image of legality as a sort of tournament in which victory is premised, at least in part, on the attributes of the contestants.

As these statements indicate, experience, either direct legal experience or experience with similar disputes, is a crucial factor in determining legal outcomes. Naïveté, lack of knowledge, or unrealistic expectations are often invoked as reasons for losses in the past. Whereas Stavros developed particular legal skills, such as knowing how to amass documentation in preparing a case, others acquired more general information, such as knowledge about legal options and rights ("We didn't know what our rights were at the time" [Jamie

Leeson]), or simply the jaded outlook of the experienced player ("I really didn't think people would lie in court" [Michelle Stewart]).

The price of experience is often described as a hard-won skepticism. After a number of disputes with his insurance agent over reimbursement for damages to his car, John Collier, on the advice of his lawyer, accepted the loss. He attributed his situation to his lack of experience.

> *I guess I used to be very naive . . . Now I am a lot smarter. I*
> *never thought people would deceive and things like that. You*
> *think that insurance companies are so proper and no problem.*
> *Now I know otherwise.*

In addition to experience, some character-related qualities, such as toughness or determination, are viewed as relevant in legal contests. People made frequent references to their tenacity or assertiveness; that they were not the type to be pushed around or duped. Ironically, people often explained why they had rejected legal actions by invoking the same personal qualities of self-reliance and toughness. In a statement typical of this explanation, Stanley Warshawsky, a seventy-year-old white retired engineer, explained why he didn't do anything after his small airplane crashed because of a faulty gas cap vent:

> *In a situation like that, I think nine out of ten people would have*
> *sued Cessna and come away from it with a lot of money. I*
> *refused to do it, you know? I have a curious bump. I think*
> *America is great because it was made great by the pioneers, by*
> *the farmer, by the mechanics, by the blacksmiths. The people that*
> *worked and produced, farmed and explored and achieved things.*
> *And in my opinion this country is degenerating into a third-rate*
> *place because all we want to do is sit around and bicker and out-*
> *smart and sue one another. And I'm so incensed in my spirit*
> *over that, that I don't want to be any part of that parade.*

Lawyers and Legal Games

There is one aspect of the law about which virtually all of our respondents agreed: one of the most crucially consequential resources one can mobilize in a legal encounter is a lawyer. No matter how competent the individual, no matter how much experience or informal knowledge citizens acquired, they generally acknowledge their amateur status in relation to lawyers. Lawyers represent the professional players; their skill, experience, and stock of legal knowledge are seen as daunting when compared to the episodic and uneven legal resources of ordinary people. Lawyers are seen as the go-betweens, the translators, initiated into the rules of the game.

> In the practice of law by attorneys, it doesn't seem to be as concrete as the law would have you feel it is . . . It's more or less a contest between the two attorneys involved, with the judge acting as an arbitrary referee. It all depended on the judge and the attorneys, not the basic circumstances of the case. (John Ganter)

Thus, attorneys are seen as experienced gamesmen who shape the process of justice. Although Charles Reed boasted of his skill as a consummate bargainer and businessman, he also recognized the determining role of legal representation in his negotiations over the lost compensation. Recall Reed's description. "Now, the guy knows, and I know, that my lawyer is getting paid by the hour to sit with me, and my lawyer's a good guy. He works for the largest law firm in Philadelphia . . . So he knows he's in a real live law firm. This is no small-time shyster . . . He knows he's in a major-league ballpark, and he knows that his guy next to him is in trouble."

Not having a lawyer, John Collier believed, was decisive in his inability to defend himself against charges and arrest for illegal dumping. John vehemently denied the act and appeared in criminal court without a lawyer. At the time of our interview he admitted that he "should have [had a lawyer]," but at the time of the incident he did not think that it was necessary "because I didn't feel I was guilty of a crime." John Collier's belief that lawyers are necessary only for the guilty was undermined by his experience in court.

> They had pictures of my truck with everything in it. When [the prosecutor] asked me, "Is that your truck?" I said "Yeah." And they said "Okay." And they got me. He said, "Well, he dumped all that stuff on the ground." But I actually didn't. I should never have admitted that that truck was mine. If I had had a lawyer they would really have no evidence. You know, lawyers are much smarter than the average person. So they sucked me into it.

Although many persons would disagree with John Collier that lawyers are "smarter than the average person," there is broad agreement that they are more manipulative and, for that reason, dangerous.

[S]omebody came by to write a report. They asked me how far was I away from the accident. And I said, "Well, I don't know how far I was, I wasn't too far from here to there." He said, "I have to have a number." So I said, "Well, twelve feet, if you have to have a number, about twelve feet." Went to court, and the attorney asked me how far I was from the accident and I said, "Anywhere from ten to fifteen feet." He says, "Well, under sworn affidavit you said you were twelve feet." I said, "To me that sounds the same. Twelve feet is the same as ten to fifteen." That's the kind of situation that you run up against in jury trials . . . the attorneys play games with the minds of individuals. Trying to confuse the jurors. (Andrew Eberly)

For many of our respondents who have learned this lesson, the importance of professional legal representation is so central that finding and being able to afford a qualified lawyer often determines whether they will turn to law at all.

There's something wrong when somebody who's obviously in the right like myself, when the ceiling falls in, has to spend five hundred dollars on a lawyer. Because I've seen, if you go into tenant-landlord court without a lawyer, your chance of . . . getting a fair hearing I think might be compromised. (Jamie Leeson)

There were major plumbing problems that we didn't know about, that they lied about . . . [We] could have sued, really . . . There was enough to sue about but, I really . . . I'm not litigious, I mean there was no way I was going to pay a lawyer, you know, it was probably about two thousand dollars' worth of plumbing work and the lawyer would have cost me more. (Martha Lee)

The refrigerator was terrible. The food rotted for eight days . . . This was a rental house, but still, we lived there. So they gave us five hundred dollars. The refrigerator stunk for months. I couldn't eat anything out of there because everything tasted like, ugh! . . . For five hundred dollars you couldn't pay me for the aggravation. When he came to pay me he said that if I wanted any more I'd have to sue and they had good lawyers. So, what was I going to do? (Mike Chapin)

It's not the courts so much as the damn lawyers. I mean who can afford these guys who make half a million bucks a year? A poor slob like me? (Stanley Warshawsky)

Although law itself was only sometimes seen as a commodity, almost without exception people perceived lawyers in the context of a commodity relationship. Being able to "get" or afford a good lawyer, or alternatively being up against an opponent with a good lawyer, exerted a profound effect on their decisions in regard to disputes and grievances. It was not simply getting a lawyer that was significant, however. As with all sorts of commodities and services, the quality and value of legal representation was seen as varying in relation to scarcity and cost. People expressed the view that legal aid or volunteer legal representation was less valuable than having a private or personal lawyer. One woman told us she considered appealing an administrative decision that denied her son a military pension but could not afford a lawyer. When asked if she had considered seeking legal aid, the woman responded, "Yeah, but they're not that good, are they?"

Nell Pearson was involved in a dispute over the control of a feminist writer's workshop when we interviewed her. She told us of a case similar to her own. One group of writers

> was represented by a volunteer lawyer . . . The Inter-Arts Center
> [the other party to the dispute] somehow got a pro bono attorney
> from some major law firm who just hit them with everything
> they had. And, you know, I don't know if you've ever dealt with
> volunteer lawyers for the arts. They're pretty good guys, but
> they're basically letter writers. You know they don't get involved
> with lawsuits per se. And this poor guy was overwhelmed.

Recognizing the central role of lawyers in shaping outcomes, people relied heavily on lawyers to define the situation for them, assess its legal character, and pronounce whether it was a case. Not having a case or a case worth pursuing was often related to a person's decision to accept a loss or tolerate a situation.

For some respondents the significant role of lawyers in interpreting and promoting their interests within legal spheres was accepted as a self-evident part of the game. For others it was a source of dissatisfaction and disillusionment. Lawyers facilitated certain outcomes, but insofar as individuals were dependent on them, lawyers were also viewed as creating obstacles. Many citizens believed that the legal system has become so professionalized that the game is no longer open to ordinary people. For instance, one man described a case in which he was denied access to a transcript of a court case to which he was a party.

*I had the date and document number. I went to the court
reporter and asked if I could please have a copy of this transcript
of that case. He looked it up and said that I couldn't have it
unless I am a lawyer. I don't understand that. I mean, if it pertains to you . . . I can understand that if you were sticking your
nose where it didn't belong, but if it pertains to you, why can't
you ask for a transcript of your own court case? Why do you
have to be a lawyer? (Leroy Tanner)*

Collective Action

In addition to the advantages of having a lawyer, people recognized
the benefits of groups. In a world in which their opponents are likely
to be resource-rich corporations or anonymous bureaucrats, there is
clearly strength in numbers. Identifying others with mutual interests
and organizing around those interests were crucial in determining
whether people took any action at all. As Nikos Stavros observed,
"You can't do much, you know, as an individual unless you join forces
with other people."

For the most part, when people in our sample joined forces with
others, it was around local issues. They established block associations to fight crime or in response to the lack of police protection.
They circulated petitions and sometimes, like Charles Reed, entered
into lawsuits to save their neighborhood from undesirable development. And much less frequently, they became involved in strikes,
class-action suits, and other forms of work actions.

Their collective experience tends to confirm the view that groups
lend strategic advantage in conflicts. In the course of telling us about
a legal action in which he and his neighbors successfully fought the
development of a condominium complex, Mike Chapin described the
developer as a formidable, but not invincible, opponent.

*They had lots of money for their lawyer. And a lot of time to
spend because they knew they could make a lot of money . . .
They brought in all these experts, traffic experts, surveyors. We
had nobody; just ourselves and our lawyer. It cost us about
$1,200.*

Even without lots of money or time and lacking expert testimony,
Mike Chapin's neighbors persevered and prevented the construction.
Others, Christopher Mitchem for example, also shared stories of the

strategic potential of collective action in defense of home, property, or a way of life.

> *Everybody wants clean living, the best you can get. We don't have any bars in our community. A track star tried to put up a bar. We all got together and started a petition and put him right out of there. We had a meeting on it. It ain't going to be here. The outsiders coming in. So we cut that off. So that's the way I think, if you can't get the police, if you think it's out of the policemen's hands, petition!*

Mike Chapin remarked again on the crucial role of collective action, especially when a problem or situation is beyond the compass of the law. Relating his frustration over his coworkers' acquiescence in the face of union corruption, Mike Chapin commented,

> *Somebody said to me, call the state police or something. I said they're not going to do anything. It's too deep rooted. You have to get the people themselves involved. If you don't want to stick your neck out, why should anybody else?*

At the same time that people recognized the benefits, or even necessity, of organizing and presenting their interests collectively, they acknowledged the difficulties and obstacles in doing so. Collective action may be effective, but it is not easy. A number of respondents commented, almost despairingly, that unless personal interests were at stake, too many people were reluctant or unwilling to take the time or effort to engage in collective actions. Gretchen Zinn suggests that collective action is too often seen only as a means to achieve individual benefit.

> *I don't think American people energize themselves. I mean, [the lack of national health insurance] is on TV every day of the week, people are dying, but if it's not somebody in your family dying, or being refused medical treatment, people don't do that much about it.*

Others remarked on the difficulty of organizing people in an unstable world where people are constantly moving and interests are changing.

> *We tried to organize the tenants. But the turnover rate is so high. It's hard. There's only about four people who have been in the building for five years or so. (Ambrose Grant)*

Mike Chapin summed up the obstacles to collective action:

*People are too scared, or just don't care enough, or don't see the
end result as being worth it, I guess.*

Thus, while many people reported some experience with some
form of collective action, and typically saw it as a powerful option,
their experience was limited. What experience they did report over-
whelmingly involved local issues or disputes concerning individual
interests such as real estate. As many of the respondents lamented, a
sense of impotence in the face of disproportionately powerful opponents, or a narrow sense of self-interest, or even fear, seems to daunt
group, as well as individual, action.

Time and Space

How is legality distributed across time and space in the schema of the
game? In what way is its character embedded in its spatial and temporal organization? In "Before the Law," we observed how the material
and symbolic ordering of time, and specifically processes of spatializing time, provide a framework for contemporary social experience and
its interpretation. In particular, the reification of the law, that is, the
apprehension of legality as remote and dehumanized, was accomplished in part by dissociating legality from the flow of everyday life.
The law was elsewhere, housed in granite courthouses, entombed in
law libraries, or awaiting its supplicants at the end of long queues at
various administrative and bureaucratic agencies. The distance constructed between everyday life and the law functioned as "both a barrier to, and a defence against, human interaction."[17]

Legality is not always or universally experienced this way, however. In those situations and encounters in which legality assumes
a gamelike character, its ludic quality derives from a very different
spatiotemporal organization. Legal players perceive and experience
the law less in terms of its discontinuity and distance from everyday
life than in terms of its simultaneity. In much the same way, card
players can maintain a consciousness of the real world with all of its
concerns and constraints and yet suspend their involvement in that
real world for the duration of the play. For example, parents engaged
in an evening's card playing with friends may attend to the game
while keeping an eye on the coffeepot and an ear cocked for the
sound of a child's cry. The various rules of irrelevancy that define the

game and filter out the real world are, Goffman notes, more like a screen than a solid wall.[18]

Simultaneity and Strategic Use of Time

As people talked about legality in gamelike terms they expressed the understanding of it as both something different from and yet coexistent with everyday life. By providing an arena of articulated rules and constraints, legality is understood as suspended in time and bracketed in space. Yet the suspension and bracketing do not eclipse the other reality. Thus, we often find respondents referring to multiple realities and characterizations for the same event or person.

When Jamie Leeson and his landlady were regularly sparring with each other in housing and small-claims court, he told us that he "liked her as a person." And when his lawyer advised him to stop talking with someone whom he was suing, Jamie assured us he would resume their relationship once the suit was over. As these stories illustrate, the suspension of affective relationships is continuous with their legal construction. Legality and affect are simultaneously available, to be avoided or invoked, as situations demand and make plausible.

This recognition of multiple roles and alternative normative contexts was neatly expressed by another respondent, Louis Napier, who was having difficulty getting the town building inspector to approve an application for an aboveground swimming pool he wanted to install in his backyard. The official insisted on four resubmissions of the application with new plans drawn for each. Because he never made the grounds of rejection explicit, it was only by trial and error that Louis Napier discovered that the inspector was applying the rules for in-ground, permanent structures rather than the rules for the aboveground pool he was planning to build. "I don't think he did his job very well," Napier said. Yet despite the error and all of the difficulty the inspector caused, Napier assured us that "he was very nice. He wasn't rude. I just don't think that he knew his job."

Whereas the reified law is sustained as remote and objective through processes of juxtaposition and spatialization, the law as game is maintained through the simultaneity of experience. In the schema of the game, legality runs concurrently with everyday life. People like Louis Napier frequently behaved toward and defined others in seemingly contradictory ways. They would characterize a town official as nice, but incompetent; a judge as nasty, but only doing his job; or they would express empathy with someone whom they were currently suing. One can, at the same time, be both a nice man and an incompetent inspector, a bully and a protector of the weak, a caring friend and a litigious lawyer. The complexity of these characterizations reveals the multiple and parallel contexts in which people interacted with others. The fact that people do not experience these differences as incompatible further reveals their embrace of these multiple contexts.

In these multiple contexts, time is one of the chips in the legal game, something to be used and strategically deployed, as opposed to something that is spent or lost. Seeing law's time as simultaneous with everyday life, some respondents actively marshaled time to enter this alternative space. Jules Magnon, a forty-seven-year-old health professional with a daughter in elementary school, actively uses time to achieve very specific and concrete results. Jules emigrated to the United States from France when he was a very young man. He is a member of his local school board and a trustee of the condominium complex in which his family lives. He is quite proud of the town in which he lives, believing the school system to be "quite unique" and the town "free from major problems."

Jules Magnon associates effort with time and believes that if you work at something, you can achieve a great deal. For example, he believes that the hospital for which he works is regularly making errors in his overtime, and as a check on this, he keeps his own careful records. He would like to get the problem resolved and says that

> in the future, I'm just going to have to take action . . . I am definitely going to give this problem more attention in the future.

Later in the interview he articulated a similar view regarding the importance of perseverance: "I believe if you want something you go after it and you go after it consistently."

With regard to a doctor whom he believes billed an insurance company for visits never made and service never provided, "I will pursue this until justice is done," he said, indicating that the time would not be a waste. Rather, Jules suggests that the time spent is itself a benefit or a good.

Jamie Leeson also expressed this sense of time as a deployable resource, with a more explicit sense of strategy and tactics.

Not too long ago, an old girlfriend of mine was in a jam and bor-
rowed five hundred bucks. Promised to give it back within thirty
days and didn't. At sixty days, or maybe it was seventy-five, I
took her to small-claims court, tacked on that extra hundred dol-
lars for aggravation money. It didn't go to small-claims court.
When she got the notice, that morning she came over an hour
later with a check, you know, for six hundred.

In this story, Jamie Leeson relies on time to mark his changing relationship to this woman, tracing her transformation from girlfriend to debtor. Initially, he reckons times vaguely and informally ("not too long ago, an old girlfriend") when he names the person and their affective relationship; but he measures time in standard and precise units—thirty days, sixty days, seventy-five days—when he refers to the financial debt and his sense of legal entitlement to payment.

Strategic Textualization

In the analysis of time and space in the schema "before the law," we noted the centrality of spatialization and inscription to the construction of legality. Inscription and textualization also play a role in the legality-as-game schema of legal consciousness, but again with a difference. Just as time becomes a deployable chip—pieces of everyday life that are simultaneously available for the legal game—space is no longer so fixed or concrete but also constructed as the game demands.

Because people recognize the authority of texts, they often reported acting strategically, ensuring against future contingencies by preparing a record or simply, "getting it in writing."

I took X rays and just made sure everything was reported in case
there were any subsequent complications . . . I just made sure
documentation was in order . . . even though the doctor said
there'd be no lasting consequences, I would document everything
just in the event that down the, you know, years later there were
some residual consequences, that it would be on record. (Jamie
Leeson)

Recall that Nikos Stavros's suit against Isuzu was constructed primarily through the record he personally manufactured and assembled.

> *My experience is that if you have this case like that documented*
> *in a very precise way, then the law can, um, you can use that law*
> *in . . . in your favor. [Interviewer: What do you mean by docu-*
> *mented?] I mean from the time that the problem started to the*
> *minute you file the complaint and you have the judge to decide*
> *upon this case, like all the documents, whatever happened to the*
> *car, take it to the mechanic, the dealers, whatever they said, all*
> *the letters that you sent to the company.*

After her landlord took her to court for nonpayment of rent, Doris Milford defended herself and won the case. The judge ordered the landlord to make repairs to the dilapidated building and he awarded Doris fifteen hundred dollars of the rent she had not paid. Doris Milford attributed her success to the care she took constructing a record.

> *My judge heard the case. I took him documented problems and*
> *took pictures and so forth and everything and kept records. And I*
> *displayed it and he saw things were in my favor.*

The objectification and distance between authors and their audiences that is created by writing frees them from the fear and discomfort that often arise from face-to-face conflict. People are often able to write what they might have difficulty saying.

> *I must have written about fifteen letters. Some of these letters*
> *were very nasty ones and believe me when I write nasty letters, I*
> *write nasty letters. (Jules Magnon)*

The pleasure of "becoming inscribed in a symbolic order"[19] is anticipated in playful amusement. For example, Jules Magnon, a frequent and effective letter writer, summarized this view of the strategic use of writing and inscription.

> *In my own experience, I'm not sure it's unique, but whenever I*
> *have a problem with a product I always write them and it gets*
> *resolved right there. It doesn't go any further . . . I believe in the*
> *power of letters.*

These conceptions of both time and space in the gamelike consciousness of law suggest connections with the perennial divide between the sacred and the profane. According to Durkheim, "the sacred and the profane have always and everywhere been conceived by the human mind as two distinct classes, as two worlds between which there is nothing in common."[20] To maintain this conceptual distance and in effect prevent any moral confusion, these spheres have often been radically separated in time and space. The reified vision of law invokes a sacred conception of legality. By contrast, legality-as-game is relegated to the sphere of the profane. As a profane, irreverent, and worldly enterprise, the legal game recognizes porous boundaries. It refuses the distinctions upon which a reified law insists. Thus, when one plays with the law, the time of law is human rather than eternal time. The space of law is something people create. It is common rather than hallowed, vulgar rather than magisterial. It is like a game.

Conclusion

In a compelling account of the nineteenth-century struggle between pig keepers and those who sought a pig-free New York City, Hartog describes Americans actively, and at times very self-consciously, engaging the law in gamelike agonistic contest.[21] Following active lobbying and opposition to a campaign to control the free-ranging pigs, ordinances were passed by the City Council to restrain the pigs and at the same time to exempt various districts from the regulation. In addition to a pound system for confining loose pigs, several other enforcement schemes developed, including licenses and fines. Despite a successful criminal prosecution in 1819 against a butcher for letting his pigs roam the streets of the city,[22] the practice continued for thirty years, during which time a number of legal encounters kept alive the question of the right to keep pigs in the city. These hesitant and uneven efforts to regulate pigs should not, Hartog argues, be interpreted as evidence of the failure of law to rid the city of pigs. The series of related legal episodes, and the enduring practice of pig keepers' letting their pigs roam the streets, suggests instead that there was no single, objective "law of pigs." Rather, the ongoing, open-ended dispute illustrates something about the legal consciousness of those pig keepers who participated in these various episodes.

> To the pig-keepers . . . the law was a domain of conflict in whose construction they participated . . . the law was both an external force imposing itself on them and also, and at the same time, a structure within which they resisted and worked to control their traditional social practices.[23]

The pig keepers engaged the common council, the mayor, and the lawyers in a series of moves and countermoves in which they knew that each move prolonged the engagement and the possibility of continuing to play. The various legal settings offered an arena of contest, a contest that provided both the opportunity to play and the constraints under which play had to occur.[24] Like the legal conscious-ness expressed by our respondents, the pig keepers' consciousness of law as a venue for contest underwrote their legal and extralegal practices, shaped the events and decisions that came to be, and in turn influenced the practices of legal officials and decision makers.

If "before the law" can be read as law's own story, "with the law" is the realist tale, or perhaps the cartoonist's account signaled by the postcard with which we began this section. To the extent that the perception of law as contest leads to strategic engagement, or disen-gagement, law may become even more gamelike. The success of the game attracts more players: those with knowledge, resources, and interest.[25] The public, players and spectators, joins in with more or new demands and understandings (e.g., tort litigation, gender dis-crimination and sexual-harassment suits) that create pressures of volume and substance.[26] Those additional players lead to additional engagement, feeding ever more contingency and uncertainty, and at the same time feeding challenges to the legal profession's exclusive access to professional play.[27] "Curiously . . . more contingent and more expensive, it becomes more accessible and more participa-tory."[28] This has the effect of producing yet more players, escalating the feedback between action and reaction. By losing some of its al-ready precarious predictability, law becomes even more gamelike. In short, the realist tale is no more illusory than the story "before the law."

CHAPTER SIX

Against the Law

Bess Sherman

Two of the five buildings remaining on Bess Sherman's block are empty or boarded up. Standing virtually alone, with vacant lots on either side, Bess's building seems, at first sight, empty as well. The ground floor of the building is covered with a wall of plywood, painted a bright blue. The door is over to the side, hidden in a recessed foyer. A makeshift buzzer system (a loud doorbell shared by the tenants) summons two young children, who let us in. In the dimly lit hallway, the paint is peeling and the stair treads are badly worn.

Bess Sherman lives at the top of two flights of stairs in a one-bedroom apartment. She's black and sixty-four years old and has lived in this building for the past twenty-six years. Sitting in her living room, windows open to the street and door open to the hallway, Bess told us, "I got old in this building." This statement lies somewhere between a boast and a simple report of fact.

The number twenty-six is an important milestone to Bess, marking not only the length of her residence but of her most intimate relationships as well. Her best friend, Agnes Ross, moved in at about the same time twenty-six years ago. Agnes has since moved three times within this relatively small building (with eight apartments), each time to be closer to Bess. When we spoke with Bess, Agnes sat across the hall, her door also ajar, watching TV and occasionally participating in the interview.

> My friend lived in this apartment, but she lived in front, and she lived downstairs, and she moved two years ago, then she moved upstairs. [Interviewer: Found a nicer apartment up here?] No, it's not nicer. I guess we wanted to live closer to each other. See how our doors are open all of the time? As long as we're both

here, we leave them open. When we're not here we don't leave them open because it's still bad, it's a jungle out there, don't you know.

Compared to the "jungle out there," Bess Sherman described the apartment building as a familiar and safe place. A couple of children sat playing on the narrow staircase. A number of apartment doors were open, the collective hum of televisions and radios muffling the traffic outside. Speaking of her building, Bess said,

See, that's the way we live. In this house we look out for each other, I put it that way. That's why we don't just let anybody move into the building. And I'm supposed to be the superintendent . . . That's why I know what kind of people we have. The landlord, he don't care. He don't live here, he lives in [New York], what did he care, all he wants is the rent.

Bess made a number of references to her job as superintendent. She performs a variety of jobs—taking out the garbage, sweeping the halls, and collecting the rents every month—and seems to take her job very seriously, particularly the responsibility of screening prospective tenants. As a rule, she doesn't like tenants with children, because children bring other children, who, she told us, tend to bring trouble.

The landlord always asks me, "Bessie, this lady is without any children, just grandchildren." But we don't want any more than two children, there are only two children in this building now . . . Agnes had a son who . . . when I moved here he wasn't quite a year old and he's twenty-six, see that's where this twenty-six comes in, and he was the only child raised here.

Despite her ambivalence about children, and more or less contradicting her claim that Agnes's son was the only child raised in the building, Bess and Agnes have an eleven-year-old "nephew" who lives with them. He is actually the son of Agnes's cousin, and no kin of Bess. Agnes "got him from the hospital, when he was a baby" and she and Bess have raised him ever since. Bess calls him her adopted nephew, although there have never been any legal arrangements made formalizing Kevin's relationship to Agnes or Bess. Nevertheless, Bess takes responsibility and some pride and pleasure in her role as one of Kevin's adopted guardians. "He lives between [Agnes] and me, but he likes to stay whenever I ask him, so he stays all night here."

Kevin is, according to Agnes, a "real jumping jack." Bess agreed, saying that he gets into trouble at school because he wants to play all of the time. According to both of them, Kevin never sits still and consequently often needs extra help, especially with his math skills. That summer, Kevin was enrolled in summer school and away every morning. Concerned about his schoolwork and his conduct, both Agnes and Bess are in frequent contact with his teachers, having given them "the privilege of calling anytime."

After so many years, Bess said, the people on the block know each other too. But it is a different sort of relationship than she has with Agnes or with the other residents in the building. Agnes describes them as "friendly, without being friends." Bess concurred with this description and gave an example:

> Next door it's a Spanish family, naturally I don't deal with them, but they are good neighbors. We know each other, sort of like the mailman knows them and he knows me. You know, in that fashion.

Even though Bess characterized her neighborhood as a jungle, at another point in the interview she described it as comparatively quiet, not like it used to be.

> It's quiet now, but there was a time when it was very bad. There was a riot in Newark in '67, yeah, '67. They hit a lot of stores in this neighborhood across the street and they had fires. They tore a lot of them down.

Nowadays the problem that concerns Bess the most is the noise: loud music, horns blowing, and the "cursing" you hear walking down the street. Although the radios are not as dangerous as the riots that devastated her neighborhood, the noise is alien and frightening.

> The only objection I have, at night they blow horns, and this loud music that I don't even understand, maybe if I [could] understand it I would enjoy it, but it's Spanish music, not any

*reference to anybody, not, you know, trying to make them dumb
or anything.*

For the most part, Bess and Agnes ignore the noise and
cursing and keep to themselves. Sometimes, when it is really
hot, they sit on the front steps. They go to church a few times
a week. They attend PTA meetings during the school year. But
they spend most of their time in their apartments, watching
soap operas and game shows and talking to one another
across the hall through the open doors.

According to Bess, her life has few, if any, problems. No
problems with neighbors (because she "keeps to herself");
no problem with merchants (because she has "no money to
buy things"); no problem with losing or lending property ("No,
because I don't have nothing to loan"); or with fences ("No,
you see how this apartment is made, no yard to fence");
no problems with insurance ("They tell me a lot of people have
problems with car insurance and different things and with different payments and whatever, but I don't have that
problem.").

Bess Sherman told us that she has little experience with or
use for the law. The last time she had anything to do with the
police was fifteen years earlier, when her apartment had been
burglarized. Bess had been away at the time visiting relatives
in the South. Agnes was living downstairs; she heard noises
above in Bess's apartment.

> Agnes was living downstairs at the time. She heard someone
> walking up here, and she called up here, knowing I wasn't there.
> That made them go back out. Faster then calling the police.
> [Interviewer: Did anyone call the police?] Hmmm [with affirma-
> tive tone]. They didn't catch them, though. They left so fast they
> left their hat, and I could see the sneaker prints on my chair in
> there.

Neither has Bess seen or talked to a lawyer in twenty-five
years, since the time when, visiting New York, she had fallen
down a flight of stairs that "weren't right." She hurt her leg
and thought about suing the landlord, but the insurance company's lawyer met with her and she "settled for money." That
was the closest Bess ever came to going to court.

Still, her life has not been totally problem free. A few years *ago, Bess became ill. She had been on welfare since she had left work at an umbrella factory some years before. On the advice of the welfare office, she applied for SSI.*

> *I had to apply so many times, they had sent me from welfare to Social Security and then Social Security sends you to their doctors, and their doctors . . . it seems as if it's a clique and their doctors work with the Social Security, it's money that they don't want you to have . . . I mean I go to them, and they examine me, they give you a physical and everything, and if you are there and complain it don't make any difference, they put what they want to put.*

It took seven months and five or six doctor visits before Bess received her SSI benefits. She assured us that what made the experience difficult wasn't that she was treated badly, but that she was never sure what exactly was going on.

> *Oh, they treat me okay, but that wasn't the problem. I'm not going to, I'm not knowing what they are going to put on the paper, I'm telling them the case but still I'm not knowing what they going to put on the paper and turn back to the Social Security, and that's the way it works.*

Eventually Bess was diagnosed with breast cancer and had to have a mastectomy. In the course of her illness and surgery she met a different, "community" doctor, one who was able to expedite her receiving SSI benefits.

> *It didn't come to a head until I had this [mastectomy]. The doctor in the hospital asked me what was I on, I told him welfare, that's what we call it . . . and he said, "You should be getting SSI." And then he made a recording, because I heard him in the other room talking to someone and evidently he sent it to Social Security. He was talking through something, he made this tape and then he wrote it in writing, on paper.*

As with the Social Security doctors, Bess didn't have any say in what this doctor recorded. In fact, she wasn't even sure what it was he wrote or said. But he said something, and it was effective. Bess was once again mystified by the content of the doctor's message, but she did recognize it as evidence of his power and authority. Only this time, it worked to her benefit.

*Reflecting on her own powerlessness, Bess Sherman under-
stood that if she had had money or connections, she wouldn't
have had to rely on the fortuitous intervention of her doctor.*

> *I knowed, if I had had money or had been familiar, I probably
> would have gotten on it earlier, like the system is now. That's
> what they have to do. If people want to get on there, and they
> know themselves that they're sick, they go to this lawyer, Shelley
> Silverberg. [Interviewer: Did you ever see Shelley Silverberg or
> any lawyer about this problem?] No. Because I didn't have
> enough money. People say, "Well, why don't you go to a lawyer,
> Bess? Why don't you go to Shelley Silverberg?" Bess can't go,
> because Bess don't have no money.*

*Being without resources, Bess understood that she had
little or no choice but to submit to the round of appointments,
forms, diagnoses, and hearings. She believed that eventually
she would have received her benefits even without the intervention of the community doctor, but she knew that he (not being
part of the clique) facilitated the process.*

*Bess told us that she knew lots of people who had had sim-
ilar frustrating experiences with welfare and Social Security.
During the seven-month period when this was going on, Bess
dealt with her frustration and confusion by talking to people:
friends, neighbors, fellow church members. That's how she
heard about Shelley Silverberg. What else, she asked us, could
she do?*

> *Not much. Nothing to do. Just talking, talking like I'm talking to
> you. Talking off the nerve part, you know.*

*Bess Sherman clearly felt secure in the narrow compass of
her life. Over the years she had carved out a small space of freedom and control within a much broader network of depen-
dency. But she also seemed to sense the fragility of her security. It could be shattered by strange and noisy neighbors,
the troublesome children, or the frustrating rules of welfare bureaucrats, or even the questions of two sociologists.
Although she was talkative and forthcoming in the interview,
Bess seemed guarded at times, concerned about revealing too
much. In some instances, the information about which she
was concerned seemed, to us, benign and even trivial. For*

*instance, when we asked her whether she had ever had prob-
lems with her landlord making needed repairs or providing services, she was apprehensive. The significance of the apartment, as the central fact organizing her life and relations for
the past twenty-six years, transformed what most people
would see as a question of little consequence into one fraught
with potential to disrupt that life.*

> *Now, will my name . . . will [the landlord] know this? [Inter-
> viewer: No, he won't see your answers at all; he'll have no access
> to this information.] Okay, then, yes. There's a leak upstairs and
> it was raining in, and my apartment in the living room here and
> he's supposed to fix it, and he always promises things and don't
> do them.*

*A number of other times during the interview, before de-
scribing a problem or voicing a complaint, Bess would again
ask whether "this tape will get turned in." Like the community
doctor, and all of the other doctors and welfare officials, we
were writing and recording information with some authority
and purpose. What we were scribbling and what use we would
make of it weren't completely clear to her. And, despite our
assurances of confidentiality and anonymity, she believed, perhaps correctly, that whatever it was we were writing was out
of her control. Not sure who would read her accounts or hear
her complaints, she seemed understandably anxious about
voicing them. She was eager, but wary.*

*Viewed in one way, the law and legality play an insignifi-
cant role in Bess Sherman's life, as she claimed. Living within
the intimate confines of her apartment, deriving pleasure and
comfort from her relationship with Agnes Ross and her
"adopted" nephew Kevin, Bess's life rarely intersects with the
law. With little or no property to lose, lend, fence in, acquire,
or insure, it seems as though she has little need for the law.*

*The apparent irrelevance of law in Bess Sherman's life is
an illusion. In fact, Bess's life is shaped by law in many ways.
Indeed, the apparent irrelevance of law to her everyday affairs
reflects its defining power over her life. In describing her
adopted nephew Kevin, Bess willingly appropriates the legally
sanctioned designation to define her relation with Kevin. Here
legality fulfills her desire. Her lack of property, her sense of inse-*

curity outside of the apartment, even the terms within which her illness was diagnosed similarly are shaped by the operation of law. In this sense, the law is not so much absent from Bess's life as it is often camouflaged and inaccessible, lying just beyond her vision or her reach. Most important, Bess Sherman understood all this. For Bess, unlike Rita Michaels, the gap between the law and her life is not a source of law's majesty. In the gap, Bess Sherman recognizes the power, but not necessarily the grandeur, of law.

Bess expressed her appreciation of law's power most clearly when we asked her how she might react in a number of hypothetical situations. One situation had to do with noisy neighbors, a version of an actual problem Bess described to us earlier in the interview. Whereas her actual response to noise in the neighborhood was to lump it (fearing retaliation and police nonresponsiveness) and rarely leave the apartment, her response to the hypothetical situation was emphatic:

> *I would really call the cops! [Laughs] I would really call them, I might feel a little frightened calling them . . . but I would really call them.*

In another hypothetical scenario involving a car accident in which no one was hurt but a child's bicycle was damaged, Bess boldly and confidently asserted,

> *I would call me a lawyer. And find out if he had any insurance. Sue him, if he don't have any, that all I know. That's what I hear about.*

There is a clear contradiction between Bess's previously expressed resignation to problems and her realistic assessment of law's inaccessibility ("People say, 'Well, why don't you go to a lawyer, Bess? Why don't you go to Shelley Silverberg?' Bess can't go, because Bess don't have no money") and her eager, almost joyful, litigiousness in the context of the hypotheticals. In these hypothetical situations, without the constraints that routinely operate to limit her actions, Bess Sherman derived pleasure from imagining a very different relationship to law. Her responses, punctuated by laughter, claimed an identity as a fully endowed and legally competent actor. Ironically, the hypothetical problems we posed were not hypothetical at all. It is the power she imagined having in these situations that was unreal. No longer disqualified by her lack of resources, information, security, or familiarity, Bess Sherman invokes the law almost triumphantly. She shows no restraint, assuring us that, despite her fear, she would "really" call the cops.

In stark contrast to this imaginary space of legal mobilization, Bess lives out her powerlessness. She doesn't call the police, she shuts the windows. She doesn't get herself a lawyer, she goes through another round of doctor's appointments. She is resigned, but it is not a silent nor total resignation. By hearing and sharing stories of law with friends, by comparing notes, giving advice, suggesting the names of lawyers, and generally "talking off the nerve part," Bess Sherman testifies to law's power to limit her participation.

Jamie Leeson

Jamie Leeson is white, forty years old, and unmarried. For most of his adult life he has been in helping professions, working as a teacher, counselor, hospital attendant, and advocate for abused children. His involvement in these social service jobs grew out of an earlier religious calling. As a young man he spent time in a seminary preparing for the priesthood. He decided only at the very last minute, he told us, not to take his vows. "I said no right before the ordination."

Jamie Leeson currently lives in Hoboken, part of the New Jersey urban sprawl that looks across the Hudson River at New York City and provides convenient residences for commuters who work across the river. The street on which Jamie Leeson lives is lined with narrow one- and two-story houses, separated by walkways and an occasional driveway. It is crowded with children and teenagers playing in the streets and cars closely parked along the length of the block. Jamie feels fortunate in this densely populated and lively neighborhood to have a garage. When we interviewed Jamie, he lived alone with his cats. Indeed, he made numerous references to his "kittens," whom he has had occasionally to protect from kids in the neighborhood. He likened his kittens to children he never had.

Jamie admits to "calling the police a lot . . . just for basic stuff." He believes that calling the police is part of his responsibility as a citizen. Once when he saw a teenager carrying a stereo, he alerted the police.

> Ninety-nine percent [chance] it was his own stereo but the police can't be everywhere. So I just called them, gave a description, said which way he was going, and had them go and check it out to make sure it wasn't somebody else's stereo.

Jamie Leeson also told us about a time when he found a young girl "wandering in a fugue state," disoriented, and unable to communicate very well. Interpreting her distraught and disjointed Spanish, Jamie believed that she'd been sexually abused, "you know, sexually assaulted within the last twenty-four hours." So he took her to the hospital.

> When I checked back on her I found out they'd committed her. And I found out that the doctor who had committed her . . . didn't speak very good English, and didn't speak any Spanish, and I just didn't feel that a person should be committed unless they've been interviewed by somebody who speaks their primary language. So I called the public advocates and said I wanted an investigation. So they did.

To describe Jamie Leeson simply as a former seminarian, pastoral counselor, and vigilant citizen is to misrepresent him by depicting only one side of his character. He is also a "biker." He drives a Harley-Davidson motorcycle and wears a black leather jacket. He told us that he self-consciously cultivates the image of the Hell's Angel as a way of interacting with others.

> I have a new motorcycle which is big and very loud, it's a big Harley-Davidson. And I leave that parked out there a lot and I think people figure they don't want to bother upsetting me . . . It's the weight and intimidation factor.
> Sometimes if I've been out riding the motorcycle with eight or ten other guys, it'll look like hell, you know, cause we're all wearing leather jackets and we look pretty scary.

Verbal, not just sartorial, threats and intimidation figure centrally in Jamie Leeson's repertoire of social interaction. The *contradictions in his character converge in this account of his kittens.*

> I've seen people almost hurt my kittens. I've taken that into my own hands. And I go, and it may be illegal and it may not be right, but I threaten the people, and I tell them I'll chop their hands off if they do it again.

Another time, Jamie said, some neighborhood kids shot off firecrackers near his door. Worried about potential harm such pranks might present to his kittens, Jamie again used the threat of excessive violence to scare off the offenders.

> I found the kid who shot the firecracker, and I told him I better not ever catch him doing that again. I was going to tell him I'd shoot fireworks off in his mouth, if I caught him doing that again near my kittens, but I don't want to get the reputation of being, you know, a crank . . . So, I just said if I ever see them doing anything to hurt my kittens I'll cut their hands off. I said they'll need somebody to tie their sneakers for the rest of their lives.

The unusual synthesis of predator and protector could also be heard when Jamie complained to us about dogs messing his front lawn. An acute sense of justice seems to animate and constrain his threats. Contemplating what he was going to do about the dogs, Jamie told us,

> I'm thinking of putting up a big sign, says I'll shoot the dog. But then I thought that's not fair. The dog doesn't know what he's doing. So I thought that what I'd do is shoot the person. You know, a sign would at least let them know that this person might be crazy, I better not let the dog go to the bathroom here.

Jamie Leeson admits that his verbal threats, like his jacket and motorcycle, are largely "for show." Again, enacting his strong sense of justice and desert, he admitted that he would probably never actually carry out the threats.

> There are times when I do believe in direct intimidation, not even intimidation, just stating a fact. To be honest, I couldn't chop their hands off, you know.

*Throughout his interview, as each of these examples illus-
trates, Jamie Leeson juxtaposed accounts of cultivated meanness with gentleness toward the weak or less able. Moreover,
he was self-conscious about what might appear to be contradictions in his ways of behaving. At one point in the interview,
Jamie pointed his finger and advised us, "You can write either
nice guy or sucker."*

*Jamie Leeson traces his contradictory and ambivalent atti-
tudes toward the law and violence to a time when he was
mugged. According to Jamie, the crime and its aftermath
"definitely was the turning point in my pacifist attitude. There
was a time when I did everything the legal way . . . and now
I'd just kill 'em."*

*A few years earlier, Jamie caught someone breaking into
his car. When he arrived on the scene, the lock on the trunk
had already been broken and the man was stealing a chain
saw that Jamie was taking to his parents' place in the
Poconos. According to Jamie, the thief was a junkie, high on
drugs. He returned the chain saw and asked Jamie just to
leave him alone.*

> *I said, "No, you broke my lock, you were stealing from me; I'm
> not going to leave you alone, we're going to a cop." So I grabbed
> him by the scruff of his neck. He was small and I had mace with
> me . . . I told this junkie that I would mace him if he tried to get
> away.*

*Jamie felt secure in the righteousness of his action and
confident in his ability to bring the fellow to justice. It turned
out, however, that his confidence was not justified. The thief
had a steel pipe hidden in a cardboard tube, "the kind you get
posters in. He swung it around real quickly and cracked me in
the skull and gave me a concussion."*

*The thief ran away and ducked into a doorway, where
he was discovered and arrested by a police officer. When
Jamie Leeson finally caught up with the gathering crowd,
he explained that the man had just mugged and tried to
rob him.*

> *So I pressed charges. There was a grand-jury hearing. It went on
> and on, it was just a big pain in the ass. I mean he went to jail,
> did about six months. Then he was out, and the court called me*

again because he had done it again. It took me forever to get my chain saw. It took me months and months of bureaucratic red tape to get my chain saw. I had to take a day off from work to go to the grand jury. Then I had to take another day off to go and get my chain saw after multiple attempts on the phone to even find out where it was. It was trying just to work my way through a bureaucratic labyrinth.

But the evidence room doesn't have late hours, so I had to take off from work in order to go and pick up my chain saw, out in the middle of Brooklyn; so that took almost a half day to a whole day. It's just really a real inconvenience, the whole situation. I would've been better off if I had killed him.

It was not simply the time wasted and difficulty of recovering his chain saw that disappointed and unsettled Jamie Leeson's attachment to and faith in the law. The experience made Jamie reevaluate the meaning of justice. He expressed a deeper sense of futility about the process and its outcomes.

All it did was put a junkie in jail for six months; you know it didn't rehabilitate him. He was out again doing the same thing about seven months later. I was trying to be a pacifist . . . I was going to take him to the police. Now what I would do if I ever caught anybody, I would just smack him in the head, handcuff him to a telephone pole and bring the police to them. I wouldn't put myself at risk bringing anybody to the police.

So maybe what I would do is I would just knock him unconscious, take his clothes off, and with an indelible marker write "thief" across his face and then leave him there. And maybe steal whatever money he had. Is that for the pot calling the kettle black?

Despite all his bravado and threats of violence, Jamie Leeson does not believe that the law should seek retribution. Nor was Jamie disappointed because the law doesn't punish more severely. For Jamie Leeson, the system fails because it does nothing.

True justice would have been for him to get rehabilitated. And he had a long rap sheet, you know. Multiple B&Es, breaking and entries, robberies, assaults. And just to have him sit somewhere and watch cartoons for six months really wasn't the answer. So justice would have been for him to go into a mandatory drug pro-

gram for minimally a year. Six months just starts to scratch the surface with any type of addiction.

In fact, Jamie observed, the process "perpetuates their trauma." As he told this story, it was not always clear who was the victim, whose trauma was perpetuated. The referent slipped, at times alluding to Jamie as the victim of the crime and, at other times, to the perpetrator as the victim of the system of justice. "You know, I was thinking, this guy's got problems. He's a drug addict. He needs help." In the end, though, Jamie abdicated the label of victim, denying his own trauma. "It was not traumatic, it was more annoying . . . That kind of stuff is no big deal."

This same complex relationship with his adversaries was expressed in other stories Jamie Leeson told. Years earlier his landlady tried on a number of occasions to evict Jamie and his roommates from their apartment. In retaliation, Jamie sued the landlady for damages to his living room rug that resulted from a fire caused by a faulty heater. Jamie described the legal encounter:

> The court assigned a mediator, and neither of us were going to back down, and then finally my old landlord who I liked as a person said that the mediator wants a compromise, wanted her to give me back half of my security deposit [as partial payment for the rug]. [The landlady] said, "I can't, my mother just died, I had to take out a loan for the burial." And when I heard that, I said, "Look just keep the money. Let's forget the whole thing." Then she and I went out for coffee together.

Despite his disappointment in the capacity of law to achieve justice (and despite his insistence on taking matters into his own hands), Jamie Leeson is an active and regular user of law. In addition to routinely calling the police, he has been in housing court repeatedly because his landlords failed to make repairs to his apartment or withheld security deposits. He has sued his employer over unpaid wages. And at the time of the interview, he was contemplating a suit against his insurance carrier for reimbursement for his dental bills. "I'm going to small-claims court on Monday," he said. He believes that once it gets to court, "it will be resolved."

His faith in resolution, if not justice, is grounded in his

*previous successful experiences. Earlier in his life, he told us,
he and his roommate withheld their rent until repairs were
made to the apartment.*

> *What we do is . . . we withhold rent until the repairs are made.
> And made them take us to court. And then we tell our side to the
> judge . . .*
>
> *We'd win and he'd have to make the repairs; and he'd make
> a real crappy repair. And so we'd withhold the rent, go back
> again and show—I would always videotape, and videotape what-
> ever was found—and so, you know, we'd always win.*

*More recently, his new Ford Taurus needed five transmis-
sion repairs within the first year or so.*

> *And I went all the way up right up the ladder with the whole
> grievance procedure with the Ford appeals board. And then
> finally the dealership where I bought the car lied, and so my case
> was just written off. So then I went and got a lawyer. And I guess
> it cost me about five hundred bucks. And finally . . . he negoti-
> ated with the Ford Company that they would take the car back
> and I would get an excellent deal at any Ford dealership, on any
> new car I wanted if I would choose to stay with Ford. So that's
> what I did . . . I got a new car at a very good discount.*

*Despite his success in realizing his interests through legal
means, Jamie Leeson is disappointed that he and others have
to use the law so much.*

> *It's a shame that it's becoming such a litigious society, you know.
> I mean I happen to have some money and I can get a lawyer
> every time something goes wrong.*

*Not only is Jamie Leeson able to afford a lawyer whenever
he needs it, he also believes that turning to law to manage conflict has only a temporary effect on his relationship with his
adversary. In regard to the potential of the law to disrupt relationships, Jamie assured us that if a lawyer told him not to
talk to someone that he was suing, he would "say, okay, fine.
I'll talk to you afterwards." Thus, Jamie envisages an after-
ward to legal disputes, a time when he could simply resume a
relationship with his opponent.*

*Thus, Jamie Leeson often sees the law as a game that he is
forced to play because of others' litigiousness. He can play,*

and play better than many. It is a shame, nonetheless, that the game needs to be played and that others are not as able as Jamie.

Despite his resources and skill at using legal devices to realize his interests, Jamie Leeson recognizes that there are times when the law is unlikely to be effective or just. In those instances, he is willing to take matters into his own hands to see justice done: writing across someone's face with a marker or threatening to cut off the hands of young punks. It would be too simple to suggest, however, that Jamie Leeson operates from a personal code of justice that he invokes to protect only his own interests or his own physical safety. He goes out of his way to ensure that others' welfare—that of a confused young woman or a drug-addicted thief—is considered.

When asked the hypothetical question regarding what he would do were a child of his hit by a car, but without injury, Jamie once again voiced both aggressive self-interest and mea-sured restraint.

> *I'd tell them I'd sue for a million dollars. I would probably also at the time, even though the doctor said there'd be no lasting con-sequences, I would document everything just in the event that down the . . . years later there were some residual consequences, that it would be on record. But I wouldn't try and bleed them for money or whatever.*

Jamie Leeson summed up his contradictory orientation toward law, legality, and justice: "I range," he said, "anywhere from, you know, the very law abiding to where I think the Islamic code works."

Up against the Law

> I needed money and I had none.
> I fought the law and the law won.
>
> SONNY CURTIS, "I Fought the Law"

> We find a multitude of homely little histories, each in its way a movement of liberty. Whenever worlds are laid on, underlives develop.
>
> ERVING GOFFMAN, *Asylums*

It is important to stress that counter-hegemony is not some purely oppositional project conceived of as if it were constructed "elsewhere," fully finished and then drawn into place, like some Trojan horse of the mind ... Counter-hegemony has to start from that which exists, which involves starting from "where people are at." Such a conception of counter-hegemony requires the "reworking" or "refashioning" of elements which are constitutive of the prevailing hegemony.

ALAN HUNT, "Rights and Social Movements:
Counter-hegemonic Strategies"

In the 1940s, Theodosia Simpson worked as a stemmer for Reynolds Tobacco Company in Winston-Salem, North Carolina. Most of the ten thousand workers in this facility were black women who, like Simpson, worked in the hardest, dirtiest, and most dangerous jobs under supervisors who were described as "no better than chain-gang overseers."[1]

For almost twenty years various unions had attempted to organize the workers at Reynolds. In 1943, Simpson and a few other workers began meeting with representatives of the Agricultural Packing and Allied Workers of America. After initially failing to sign up more than a handful of coworkers, Simpson eventually found a way of mobilizing support for the union. Here she describes how she was able to do this:

We wore uniforms that buttoned down the front. One day I tore all the buttons off my dress and buttoned it up with union buttons and went to work like that. The foreman didn't know what to do about it. So he just asked if I would go home and change uniforms please, and he paid me for the time I was gone. Then a memo came out the next day. No pins in your clothes. No pins, no earrings, no rings but your wedding rings. They were afraid this stuff would get into the tobacco; that was the excuse they give. After that I was able to get people to sign up, when they saw that I didn't get fired for it.

Theodosia Simpson's story illustrates two sorts of oppositional practices that are employed by subordinate persons against the powerful institutions or organizations in which they find themselves living and working. On the face of it, hers is a story of subversive collective action in which the distribution of resources and cultural legitimacy was challenged. Read from today's vantage point, this anecdote stands as part of labor history, a narrative of American labor that describes the successful challenges by workers through which the organization and conditions of work were altered and the relationships among employers and employees fundamentally reshaped.[2]

Before Theodosia Simpson mobilized that collective challenge, however, she took a different, solitary stand against power. When Simpson ripped the buttons off her dress and replaced them with union buttons (buttons she had tried to distribute earlier without success), she literally refashioned, as Hunt suggested, elements of the prevailing hegemony. The desecration of her dress and the incorporation of the union buttons transformed her uniform, the material sign of her subordination, into a potent symbol of resistance. Through her individual act of subversion she stunned power, rather than challenged it.

It is easy and tempting to collapse these two acts of resistance into one, to interpret Theodosia Simpson's individual stand as part of the subsequent collective action, rather than an act preliminary to it. Such collapsing is of course the danger of narrative history, where the moral and causal meaning of events is conferred retrospectively depending upon the ending we write to the story. Although motivated by a collective vision, at the moment Theodosia Simpson took her stand, tearing off the buttons of her uniform did not constitute a collective action. At that point, her opposition was individual. It did not openly challenge or question the authority it defied. Rather, to paraphrase John Dewey, Theodosia Simpson proceeded by remaking the situation as it stood.[3]

Scholarship has traditionally focused on the more collective forms of challenge and resistance epitomized by Theodosia Simpson's subsequent success at organizing a union. It has looked at revolutions, rebellions, strikes, boycotts, petitions, class-action suits, sit-ins, marches, and the like.[4] The reasons for this focus are obvious and defensible. These forms of collective action often mark ruptures in the historical record. Because they are understood as being responsible for history's "veering off course,"[5] such acts seem to warrant study.

More recently, however, scholars have claimed that the seemingly small acts of defiance engaged in by persons in subordinate social positions also make history, albeit a history that often seems to remain on course. Still, insofar as they too are world-making activities,[6] these acts of resistance also warrant our attention. Variously referred to as secondary adjustments,[7] tactics,[8] or weapons of the weak,[9] these commonplace acts of resistance represent the ways relatively power-less persons accommodate to power while simultaneously pursuing their interests or protecting their identities. Indeed, the accumulated record of institutional ethnographies provides us with evidence of the universality of such practices. As Goffman observes, "[W]henever worlds are laid on"—in the wards of mental hospitals, on the assembly lines, in classrooms, barracks, prisons, and courtrooms—"underlives develop."[10]

Given their ubiquity, these daily acts of individual resistance defy easy summary or description. They include such practices as pilfering, violence or threats of violence, tricks, institutional disruptions, foot-dragging, humor, storytelling, and gossip. However, not every joke or act of petty theft is an act of resistance. In order to be understood as resistance, such acts must invoke a particular interpretation of the situation in which they occur. According to Linda Gordon, "[t]o resist is to experience autonomy, to experience oneself as planning against one's [opponent], and to interpret the [situation] as avoidable or controllable."[11]

In this understanding, resistance is not defined by the means that are employed, nor by whether the action effectively realizes its objectives. Rather, three features distinguish resistance. First, resistance entails a consciousness of being less powerful in a relationship of power. Resistance thus implies a particular understanding or positioning of self and other, of being up against something or someone. Second, resistance requires a consciousness of opportunity, a situation in which one might intervene and turn to one's advantage. Thus, resistance represents a consciousness of both constraint and autonomy, of power and possibility. Third, resistant acts involve assessments that power has produced unfair constraints and opportunities. It involves a justice claim and an attribution of responsibility for the unfair situation.

Given the pervasive authority of law to define, organize, and violate the lives of individuals, it is not surprising that many persons described themselves as caught within a foreign and powerful system against which they acted. In these moments, rather than understanding legality as an arena of transcendent authority to which one defers, it is understood to be an ascendant power to which one conforms. Rather than perceiving legality as a game that one plays in order to seek one's interests and values, people described legality as a net in which they are trapped and within which they struggle for freedom. Rather than apprehending the law as distant from and incommensurate with mundane affairs, or as operating alongside and simultaneously with everyday life, at moments when people express a resistant consciousness, they experience legality as palpably present, substituting its here and now for all others, limiting movement, and curtailing meaning and action. Thus, in plotting to remake an unfair situation as it stands, resistance lies at the intersection of the power of legality and the possibilities for escaping it.

Making Out by Making Do

> By the art of being in between, [they] draw unexpected results from their situations.
> MICHEL DE CERTEAU, *The Practice of Everyday Life*

While sociologists have long documented the mundane practices and secondary adjustments of powerless persons, scholars have given these activities considerably less attention and attributed to them less significance than more organized and collective challenges to power. In part, as we mentioned above, this relative neglect by scholars reflects what seems to many to be the limited role of such acts of defiance in producing social change, as opposed to producing social life. Two additional features of resistant practices make them difficult to study.

First, tactical resistance rarely announces itself as such. By not labeling itself, resistance is less likely to be avenged by those in power or noticed by those who would study it. Because resistant practices are typically enacted by those who lack the authority to openly challenge or contest power, these practices are often hidden, intentionally designed and executed to remain unrecognized and undetected by those against whom they are directed. According to Scott, the resistant tactics used by peasants of Sedaka against wealthy landowners—practices such as sabotaging combines and other machinery that would replace their labor—tended to be nocturnal and anonymous. By remaining clandestine, resistance "preserves, for the most part, the on-stage theater of power."[12] Even in those cases where tactical resistance is open and traceable to an individual, it tends to be practiced so that it can be denied if called to task. Much like courting a new lover, a certain ambiguity of intention is built into the act so as to allow for disavowal or retreat if the situation requires it.[13]

In the modern world of bureaucracies, however, the invisibility or deniability of an act may be less important than its indecipherability. In highly rationalized contexts, indecipherability means that there are no standard operating procedures anticipating, no taxonomies classifying or forbidding, such practices. Nonetheless, while there may be no rules acknowledging and attempting to regulate specific acts, superordinate authorities are not necessarily unaware of or bamboozled by such practices. It is just that the absence of such rules or classification schemes makes these actions officially unreadable. The fact that they cannot be deciphered by the formal rational organizations in which they often occur ensures that when and if they are detected, they will incapacitate power, if only for a moment.

For instance, Theodosia Simpson's subversion briefly stunned power ("The foreman didn't know what to do about it"). Although a rule was quickly formulated ("no pins, no earrings, no rings"), the moment of incapacitation lasted long enough that Theodosia Simpson was able to demonstrate to those watching that power (in this case exercised by the foreman and R. J. Reynolds) is vulnerable and can be ruptured in different ways. Similarly, whether the court officer who arranged for Millie Simpson's community service knew about her ruse is neither clear nor particularly relevant to our interpretation of its resistant character. Had the court officer been wise to her trick, the rules would still apparently neither define nor prohibit the contingency. The indecipherability of resistance means that it is often beyond the capability of powerful actors (including scholars) to recognize and control.

A second feature of tactical resistance that makes it difficult to study is that it often involves making do with what a situation offers.[14] Almost by definition, those who practice tactical resistance have limited access to resources that otherwise might be converted into power within the situation, such as money, office, social networks, education, or other forms of cultural capital. As a consequence, resistant acts use, in unforeseen and inventive ways, the resources that are at hand. This bricolage may involve a reworking of the material world, such as Theodosia Simpson replacing buttons with union pins. It may also entail a cultural bricolage, that is, importing into a situation or interaction statuses, relationships, or meanings that are foreign to it. In this way, Millie Simpson invoked her status as churchgoer and volunteer in evading the penalty imposed by the court. Although generally and legally irrelevant (as opposed to illicit), fortuity made these roles highly relevant to the specific situation she encountered.

Resistant acts are almost always opportunistic, dependent upon a crack or opening in the face of power. Operating with few resources within a context of power, persons who would resist are typically unable to arrange situations so as to be able to consistently or predictably realize their objectives. Aware of the possibilities afforded by lapses in the institutional order, however, they are able at particular moments to turn the situation to their advantage.

Making do with available resources and refashioning cultural symbols renders the meaning and significance of these acts ambiguous. Commonplace objects, words, statuses, or other cultural artifacts are encountered in unexpected or undefined, as well as apposite, ways. In other words, cultural objects do not come with fixed, uniform meanings. Those meanings are made and remade through actions in specific contexts.[15]

Many forms of female resistance, for instance, play aspects of patriarchy to women's advantage.[16] Hoodfar, for example, reports that some lower-middle-class Egyptian women have returned to wearing a veil in order to continue working in the public sphere without censure. Many of the women with whom she spoke reported that they wear a veil in order to avoid criticisms by family members and neighbors of their working outside of the home and moving about in public. Ironically, these Egyptian women rely on a traditional symbol of female subordination in order to achieve a level of autonomy and financial security.[17]

A debate has recently emerged among scholars about whether it is not merely difficult but actually useful to study these sorts of resistant practices. At the heart of the objections to studying commonplace resistance is the claim that these acts of defiance are individualistic, self-interested, and inconsequential, as opposed to collective, principled, and effective.[18] Unlike the example of Theodosia Simpson, resistance is rarely motivated by a collective ideal of social justice. It is more frequently enacted to achieve individual benefits and advantages: a sense of pride or dignity, extra money, food, or time.

Indeed, acts of resistance often seek precisely the sorts of material and social resources that are denied to individuals by the relationship of power in which they occur.[19]

Moreover, because these acts are often practiced to escape, rather than change, a structure of power, their effects are typically temporary. Indeed, some critics have observed that such individual acts of resistance may do worse than simply fail to challenge power and inequity. By providing temporary relief of the burdens power imposes, tactical resistances may make insufferable situations tolerable. In doing so, they actually inoculate power from sustained and collective challenge. Based on these criticisms it has been claimed that scholars, in attending to such acts, are at best elevating the trivial and at worst serving as handmaidens to power by romanticizing powerlessness.[20]

Yet to dismiss everyday forms of resistance on the grounds that they are individualistic, unprincipled, and temporary is to foreclose crucial questions about the relationship between power and resistance. Although resistance may be opportunistic and individualistic, it is neither random nor idiosyncratic. The opportunities for resistance emerge from the regular exercise of power. Resistance does not, in other words, opportune on lapses of power as much as it relies on (and its study reveals) a particular social organization of power. Through everyday practical engagements, individuals identify the cracks and vulnerabilities of organized power and institutions such as the law. Goffman makes just this claim for the study of resistance, or what he calls "secondary adjustments," as a diagnostic of power relations.

> From a sociological point of view, the initial question to be asked of a secondary adjustment is not what this practice brings to the practitioner but rather the character of the social relations that its acquisition and maintenance require. This constitutes a structural as opposed to a consummatory or social psychological point of view.[21]

Although individual tactical resistances may provide emotional and material benefits, the understanding of power upon which they depend and the analysis of power they reveal is "the sociologist's first concern."[22] Thus, it is possible that the recent increase in scholarly interest and documentation of everyday forms of resistance may itself reflect modern changes in the operation of power.[23]

Foucault, among others, provides us with a theory that would account for such a change in the organization and experiences of power.[24] He describes the transformation in the exercise of power as "a reversal in the political axis of individuation"[25] whereby disciplinary control circulates "through progressively finer channels, gaining access to individuals themselves, to their bodies, their gestures, all their daily actions."[26] To the extent that modern power operates by constituting and disciplining individual bodies and minds, by creating desires and then naturalizing those as drives, it has implications for the possibilities of protest. Power that is public and visible is more vulnerable to collective forms of protest. For instance, the public hangings, decapitations, and mutilations of the seventeenth and eighteenth centuries were designed to instill fear and awe in the observing population. They often succeeded, "but protest and revolt were also incited by these public demonstrations . . . The site of power could easily become the site of social disturbance, or even revolt."[27] By contrast, the technical, faceless, and individuated forms of contemporary power defy the possibilities of revolt or collective resistance.[28] The spatial and temporal restructuring of the world in a disciplinary regime disables the very communities that were once the site of social disturbance.[29]

Finally, we ought not to assume that everyday forms of resistance are entirely individual or unrelated to more organized social protest (although they may first appear to be). A consciousness of the structures of power, and an experience of its openings and lapses, may be a necessary, if not sufficient, precursor of political mobilization.[30] Minimally, research on everyday tactical resistance allows us to inquire whether such acts do prefigure or even provoke more collective contests of power.

To examine these empirical questions, we must acknowledge and seek out the often unseen and unrecognized practices of the weak against the strong. We now turn to stories of legality and resistance. These are stories of daily confrontations with power. They reveal individuals' consciousness of an opposing "other." They also illustrate how, when opportunities present themselves, people invent and try out forms of practical opposition. Although resistance is often described in terms of action, it is important to remember that a resistant understanding of legality (or of being against the law) is expressed in silences, refusals, and absences as well as in acts of defiance and disruption. Our respondents' stories reinterpret those events and in the telling enact a resistant consciousness.

Normativity: Might Makes Right

To express or enact a resistant consciousness of legality is to understand legality, and its normative claims, as a product of power. In this sense, resistance inverts conventional understandings of legal authority and its relationship to morality. Rather than seeing legal authority as deriving from some moral principles, principles that legitimate power, this view of legality understands power as producing the normative grounds upon which power is exercised. Might, in these stories of resistance, makes right.

Arbitrariness

In the course of our interviews, we asked respondents a hypothetical question regarding what they would do if a judge were to treat them unfairly. Many respondents answered the question by describing the self-defining and thus arbitrary power of the law as it is embodied in the judge.

> What other levels do you have? The only thing you got is the court. Everything is settled by the court. Somebody's opinion. And the people that are in power make their decision. (George Kofie)

> There is nothing you can do. Just grin and bear it. Who can you complain to? You can't . . . there's nobody you can talk to. There is nobody higher than the judge. (Mike Chapin)

> What can you do? They're always right . . . Who you going to complain to, who cares? Truthfully, you know, and if they cared, what do they do about it? (Claudia Greer)

> Not much you can do about it. Except complain. [Interviewer: Complain to whom?] To no one. [Laughs] To complain to yourself about the lousy court system. (Andrew Eberly)

Several respondents sarcastically alluded to the unrestrained power of judges by suggesting that they are God-like.

*File complaint with? [Laughing] I have no idea. God, his supe-
rior? I don't know. (Michelle Stewart)*

*In court you are treated as a person of less value than the court
officials or the judge. At that point, he's God. So, if you don't like
this God, you go to another God. (George Kofie)*

The arbitrary power of legal actors—bureaucrats, public officials, police, and judges—was also described in terms of their lack of
empathy or sympathy. Whereas a reified view of law expects justice
to be blind to the particularistic exigencies of biography and circumstance, here people rejected this ideal. Finding themselves facing the
mundane and tragic contingencies of life—family illness, poverty, ex-
haustion, confusion, and misunderstanding—they experienced the
law's failure to acknowledge or take their situations into account as
subverting, rather than ensuring, justice.

Claudia Greer's account of her experience in traffic court illustrates this frustration.

> *[The policeman] said, no, that was a red light, so I got a ticket
> for that, now . . . my mom was terminally ill with cancer. I was
> working two or three jobs, and going to school at the same time
> and, you know, try and make time. Then I go to court. Now, my
> mom needs me at home, and I'm sitting in court from the time it
> starts. I think it started at seven o'clock, I don't know. But any-
> way, I'm sitting there for hours, and I see all these people go
> before the judge, and I see the bias in him, right? And then, by
> the time he gets to me, he's unreasonable, and whoever I had to
> speak to was unreasonable. In other words, when they ask you if
> you're pleading guilty or not, not guilty, why ask you if you're
> pleading guilty? They're going to fine you anyway? You're guilty.
> Why don't they just tell you you're guilty, pay at the door and
> leave!*

The difficulties of working multiple jobs, going to school, and
dealing with her mother's illness are a central part of Claudia Greer's
assessment of the court. These biographical facts establish a temporal and emotional framework for Greer's legal encounter. A just system, she suggests, would take similar notice of her life circumstances.

Nell Pearson, a writer and editor, was accused of absconding with
the funds of a journal she was editing. Nell had been the administrator of several writers' workshops, managing both the NEA funding

for the workshops and the publication of the workshops' quarterly journal. At one point, while she was hospitalized for an ectopic pregnancy, long-simmering animosities and jealousies among the various collectives erupted. In her absence, the board voted to cancel the specific issue of the journal to which Nell was personally contributing work, not only overseeing production. Incapacitated and emotionally distraught, Nell, in her own words,

> did something very, very desperate. From my sickbed, I trans-
> ferred the [magazine's] funds for that particular issue into my
> personal account with the idea of, when I got stronger and better,
> and we could talk, we would work this out.

Her physical immobility, emotional distress, and good intentions, she thought, should have influenced the interpretation of her action. She had no intention of keeping the funds, merely forestalling any decisions until she got out of the hospital. "Since I was in my sickbed . . . I couldn't set up a separate account."

Although she returned the funds, neither the lawyers, the opposing parties, nor the legal definition of culpability seemed to take account of or empathize with her situation.

> So the upshot of all that was that I did eventually return the
> money and the materials to them, but they're still going after me
> for punitive damages.

For these and other respondents, legality is whatever those with power—the judge, the police, the utility company, the supervisor—say is legal. Steven Wager expressed this view explicitly.

> Well, that's the question. What's unfair? The judge is going to
> pass judgment on the law, so it couldn't be considered unfair.

Avoidance and Resignation

By defining events, relationships, and interactions as legal, people reveal their understanding of the normative terrain of legality. The normative dimension of legal consciousness not only describes the distinctive moral bases of legality, in doing so it also determines the conditions under which people think law should or should not be mobilized.

In the form of consciousness we referred to as "before the law," you will recall, legality was equated with collective interests. To seek legal remedy, whether that involved calling the police, instituting a lawsuit, or complaining to a government agency, required defining problems in such a way that the harm that these problems produced reached beyond the individual. By conjuring up either some future or current harm to others (e.g., elderly shoppers or innocent children), people felt authorized to mobilize the law. Alternatively, those expressing an understanding of law as a game perceived legality as applicable to situations of explicit self-interest. In these instances, what made something legal was the operation of a distinctive cluster of rules and procedures—the "rules of the game"—that one followed in seeking those self-interested ends. In contrast to both the reified and gamelike versions of legality, when people describe themselves "against the law," legality is characterized as something to be avoided. Because it is a product of arbitrary power, legality is seen as capricious and thus dangerous to invoke. Rather than conditionally appropriate or useful, in this form of consciousness, legality is condemned.

This understanding of legality as untrustworthy, and thus to be avoided, was most poignantly expressed by Aida Marks in her account of her son Ronald's arrest. The mother of eight adult children, Aida Marks had worked hard to maintain a sense of herself as "ordinary," "decent," and "well respected." Despite her poverty, Aida Marks succeeded in keeping the crime, drug dealing, and physical degradation of her neighborhood at bay. The outside of Aida Marks's still-sturdy house was unremarkable next to its neighbors, displaying signs of its former more polished self amid more numerous indicators of advancing decay. The inside, however, was remarkable among the homes we visited in the degree to which it was a self-conscious record of Aida Marks's relationships and respectability. She commented explicitly on this fact, describing different pieces of furniture, how they were acquired (as gifts or purchases), and what they meant to her.

> You see that breakfront? I bought that from Macy's. It's older than my son, my son's thirty-eight and I have it that long . . . put wood in there and glass . . . Now I bought that one at a flea market for fifteen dollars and the rabbi's wife gave me that bookcase . . . This set I've had for years. I bought it from a white lady, where was it? Somewhere she sold me the whole set and you can get chairs and things like that for eighty dollars.

This house is a glistening space fragrant with wax and moist green leaves and alive with the sounds of Aida Marks's grandchildren running in and out. The living room and dining room opened to each other with the kitchen to the rear and the stairs to the upper floors at one end of the dining room. The upholstered furniture was wrapped in fitted plastic slipcovers, a phalanx of couches, chairs, buffets, and tables bordering each room. The walls were massed with framed photographs of several generations of the Marks family. Lodging her hard-won and fragile sense of respectability in various public roles, such as the presidency of her block association, as well as these material objects, Aida Marks told us, with some measure of pride, that she was "known throughout the city."

When her son Ronald got into trouble (for use and distribution of controlled substances, breaking and entering, and assault and battery), Aida Marks tried to insulate and protect the rest of her family, especially her "good son, David," by taking out a restraining order against Ronald. This, she believed, should have clearly established her honesty and respectability. Having officially positioned herself on the side of the law, she believed that the restraining order should have certified her credibility and protected her from being treated as a criminal.

Aida Marks's eventual rejection of law was borne of a betrayal of this trust. Despite her record of decency and social position, and her efforts to disassociate herself from Ronald, Aida claimed that when the police came looking for Ronald, she was "treated like a common ordinary criminal." The police, she told us with much bitterness, did not believe her when she told them that Ronald was not in the house. The police entered her home forcibly, handcuffed her to a radiator, and then arrested her and her son David.

> Right now the way I feel now I said I couldn't call the police on my worst enemy, but if it was before the set-up I would call the police . . . now, I don't trust the police.

Other respondents also described encounters that undermined their sense of any connection between legality and justice, supporting their notion that as far as law is concerned might makes right. Olive Washington, mother of six grown children, described herself to us with a short harsh laugh, as "black and poor." When her son Steven had been walking home from the store one day, the police stopped him. Mistaking him for someone for whom they had an arrest warrant, the police made Steven strip off his clothes.

> *Would you believe they made him strip? They made him, they*
> *pulled his pants down in the middle of the street.*

Although she was enraged, she decided to let the matter drop.

> *I was totally upset . . . [Steven] had the badge numbers of a*
> *couple of them, and everything. But I said, we'd just leave it alone.*
> *We might need a policeman here one day, and they might not*
> *show up. He was scared because he said, there was like five of*
> *them. And they were all white, and that was what scared him so.*

In the face of arbitrary power, "He just didn't say anything . . . [He] knew he better keep shut."

John and Janet Collier, a young white couple living with their newborn son in a neighborhood of small, closely built single-family homes, told us a similar story of arbitrary police power.[31] While driving through Newark one evening, Janet Collier was pulled over by some police.

> *He just stopped me for no reason. I said, "Well, what did you*
> *stop me for? I didn't go through any lights. I didn't disobey any-*
> *thing." He just pulled me over. I guess maybe he just thought I*
> *was cruising around looking for some dope or something . . . I*
> *figure it's a typical cop reaction . . . They like to hassle people.*
> *Even guys I work with, friends feel the same way about them.*
> *They just like to hassle people, and they get away with it. And*
> *there's nothing we can do about it. So you lose all respect for the*
> *police. I do. I have no respect for them. I have relatives who are*
> *law officers. I like them not a lot.*

Not surprisingly, given this view of legality as inextricably tied to power, many persons, like Aida Marks, Olive Washington, and Janet Collier, reject law. For them, given the choice, one avoids law and legal constructions as much as possible. If necessary one tolerates one's "worst enemies," one accepts losses, "keeps shut," lumps indignities and even what appear to be clear illegalities. As Raymond Johnson told us,

> *I would have to say that I want to stay away from courts as*
> *much as possible. Well, that's the way I feel about the legal sys-*
> *tem in general. Sue, only as the last resort, better negotiate, com-*
> *promise, settle.*

Of course, avoidance of the law is not always possible. When encounters with legal agents are inescapable, the strategy many respondents adopt is resignation and deference. This stance was described by Michael Chapin:

I have been treated unfairly at times . . . I had the cops on the
turnpike one day. And they really tried to provoke me into a fight.
They pushed me, they shoved me, they yelled at me, they
screamed at me . . . and I just said yes sir, whatever you say,
because I knew they were just looking to give me a beating . . .
There's nothing you can do, just grin and bear it.

The observations of Ralph Jeffers echo Mike Chapin's account.

You can't win . . . The problem . . . is the judge will believe what-
ever the cop says regardless of whether he's lying or not. So
there's no point in bothering with it.

Dozens of respondents offered similar comments on the necessity of bowing to what seems like the overwhelming power of police, judges, and courts. The observation of Joseph Dimato, a thirty-four-year-old hairdresser, epitomizes these accounts. In the course of his interview, Joseph recalled numerous incidents and legal encounters, everything from traffic violations to arrest for possession of marijuana. Joseph Dimato voiced his conviction that in the face of capricious power, one had to bend.

I dealt with the system enough times that I realized that you
can't be against them. You got to go with them . . . It just won't
get you nothing. You just got to yes-and-no them to death, noth-
ing else.

Sima Rah, a Vietnamese Indian woman, described a time she complained to a police officer about what she thought was an unfair traffic ticket. Not only did her criticism go unanswered but the officer issued several more tickets.

I told him that is not fair. Seems like you can't say anything.
They stop you. You have to keep your mouth shut.

Such resigned compliance and displays of deference help respondents escape or minimize the power of law. In some cases, passive acquiescence is an attempt to retain a sense of autonomy and dignity, to refuse the law's ability to further intrude on one's life.[32] In other instances, docility in the face of arbitrary power is practiced for physical survival. After the police entered her home and arrested her, one of Aida Marks's neighbors commented that he would not have allowed the police to treat his mother the way Aida's sons had let the police treat her. Imagining the possibilities of more overt resistance, Aida Marks remarked bitterly, "I would've had three dead sons if I had put up any squabble."

Unpredictable and arbitrary, the law lacks, in these accounts, any moral anchor. Rather than confining power and violence, it seems to embody it.

Constraint

> Power is bound by its very visibility.
> MICHEL DE CERTEAU, *The Practice of Everyday Life*

Although legality is seen as a product of power, even here people recognize that it is not omnipotent. In these stories of resistance, legal power is arbitrary but not unconstrained. The features of modern rational law—its size, visibility, the fact that it organizes the actions of many persons, occupies space, and monopolizes time—represent to many persons constraints on the law's ability to act. Mired in formal procedure, captured by bureaucratic structures and remote from the real concerns of citizens, the law is unable to effectively resolve disputes, recognize truth, or respond to injustice.

To say that these accounts describe the law as limited by these features, however, is not to say that people perceive the law as less powerful because of these limits. In fact, to many of the persons with whom we spoke, these limitations contribute to law's dangerousness. When respondents tell stories of resistance, they describe law as a giant, hobbled by its size and blinded by its formality. And as they see it, living in the shadow of a giant, one is as likely to be harmed by its clumsiness and myopia as by its rage.

Overwhelming Everyday Life

In many of the stories of legal trouble that we collected, people repeatedly referred to the inability of law to respond to the sorts of ordinary troubles that characterize everyday life. The very size, complexity, and grandeur of the law place it beyond the ongoing relationships of dependence and power that routinely produce trouble. At best, people believed, the law might condemn these situations; it might even intervene momentarily to unsettle the situation. But without really transforming the everyday, legality often exacerbates the powerlessness that it is supposed to remedy.

One of the most common reasons people gave for not turning to law was that "it wasn't worth it." The formal apparatus of the law and the costs it exacted in time, money, and loss of privacy had the general effect of rendering much of life "not worth it" from a legal point of view. The formal rights and processes of law seemed to erect hurdles too high for ordinary people to vault. The thirty-seven-dollar consumer scam, the disruption of having to move to another apartment, even the physical and emotional pain of unnecessary medical procedures were accepted or "lumped" because of the law's assessment of those costs. Although the law is theoretically available to mediate all sorts of social situations, and may indeed help reconcile differences and disputes, people experiencing themselves up against the law understood it as an expression of overwhelming but unreliable power.

Sophia Silva, for example, told us what dozens of other respondents also reported. When her children's cars were broken into, she did not claim compensation from her insurer. Although she reported the incidents to the police, she did not expect much from them because "they have so many other problems."

> We didn't, we don't, report anything to the insurance company unless it is something really major because we're afraid that our insurance rates will go up. My daughter's bill was $900 and my son's was $400. It is easier to absorb the cost.

According to Sophia Silva, neither the police nor the insurance company can fully protect her. The police cannot protect or redeem her property, and she feels that she cannot jeopardize her insurance by seeking compensation for these smaller injuries and losses when she fully expects bigger ones in the future.

Sophia Silva's account conveys a picture of two giant organizations (law and insurance) that, despite their power, fail her. Because the legal system is large and cumbersome, minor disputes and losses often cannot pass the boundary conditions for cost-effective action. Precisely because her problems fell within—rather than outside—these institutionalized domains, her loss appears insignificant.[33]

When people do decide to pursue remedies by mobilizing legal organizations, they face another constraint of law. Respondents acknowledge the capacity of law to radically reshape relationships, to make and unmake families, create and transfer property, and transform identities. Nonetheless, respondents see these interventions as momentary, leaving intact ongoing social relations.[34] Michelle Stewart recounted a childhood in which she was sexually and physically abused by her parents. On numerous occasions, as a child, she had called the police for help. Despite abundant evidence of violence ("blood and guts"), the police never arrested her parents. By treating the family relationships as beyond the law, legality helped to construct the content and form of those relationships. The balance of power between Michelle Stewart and her parents remained fixed, the beatings and abuse unabated. Michelle Stewart experienced the power of law by its refusal to act.

> I wouldn't go through the system, because I think that you get hung, I don't trust it at all. I have learned to trust me, period . . . I wouldn't put myself in the hands of the law. It works nice on paper, you know . . . But a paper law, from what I've seen, doesn't work.

By entering social relationships intermittently, legality's power was seen as limited. People often noted the gap between formal procedures and actual outcomes. Crimes go uninvestigated, convicted criminals unpunished, and civil awards uncollected.

After having successfully sued a restaurant in small-claims court for replacement of a $500 coat, Martha Lee gave up after receiving only $250 of her award.

> I could never collect the whole five hundred dollars. I didn't agree to it but they sent me a check for two fifty. And I never got the other half. And there was nothing I could do. I called the court and said what's my recourse, and they said, "You'll have to go back to court again and get another judgment." . . . Forget it, I'm not going back to court again . . . The court gives a judgment, and then, you still can't collect.

For Martha Lee, the combination of the court's inability to enforce the judgment, the insurance company's experienced gamesmanship, and her own lack of time and experience created a residue of resentment and distrust of legal processes.

Janet Briarly told us a similar story about winning a suit but failing to collect.

*I never got my money. So that was, kind of makes the whole
thing bogus . . . You don't get settlement after winning. What's
the point of it?*

Mike Chapin also expressed an appreciation of the futility of
court judgments; in this case, the imputed impotence worked in his
favor.

*I talked to a lawyer who said "don't worry if they get a settlement
against you . . . I have a contractor, who's a client of mine, he
has thirty-five settlements against him and he never paid a
dime." He says it's one thing to get a settlement against you—
this is where the law cracks me up. You can have a settlement
against you but it doesn't mean they can collect, you know.*

Because legality is unable to enforce its own judgments, many
respondents noted that it also fails to protect them from retaliation
on the part of others. Mike Chapin reported several instances in
which he thought that he had legitimate bases for complaint. Nonetheless, he refused to formally voice his complaints because he feared
retaliation from his landlord, the town officials, the trash collector,
or his union friends. Mike Chapin understood that the specific situations could be handled, but legal action could not intervene over the
long run. The systematic and organized power of landlords, the city,
the union, and the schools, among others, would eventually win out,
he believed.

Diana Taylor claimed that after she had won a suit for a work-
place injury, her employer looked for ways of firing her.

*What it was, it was that they were looking for little things
because I had the grievance filed about my injury. So nothing
that I did was right any way after I filed the complaint about me
being hurt. So they tried to blackball me.*

Diana Taylor did not hold her immediate supervisor responsible for
the firing. Rather, she explained the situation in terms of the company's hierarchical power structure and the failure of law to protect
in private settings. She seemed to recognize the constraints on legality's power.

*It's funny though because there were no hard feelings and you
know I see [the supervisor] and I speak to her and say "Hi" and
everything. But it was just the nature of it all. That's a privately
owned organization and what Papa Bear says goes.*

At the same time that the law was seen as unresponsive to their needs, many people believed it catered to criminals. Although he had to wait three months for his insurance company to compensate him for his stolen car, John Collier expected that the thief was probably out on the street before he received his insurance money.

> I got to dig into my savings. The whole thing wasn't my fault in the beginning. This crook probably did it ten times before. And he just goes binga binga bing through the doors—in jail and out of jail . . . They should cut his hands off when they catch some-one stealing a car. They can't steal another one . . . That's what they do in the Middle East. Don't they? Get caught stealing they remove your hand. You don't do it again, do you . . . Oooh, if I could run the world.

Here John Collier juxtaposes what he sees as the impotence of modern American law with the legendary and stereotypical version of Middle Eastern law: harsh, immediate, and effective. Jamie Lee-son offered almost exactly the same interpretation of law's capricious system of punishment and protection when he commented that he sometimes believed that the Islamic code works.

To Mike Chapin, the law has tremendous power over life and death and yet does not use it to protect innocent people from the dangerous ones. Its power is fickle; it is not, he said, "committed . . . to do the right thing." Rules, technical procedures, repeated trials and appeals constrain legality.

> They had twenty-three appeals in the last few years to the death sentence, and they've all been commuted to life sentences. So they might as well just get rid of the sentence . . . We have the death penalty in New Jersey but they're not using it. They haven't used it since we reinstated it. I don't know how many years it's been . . . My friend's father was a police officer who was killed and that guy got commuted to life. He originally was supposed to get the death penalty and he never got it . . . They keep trying to get him out of jail . . . This guy's got a wife and kids, this bum! What about my friend's father? What about his kids? That screwed his kids up good . . . This guy comes along, kills his father who's a police officer and gets off the hook. He has conju-gal rights with his wife. Is that right? I mean, to me that just says . . . some lack of some kind of commitment to, you know, to do the right thing.

Violence and Self-Help

Because the law is seen as powerful but ineffective, creating barriers that ordinary people cannot surmount, people sometimes describe themselves as having to take the law into their own hands. Taking the initiative for securing their own remedy, restitution, or retribution for injuries suffered, people report engaging in violence or threats of violence.[35] Many persons, like Mike Chapin, believe that they are authorized to do violence by the law's apparent refusal to act. "That's what they're telling me. Because the court is not going to do the job."

Jane Elliot told us that although she often wants to call the police when her neighbor plays loud music, she does not feel safe doing so. Fearing retaliation were she to call the police, instead, she said,

[I turn] on my radio with the easy listening. I turned it on loud too. Let them realize, you know, how loud music can disturb next-door neighbors. This is the way I handle it rather than call the police . . . Let them know how it feels. Retaliate like that.

Sometimes people explicitly describe their own actions as a response to the inaccessibility of law. In regard to a dispute with a building contractor, Robert Tisdell observed, "I really couldn't afford litigation. But I could afford to keep bothering the guy day and night."

Citizen self-help and retaliation are sometimes less benign. They may involve criminal acts[36] or, more often, the imagining and threatening of violence. For example, Joan Kinsler told us that she would "kill their cat" if a neighbor refused to return an expensive appliance they had borrowed. She also warned that her husband would be "talking three octaves higher" and "wouldn't have that thing anymore" if she caught him having an affair. These allusions to such extreme but improbable acts of violence peppered more than a few people's accounts.

Jamie Leeson, you will recall, commented repeatedly that because the law is slow and ineffective, he pursued other, more violent means for handling routine problems. He said that if anyone tried to hurt his kittens, he would chop their hands off. He could not be bothered with the kind of drawn-out and costly processes that he faced when he was mugged. Next time, he said, "I would just knock him unconscious, take his clothes off, and with an indelible marker write 'thief' across his face." These kinds of comments reveal our respondents' sense of hopelessness in situations they are unable to lump.

Many others expressed similar sentiments of frustration and violence.

> *I wanted to hit him. (Paul Dyson)*

> *What's to pursue? I mean, give him a bat over the head, maybe. (Mike Chapin)*

> *I would have done more if I could have. But there really wasn't much else you can do . . . I personally wanted to do her bodily harm. (Martha Lee)*

> *I'm going to get a gun. Anybody comes in here, he's going to go out of here carried. You see, that's another thing. If you don't kill him, you are in trouble. He can sue you. Why should he sue you when he is on your property? Are you supposed to sit there and let him go? I don't buy that. Maybe I'm violent, but I don't buy that. He's on my property and if I can get him, I'm going to get him! I don't have a gun, but I might get one. Today is just like the old west, you got to carry one on your hip. (Scott Smetona)*

> *You talk about the Supreme Court. They had a guy in there who was appealing his death sentence. I don't remember all the details, but they let him off the hook. They're not using the death sentence . . . because he didn't mean to kill this poor woman when he hit her with a hammer twelve times. I don't know if it was ten or twelve. I mean, that made me sick. Because if anybody hits anybody in my family with a hammer and kills them like that, they're going to have to answer to me. That's what they're telling me. Because the court is not going to do the job. (Mike Chapin)*

> *[Referring to a dispute with a bank about a mischarge on a credit card] So they put it into the hands of a collection agent who called me up and infuriated me and then said, "Why are you cursing at me?" And I said, "I feel like punching your nose. Now get the hell out of here and don't bother me." (Stanley Warshawsky)*

Exaggerated, blustering boasts such as these express a frustration borne of limited alternatives. "What's to pursue?" "There isn't much else you can do." "If you don't kill him, you are in trouble. He can sue you." In these instances, a person opposes imagined violence to accepting some victimization already perpetrated or to preventing future victimization orchestrated through law. The hyperbole that is so often part of these threats (killing cats, chopping off hands and other body parts for relatively minor infractions) is an expression of futility in the face of legality's constraint. The very excessiveness of the rhetoric suggests that we are not expected to take these comments literally, to believe that Joan Kinsler would actually kill her neighbor's cat or castrate an unfaithful husband. Rather, the hyperbolic threats express the person's sense that there is absolutely nothing that they can do to repair the problem. Thus their very threats of violence are expressions of impotence in the face of law's power.

Violence is not, of course, only imagined or threatened, it is also enacted. In each instance where respondents described themselves as an assailant, they defined their action as a response to the wrongful acts of others: unreasonable shopkeepers, disrespectful children, or those who would threaten their neighborhood. Mike Chapin told us about an incident when some neighborhood kids were throwing rocks at his car. He drove home, put his young daughters in the house, and then went back to confront the boys.

> When I told them to quit throwing rocks, one boy yelled, "If you do anything to me I'll sue you." So I gave him a kick because I got so mad when he said "sue me."

Martha Lee told us that a former boss had regularly made sexual passes at her. He would call her at home, invite her to Florida with him, and hang around in her office. When she could not get him to stop, she took action.

> I punched him at the Christmas party and called him an asshole. [Laughing] He comes up to me, and asked me to dance, and I said, "I don't want to dance with you." He grabbed me and starts singing and dancing with me, and wham, I punched him. I said, "You're such an asshole . . . What would your wife think of this?" And he walked away.

Olive Washington talked about how her neighborhood was infested with drugs and how difficult it was for her to keep her children safe. Believing herself to have no other recourse, Olive Washington told us that she would take her "trusty baseball bat" down to the corner to clear out the kids hanging around the drug dealers. When her son asked her not to do that anymore, she replied, "If you don't want me hurt, then don't you get on the corner. Because as long as I hear you're on the corner, I'm coming up there."

Capacity: Desired Disturbances

> The study of common sense knowledge and common sense activities consists of treating as problematic . . . the actual methods whereby members of a society doing sociology, lay or professional, make the social structures of everyday activities observable.
>
> HAROLD GARFINKEL, "Studies of the Routine Grounds of Everyday Activities"

The dimension of legal consciousness that we have been referring to as capacity corresponds to people's understanding of the locus of legality: from what source(s) do legal actions and legal outcomes derive? In this sense, capacity represents a sort of practical theory of social action. As Garfinkel states above, professional social scientists are not alone in "doing sociology" or developing theoretical accounts of social life. As we go about our daily lives, we operate on the basis of understandings of how and why people behave and of how and why things happen. Moreover, we are constantly testing and revising our practical theories against our observations and experiences, even as we interpret those observed events and experiences in the context of our theories. Resistance, as a theory of social action, represents the discovery of social structure operating within the commonsense world of everyday life.

Writing as a sociologist introducing a series of now-famous ethnomethodological experiments, Garfinkel observes that "a knowledge of how the structures of everyday activities are routinely produced should permit us to tell how we might proceed for the effective production of desired disturbances."[37] A similar knowledge underwrites routine forms of everyday resistance. Premised upon an appreciation of the relationship between "the world known-in-common and taken-for-granted"[38] and larger, stable structures of power and inequality, resistance consists of breaches of these often unseen and unarticulated structures in order to produce such disturbances.

In modern American society, public power is most often organized bureaucratically. This means that people generally confront their relative powerlessness within impersonal, rule-governed, functionally organized hierarchies. Consequently, their efforts to resist and unsettle these relationships of power must engage those very same features of formal organizations. To remake situations as they stand, people make do by relying on their understanding of and using the very elements of their subjection: roles, rules, and hierarchy. As we illustrate below, resistance often involves *masquerade*, a playful or strategic use of roles; *rule literalness*, the invocation (rather than violation) of rules; and *inversions*, the manipulation of hierarchies or other arrangements of power.

Masquerade

In their stories and accounts, people expressed an understanding that social action is role based. This sociologically informed view includes two insights. First, it expresses the idea that people's behaviors (as well as their obligations, privileges, entitlements, and ability to enact power) accord with expectations associated with the statuses or social positions they occupy. At the same time, this understanding recognizes an equally relevant insight: because roles are not synonymous with the person, they can be manipulated to influence interactions.[39]

The manipulation of roles might involve some degree of deception. In these instances, persons engage in literal masquerade insofar as they pretend to be something or someone they are not. They assume whatever role would lead to more desired outcomes. What is worth noting in regard to such commonplace deceptions is that people do not typically assume roles that carry greater social status or power. Often, in fact, people assume the role of someone who has less power or greater need, thus making a different sort of claim on power.

Jesus Cortez, an elderly man living in a run-down and dangerous area of Newark, told us that his calls to the police were repeatedly ignored. Finally, he decided to change his voice to sound like that of a woman when calling. Only when he mimicked a woman, he assured us, did he get a "quick response."

Michelle Stewart reported lying about her age to a hospital in order to receive emergency room treatment. Because she was only seventeen at the time, the hospital wouldn't treat her without her parents' permission. Although she had been living independently for two years, having had no contact with her abusive parents, she soon realized that to the hospital she was a dependent minor. Since she couldn't change the circumstances of her family situation in order to conform to hospital rules, she went to a different hospital and changed her age, matter-of-factly telling them she was eighteen.

In both of these instances, Jesus Cortez and Michelle Stewart acted on an understanding of organizational behavior, an understanding acquired through experience and learning. They presented themselves as whatever they needed to be—a (presumably) more vulnerable woman; an adult without family to help or support her—in order to instigate organizational action.

Often, however, the manipulation of roles as a form of resistance is not deceptive but rather selective. People do not lie about a role as much as they selectively invoke or present themselves in a role to which they might, in fact, lay legitimate claim. Persons strategically draw from the vast number of roles they enact in attempting to mobilize and shape the direction of power. Once again respondents' choices reflect their understanding of that power and of how it might be tricked or duped to their benefit. Millie Simpson's role as churchgoer and veteran volunteer, of course, exemplifies this form of resistance. These roles provided the knowledge and experience by which Millie Simpson could deflect the consequences of punishment.

The invocation of a role is intended to define the situation in such a way as to escape the unwanted effects of power. The choice of what role to invoke in a situation, of course, is not simply a matter of freely picking from a catalog of possibilities. The ability to invoke any particular role, for purposes of resistance or conformity, draws upon people's store of cultural and social capital, their experience and knowledge of alternative roles, and the likelihood that the performance will be accepted as genuine. Some possibilities, of course, are not sanctioned, and their legitimacy and viability as role performances are not equally distributed among populations. For example, middle-aged females of any race are more likely to successfully masquerade as churchgoers and volunteers than young unemployed men. Moreover, the behavior associated with some roles may also be the privileged knowledge of particular classes.

Aida Marks relied upon a feature of racial and gender subordination—African American women's employment as housekeepers for white middle-class and upper-class families[40]—and turned it to her advantage. Unable to secure adequate telephone repair through the

normal channels, Aida called the president of the telephone company. Although such officers are insulated from consumer complaints by layers of bureaucratic hierarchy, Aida Marks was able to
cut through the organizational barriers by invoking a role that legitimated such access. By claiming to be the corporate president's housekeeper, she was immediately put through to him and voiced her complaints about her inadequate telephone service. She was soon visited
by an expert team of repairpersons. Thus, Aida Marks drew on her
racially marked speech and her knowledge of the backdoors of formal organizations to manipulate a conventional expectation that African American women serve as domestic workers for white elites in
order to circumvent her lack of power.

Without making an explicit claim regarding their role, people
may also position themselves within a relationship by using words
and phrases to convey a particular status for themselves and the situation. George Kofie continually referred to "John Doe Citizen," a hypothetical everyperson who, he claimed, was duped by government
at all levels. According to George Kofie, John Doe Citizen doesn't receive adequate police protection; instead John Doe Citizen's taxes are
used without his knowledge to fund the "war chests" of politicians.

> A person who is in politics should be a person who is looking
> out for the best interests of John Doe Citizen . . . Should his goal
> be to fatten the pockets of other politicians and his, or should his
> goals be to reduce the burden on John Doe Citizen and make it a
> more comfortable life?

"So that's politics," he concluded, "but that's the thing I think a lot of
people don't know about." By naming this generic, victimized, and
naive citizen, George not only characterizes the size and scope of the
problem (it is systemic and collective), but characterizes himself as
well. He is not naive or duped. Although he is, like all citizens, a
victim of government, George Kofie knows it. And that knowledge
distinguishes him from others.

Rule Literalness

De Certeau observes that everyday forms of resistance "do not obey
the law of the place, for they are not defined or identified by it."[41]
Based on our conversations and interviews, we might revise de Certeau somewhat: precisely because such practices are not defined or

identified by the laws of the place, neither do they disobey those laws. Theodosia Simpson's resistance, for instance, played off of the fact that there was no rule against wearing union pins as buttons. Crucial to the success of her ploy was the fact that it did not violate any rules of the organization or the state. It insinuated itself into the organization's rules and guidelines, rather than transgressed them. In fact, forms of rule literalness, or technical obedience, constitute another way in which persons manage their encounters with powerful legal organizations and agents.

Whereas masquerade relies on a recognition that social interaction is based on roles, rule literalness is based on an appreciation that all interactions are governed by rules: formal rules stipulating rights and duties as well as informal rules of ceremony and deference. Rule literalness is also based on the understanding that most interactions, while governed by rules, can run smoothly only if some rules are systematically overlooked, bent, stretched, and otherwise ignored. Recognizing this, persons create disturbances by willfully refusing to participate in these routine violations. This might involve finding a lacuna within a network of rules, a space that, by virtue of not being governed or defined, becomes momentarily free of control. Or it might involve subverting the purpose of the rule by rigidly observing it. Assuming the form of either a feigned ignorance, naïveté, or a concrete literalness, this form of resistance challenges and disrupts power by holding it accountable to its own rationality.

When he was arrested on a Saturday for driving without insurance, Mike Chapin was compelled to put up five hundred dollars in cash as bail to guarantee his return to court for a hearing. In court the following Monday, Mike Chapin provided the evidence that there had been an error in the police records and that indeed he had been insured at the time of his arrest. The charges were dismissed. At that point, Mike demanded that the court return the five hundred dollars in cash.

> Then they try to write me a check for my money back and I wouldn't accept it. I made a big stink. I said I want my cash back. I gave you cash, I want cash back . . . I said I don't care what you have to do. I don't care if you have to print the money up. I want cash money. You didn't trust me for a check, I don't trust you either. I made them open the safe. [The judge] came back to see what I was yelling at the clerk, telling her I want my money.

In effect, Mike Chapin appropriated the court's rules requiring that payments be in cash only and used them against the court. By insisting that he be treated as the organization treated him, Mike Chapin challenged the often unquestioned prerogative of the court to define what constitutes equal treatment.

By remaining scrupulously within the rules, a challenge remains invulnerable to control. Although little in the way of material benefit may be achieved, the moral claim of a challenge remains unsullied by counterclaims of deviance. Rather than challenge a credit card charge and risk losing his credit rating or worse, Stanley Warshawsky carefully calculated the disputed amount on his monthly bill and withheld only that amount.

> *I never paid that part of the bill . . . I did a little arithmetic and I figured out how much of my final bill was the fifty-five dollars. You know, multiplied by the logarithm of 1.01 and all this good stuff. And I said this is the amount of money I don't owe them and I just didn't pay it. I cut the card up in twenty pieces and sent it back.*

George Kofie claimed that he did not pay medical bills when hospitals insisted on double-billing him. With a knowing wink, he explained his approach.

> *When I go to the emergency room, I have a hospital bill, and a separate doctor bill . . . I pay the hospital. Then I get a bill from some outside source for the treatment that I received in the hospital. This happens every time you go. And I've never been able to get any response from these people who send the bill . . . I send letters telling them to explain to me the medical attention, then I pay the bill. I don't get responses, then I don't pay it. [Interviewer: You don't pay the doctor bill.] I don't pay. I pay the hospital bill . . . If the doctor is working in the hospital, why do I need to [pay him]? I go to the hospital and I pay the emergency room bill. Why do I pay twice? I don't pay unless I get the proper response . . . When I go to my doctor's office, I don't get a bill from the hospital.*

Inversions

Resistance through inversion is underwritten by the insight that social interaction is organized in hierarchies of authority. These structures of hierarchy and the expectations that sustain them, while enacted through human behavior, most often remain unspoken. Relationships and interactions among persons of vastly different degrees of power rely on a silent but mutual recognition and performance of those differences. Inversion consists of willfully ignoring this hierarchy and with it the relays of respect, deference, and duty that are attached. Because power and authority so often go without saying, ignoring these structural differences is disruptive precisely because it forces power to articulate itself, to reassert itself. By demanding power to own up to itself, it calls power's bluff.

Not wanting to remain passive in the face of what he believed was blatant union corruption, Mike Chapin plotted to invert the relationship between the carpenters' union and its members.

> My latest crazy idea was to picket the local. Get a hundred guys
> with signs. Call up the TV station, call up the newspapers and go
> down there and put them into shame. Shame them into doing
> something right. To change what's going on down there.

Had he used the social practice of picketing against the local construction workers' union as he imagined he might, Mike Chapin would have challenged the union's fiduciary relationship to workers. More important, he would have made explicit the way in which union and management interests were aligned rather than contested.

Having over the years been subjected to numerous forms of harassment and humiliation at the hands of the local police, Olive Washington described her response in one such instance.

> I was riding down Hadden Avenue one day and the cop pulled
> up in back of me. All of a sudden, turned on his lights and siren
> noise. Scared the mess out of me. I almost hit a parked car. And
> the only thing he did it for was to pass the light. Then he turned
> everything off and was cruising on down the road, you know?
> And I very nicely cruised on down the road and pulled him over
> and told him exactly what I thought about it. [Interviewer: What
> did he say?] I didn't appreciate it. He laughed. I told him you
> wouldn't be laughing if I turned his badge number in . . .
> because they are supposed to observe all speed laws just like
> we are if they are not on call.

Michelle Stewart provided a similar example of inverting the lines of authority and responsibility that define common relationships. She told us that as a teenager she feared her mother's reckless driving when her mother had been drinking. After futilely pleading with her mother not to drive, Michelle took her mother to the local police station.

> I went with my mother one time when she was really drunk, like when I was fourteen. She was an alcoholic. She was always drinking and driving and crashing her car and everything. And I would get pissed off when she would come to pick up my friends and she'd be like that. She endangered us. So, I brought her into the police department. I called her on her bluff. She told me she wasn't drunk and I called her on it. She goes, I'm not drunk, let's go get a Breathalizer. So I went there with her, and she was obviously drunk and driving a child, me.

In these examples, asymmetrical lines of authority are reversed: a union man imagines picketing his union, a citizen stops a police officer, a child disciplines a parent. In each instance, a person forces someone occupying a position of greater authority to make explicit the prerogatives of that status and to demand rather than simply expect deference. In this sense, resistant acts impose costs, they require power to use additional resources of social interaction.[42]

Another form of inversion involves less of a reversal than a refusal to acknowledge and defer to lines of authority. One of the most frequent forms of resistance entails leapfrogging over layers of bureaucratic hierarchy. Cogently summarizing the distribution of power and authority within organizations, Aida Marks described this practice when she told of us of her masquerade as a maid.

> I start at the top because the people in the middle want to move to the top and the ones at the bottom can't help you, they're in the same situation you're in. So I always, that's how I got to meet Robert A. [the president of the telephone company], I called over there first and I told them I was his maid.

Sophia Silva told us her favorite story about her experience as a frustrated consumer.

> [W]hen my children were young, my washer kept overflowing and I was doing washes by the dozen. So I kept calling the repair place. They came and they kept fixing motors in it. This was costing us, and we were a young couple. Anyway, nothing was happening and I called, I think it was the General Electric number, and I called the company and I got the president of the company. And the secretary said, "I'm sorry, he's not available." And I said, "Well, I am going to call him until he is." So she said, "Hold on a

minute." And he came on, and said how can I help you? I
started to cry, I was so nervous. And he said, "Now you sit down
and you tell me the whole story." And I told him the whole story.
That I have all these bills in front of me and I have this machine
that does not work and nothing has been done. He said, "Don't
you worry, ma'am, it'll be taken care of." And five minutes later
after we hung up, I got a call from a service company . . . out on
Route 22, or something, and they came up and they fixed it. I
mean, I don't mind paying for things, but . . . This is my favorite
story.

By going to the top, respondents achieve three objectives. First, there is a high probability of having the specific demand met. When superordinates are informed, the problem is usually remedied quickly. Many respondents discussed the routes they followed to get to the top. Gretchen Zinn cautioned, however, that it was a difficult climb. "I think you have to start through the regular channels though, or else they're going to send you back to that."

Believing that bureaucratic processes and incompetent personnel create unnecessary obstacles, respondents see leapfrogging as efficient action. Bradley Spears offered an extended analysis of how bureaucracies become unresponsive, and how hierarchy and structure underwrite power. Describing a state office, he confessed,

If you don't dot an i, you jeopardize your complaint . . . I'd like
to reorganize their hiring practices, or training practices, so that
the people who deal with the public are able to make decisions,
are able to make judgment calls. I think they have no discretion-
ary power, so consequently, if the dot on the i is upside down,
they reject it. I think sometimes, there has to be some discretion
used.

Thus, in going to the top, respondents meet a second objective. They let the higher-ups—the supposedly competent and responsible members of the organization—know about what is going on among their subordinates. Because the higher-ups often do not desire this information, the people who leapfrog through bureaucratic hierarchy not only disturb the official sequence of movement and action, they also introduce unwelcome information. David Majors, another union member, told us that the higher-ups in any organization or management "don't want any problems." Each level in the organization has its attention focused on those below and those above.[43] Respondents use this feature of organizational hierarchy as a wedge for their claims. Telling us about the state bureau of social services, David Majors commented,

> On many occasions . . . I was forced to deal with their supervisors, and I usually got satisfaction out of them. Only because, you know, they don't want any problems . . . If I couldn't get the answer that I wanted to hear, and knew that should be forthcoming . . . They were just putting it on the back of the table, and saying, you know, "I got all this work in front of me, I'm not going to do it." All you had to do was talk to their supervisor, and they're going to do it. Because that supervisor doesn't want to hear any grief from upstairs. Because if I don't get satisfaction out of him, I'm going elsewhere.

By reporting problems to those higher in the organization, respondents are able to escalate the significance of their complaint, converting it from an individual into an organizational problem. In this way, people call forth higher authority to retaliate against those who have been obstructing their attempts at redress.

Third, going to the top of an organization allows respondents to experience a measure of agency and freedom that the bureaucratic processes of large organizations normally stifle. It is no doubt this satisfaction that accounts for the fact that one of Sophia Silva's favorite stories concerned the washing-machine repair. The satisfaction of being heard is often enough for people to pursue this strategy even in situations they define as futile.

> I think on a couple of occasions [I sent] copies of the letter to the governor's office. Knowing the system, having access to the books and whatnot, it's pretty easy to find out what the chain of command is and to write. Not that it gets you anywhere. (Bradley Spears)

> I go to whoever his superior is. I write a letter, not knowing, you know, if the letter would do any good or not. But I put it down in writing, my grievances. (Sophia Silva)

Time and Space

Legality is often experienced as incongruous with the time and space of everyday life. Operating by organizational rhythms that are often inconsistent with the routines of family and work, legality is experienced not merely as interruption but as a confiscation of private life. The time of legal institutions is (as the phrase "longue durée" suggests) a temporality with a different order of magnitude from the limited, irreversible, and thus irreplaceable lifetime of any person.

As we noted in chapter 4, "Before the Law," the rationalization of social action involves converting time into units (minutes, days, weeks, years) and then using these units to organize social life. Rather than understanding time as passing in an indivisible, continuous stream, it is seen as comprising distinct elements that can be abstracted, partitioned, calculated, and rearranged. These elements are then mapped onto social life and become the basis for interaction. Through this process, relationships and interactions are transformed into static encounters that are unconnected by memory. Lacking the continuity of shared experience, one encounter may have little or nothing to do with another, as Millie Simpson discovered. People often report the experience of being transformed into a case, which may then be reassigned, forgotten, or filed away.

In addition, much of the of timelessness of law is achieved through the spatialization of relationships, interactions, and practices. Law occupies space in a variety of ways, most importantly by privileging writing. Through inscription, that which is spoken and heard is transformed into that which is seen. This feature of modern legality has consequences for the distribution of social power. Strategically entering the time and space of the law is problematic for those with few resources and little power. Unable to penetrate the legal text, many persons and groups remain unrecognizable in a world of paper, precedent, and archive.

Even those who are able to enter into the law's text often cannot control where they are placed or deployed. Having entered legality's textualized realm, as we noted earlier, they are easily confined by it. Their words, deeds, statuses, and relationships are concretized and objectified. Through such transformations, persons forfeit the ability to amend or withdraw. Through writing, words are given an existence apart from their authors. As Rosalind Petchesky notes, "Sight, in contrast to other senses, has as its peculiar property the capacity for detachment, for objectifying the thing visualized by creating distance between knower and known."[44]

Still, as de Certeau notes, many of those who are confined within the spaces of the law—inhabiting the files, records, dockets—are able to establish within it a degree of plurality and creativity. "By the art of being in between," he writes, "[they] draw unexpected results from their situations." As in all forms of resistance, drawing these unexpected results is contingent upon recognizing the operation of power.

In many of the stories we heard, the rationalization of time and the privileging of texts and other forms of inscription were recognized as central ordering principles of law. And, as with other forms of resistance, the shape and form of defiance derived from the power against which it was poised.

Taking Time: Foot-Dragging

> The first generation of factory workers were taught by their masters the importance of time; the second generation formed their short-time committees in the ten-hour movement; the third generation struck for overtime or time-and-a-half. They had accepted the categories of their employers and learned to fight back within them.
>
> E. P. THOMPSON, "Time, Work-Discipline,
and Industrial Capitalism"

One of the most common forms of resistance is foot-dragging, or "taking time." Note that we did not use the more familiar construction, "taking *one's* time." As a form of opposition, the time taken in foot-dragging is not that of the resister. It is time that belongs to one's employer, one's creditor, one's jailer, to anyone, in fact, who defines and controls behavior in terms of time. In this regard, foot-dragging is a modern form of resistance that depends upon, even as it defies, the rationalization of time.

Frequently, for instance, when people cannot resolve disagreements with merchants, credit card companies, or professionals, they accept defeat but, as Rita Michaels said, "get a little of her own back." When asked to pay a medical bill she felt was unfair, Rita Michaels purposely paid only ten dollars a month. Her motive was not to avoid the charge, but to make the hospital wait for her compliance.

> *It was two hundred and fifty dollars. And he sent me a bill for that, and I questioned it. And he told me what it was for. Every month I'd get a bill. It would say if you don't pay this bill, we're going to send you to a collection agency. I paid it ten dollars a month. I could've paid it all off in one shot, but I should have been told about [the costs up front] . . . I did it to be a pest, you*

know. You can't take me to court if I'm making at least an effort to pay.

Anticipating problems, some people use time to avoid or minimize their victimization. When asked if she had ever had problems with renting, such as having her security deposit withheld, Sima Rah laughed.

No. I laugh because we don't give the owner a chance to withhold our security. If we know we have to move, we don't pay that month's rent, which is our security. Because we know these landlords. They won't give your security back.

Recognizing the value of time, people report taking it in compensation for losses that cannot be redeemed in other ways. Although Nell Pearson could not get full compensation from the insurance company for her losses in a car accident, when the opportunity arose, she managed to make the insurance company lawyer spend the money she should have received. When the insurance company lawyer called her to negotiate a lower settlement, she used her knowledge of lawyers' billing practices (where labor is reckoned to the minute) and kept him on the phone for as long as would likely equal the difference in what the insurance company offered and she wanted.

They turned it over to their insurance company (and I got a call from the insurance company's lawyer) wanting to settle the night before the small-claims hearing. And we were haggling over fifty dollars. I had already decided that he probably wasn't going to pay me the fifty dollars but I would get fifty dollars of his time on the telephone. So, after about a half an hour, he was screaming . . . And he said, "I'm just going to have to see you in small claims." I knew he didn't want to go. It was too small an amount of money. So I said, "That's okay, you don't have to do it, I've gotten my fifty dollars out of you." And he said, "Is that what you were doing?" And I said, "Yeah. I know what lawyers are worth." And he said, "You've got your fifty dollars."

Foot-dragging is a means of exercising some control in situations in which little opportunity for control exists. As these examples illustrate, foot-dragging is less of a refusal (to pay, or act, or work) than it is an assertion of some level of autonomy in the course of complying. The possibilities for foot-dragging are, of course, premised upon compliance being reckoned according to spatialized units of time. A second type of intervention involves literally appropriating and colonizing space.

Taking Space, Camping Out

> Discipline proceeds by the organization of individuals in space, and it therefore requires a specific enclosure of space. In the hospital, the school, or the military field, we find a reliance on an orderly grid. Once established, this grid permits the sure distribution of individuals to be disciplined and supervised.
>
> HUBERT DREYFUS AND PAUL RABINOW,
> *Michel Foucault: Beyond Structuralism and Hermeneutics*

As we mentioned in chapter 4, modernization can be defined, in part, in terms of a set of distinctive spatial practices. In large part, as Dreyfus and Rabinow point out, these practices involve "the enclosure of space" and the containment of individuals within these enclaves. The control of individuals is also achieved through spatialized practices of inscription. Thus, whether we are talking about the power of inscription or the placement and regulation of bodies across space, modern forms of control present opportunities for spatialized forms of resistance.

Aida Marks recognized, and reversed, the power of written documents to initiate organizational actions. After her son Ronald had been shot, he was brought to a hospital that Aida Marks believed provided substandard care to nonwhite patients. On the advice of a family doctor, she tried to arrange for Ronald's transfer to another hospital. When she failed to persuade the doctors or hospital administrators to transfer Ronald, the medical records hanging on the end of his bed presented an opportunity to move him. Knowing that these records are the only official recognition of a patient's existence, Aida Marks was able to make her son disappear along with the papers.

> *I went up there at eight o'clock in the morning after [my personal doctor] told me to get him out of there. I had that big bag from Avon with me and this silly old nurse up there . . . she gave me all of Ronald's records so I pushed them down into my bag. . . . They didn't care whether he went, I don't think. They couldn't find those records. They was having fits.*

After the "silly old nurse" mistakenly handed her Ronald's medical records, Aida Marks seized the opportunity to do what she could not through direct means—to transfer Ronald to a better hospital. Recognizing her relative powerlessness in the situation, Aida Marks did not directly contest or question the authority of the doctors, nurses, or social workers. Yet even without openly defying the professionals, she successfully disabled them by depriving them of the records. Perhaps most revealing of her understanding of the role of textualization in the formal institutional world of the hospital was her observation that the nurses and doctors ultimately didn't care whether Ronald went, but they cared deeply whether the papers went. They were, she said, "having fits" about that.

Martha Lee described how she would respond to a good friend who did not return an expensive tool he borrowed. She could cry, she suggested, or "camp out on their front porch until they gave it back to me. I don't think I would sue my friend." Thus, to Martha Lee, intentionally and obstinately being out of place, occupying her neighbor's front porch, represents a more efficient and legitimate means of seeking compensation than those provided by law.

Sophia Silva described how she taught this tactic to a young mother having difficulty getting service at Sears.

> I was in Sears one day, and this young girl was there with all these children around her . . . She had bought a vacuum cleaner like a week before and it didn't work, and they were telling her to mail it back . . . And she was distraught. I said to her, "Don't you move." I said, "You stay there, you'll have to stay two or three hours until they give you a new one." And I kept coming back to check, and they did give her a new one.

Finally, Joan Walsh told us that she learned the usefulness of colonizing space by observing other parents who were "pushy advocates" for their kids. Sensitive about being a member of the "working class in a snooty suburb" and the fact that her son had some special learning needs, Joan Walsh decided to occupy the guidance counselor's office at her son's high school because the counselor was not providing the paperwork her son needed for his college applications.

> My son wasn't getting any place [trying to obtain a copy of his transcript]. So, one morning, I got up and I dressed nicely. Not jeans, I got dressed nicely. And I went to school with him at 7:30 in the morning and I went to the guidance waiting room and I sat in the chair and I said I'm going to sit here until I talk to him. And when he walked in and realized I was sitting with my

son—because he recognized my son—he was very friendly . . . So
I got results . . . But I feel that if I hadn't done that he'd probably,
he may have missed out on the only school he wanted to go to,
because they weren't sensitive to his needs. So I don't like to have
to interfere like that but I learned back in elementary school
when other mothers used to do it, and I used to be the type who
didn't say much and sat back, that other parents were getting
what their kids needed for them . . . So I had to change my way
and I had to start speaking up.

The spaces occupied are not only physical places, or texts. Odette
Hurley described how her neighbors got together to literally occupy
the police telephone lines in order to get help with some dog packs
running around the town. Although she had called each time she had
seen the dogs, the police never responded.

[I] called the police and nothing happened. And finally when all
the neighbors kind of formed together and started timing their
calls, and we'd just call one right after another and kept calling
and calling until they finally came and cleaned them up.

As with other forms of resistance, these acts reflect the structures
of control they defy. Unarticulated understandings about how long
one stays in a department store or how hospitals authorize medical
procedures are the grounds upon which such resistances operate. By
recognizing and using these expectations, previously ignored claims,
requests, or pleas for help are heard.

Conclusion: Storytelling and Resistance

Individual narratives of resistance are routinely circulated in the
course of everyday interactions. Indeed, Aida Marks, Sophia Silva,
Mike Chapin, Nell Pearson, and many others who told us their stories
of resistance expressed a continuing pleasure in the memory of their
tricks and deceits. Sometimes, the pleasure would be explicitly
stated, as when Sophia Silva told us that calling the president of General Electric was her "favorite story." Other times, the pleasure was
marked by winks, gestures, smiles, and laughter.

In fact, many acts of resistance deployed humor: reversing a relationship of power by refusing to take it seriously. When he couldn't
adjust an overcharge on his insurance policy, Stanley Warshawsky
"made fun of" the insurance company by parodying their claims to
be caring.

I took violent exception to that [insurance billing] and I ended
up, between myself and the insurance agency, doing every damn
thing that we could think of. Writing letters, making phone calls.
They didn't want to hear from me, they had to hear from the
agent. So the agent would call there. They'd give him the run-
around. I ended up writing a letter to the insurance commis-
sioner before I finally, I got results on that. I remember sending
them a cartoon that said, "You're in good hands with Allstate."
And the cartoon's got this pair of hands around the guy's neck. It
was turning a little purple, you know.

Even the stories that were recollected with pain and humiliation—the strip searches in the middle of the street, being handcuffed
to radiators or subjected to sexual harassment—had a narrative integrity that many of the accounts and responses we heard lacked.
Whether the tales were told with humor or despair, they invariably
characterized some as antagonists and others as protagonists. They
typically culminated in some climax, whether it was the punch line
to a funny story or the final, telling act of humiliation.

The narrative structure of these anecdotes suggests, if nothing
else, that these stories had been told before to friends, acquaintances,
coworkers, and family. In fact, sharing stories of resistance may be
one means through which individual encounters with power become
the basis for collective action. Indeed, the act of narration itself—the
telling of the story—may be conceived of as a collective act. According to de Certeau, these stories,

like the stories of miracles, ensure the victory of the unfortunate in
a fabulous, utopian space. This space protects the weapons of the
weak against the reality of the established order. It also hides them
from the social categories that "make history" because they dominate it. And whereas historiography recounts in the past tense the
strategies of instituted powers, these "fabulous" stories offer their
audience a repertoire of tactics for future use.[45]

Relying on humor and bravado, these stories recount and cele-
brate either a reversal or an exposure of power. The fact that these
tales are offered with a smug pride or moral outrage, as opposed to
shame or guilt, indicates that behind the telling of the trick or report
of humiliation lies a moral claim, if not about justice and the possibilities of achieving it, then about power and the possibilities of evading it.

PART THREE

Conclusions

CHAPTER SEVEN

Mystery and Resolution: Reconciling the Irreconcilable

> Law operates in a social world yet exists separate from and dominant over it. Law can relate integrally to that world without being existentially exhausted in the relation . . . It can transcend and yet be in time . . . It successfully demands allegiance not just to all that it was or is but also to all that it will be. The list could go on . . . but this is enough to show that here is a mystery.
>
> PETER FITZPATRICK, *The Mythology of Modern Law*

Here then is the mystery. How can legality be what it is and at the same time what it is not? How can legality be autonomous from and simultaneously constitutive of everyday life? How can legality be both sacred and profane, God and gimmick, interested and disinterested, here and not here? In the preceding chapters we have described this mystery as it has been articulated and enacted by ordinary Americans. Now it is time, as in any good mystery, for resolution.

We begin by reiterating a definition and a method. First the definition: legality is a social structure actively and constantly produced in what people say and in what they do. Proceeding on the basis of that definition, we listened to people's stories of their everyday lives in order to discover the contours of legality in the world. We recorded what people do, and how they talk about what they do. We marked when people thought they were talking about the law and what they said about it. We also paid attention to when people excluded the law from their stories. Sometimes their exclusions were explicit (asserting, in effect, "no law here"). At other times, their exclusions were implicit (no mention of law either way, here or there).

Out of the masses of detail, we identified three forms of consciousness, or commonplace stories of law: "before the law," "with the law," and "against the law." Each of these understandings of legal-

223

ity draws on different cultural schemas; each invokes different justifications and values; each expresses different explanations for legal
action; each locates legality differently in time and space; and each
positions the speaker differently in relation to law and legality (as a
supplicant, player, or resister).

	Before the Law	With the Law	Against the Law
Normativity	impartiality, objectivity	legitimate partiality, self-interest	power, "might makes right"
Constraint	organizational structure	contingency, closure	institutional visibility
Capacity	rules, formal organization	individual resources, experiences, skill	social structures (roles, rules, hierarchy)
Time/Space	separate sphere from everyday	simultaneous with everyday	colonizing time/space of everyday life
Archetype	bureaucracy	game	making do

Having thus far described these forms of consciousness in distinction to one another, we conclude by arguing that these forms of
consciousness can best be understood only as they are related to one
another. Indeed, rather than see these forms of legal consciousness
as three different, or even opposed, understandings, we need to appreciate that the apparent contradictions and oppositions between
and among them are really not so mysterious after all.

Structure, Consciousness, and Ideology

In chapter 2, we abandoned the sharp distinction that has been
drawn between the concepts of structure and consciousness. Following Sewell, we defined structure in terms of cultural schemas and
resources that together produce patterns in social interaction. We
defined consciousness not merely as an effect of structure, but as an
integral part of it. Consciousness, we argued, is participation in the
production of structures. In this sense, consciousness entails both
thinking and doing: telling stories, complaining, lumping grievances,

working, playing, marrying, divorcing, suing a neighbor, or refusing to call the police. As we go about invoking available cultural schemas and deploying resources, we literally (re)produce social structures.

Reconceptualizing these two terms involved blurring the lines between them. Consciousness can no longer be understood as something that is individual and merely ideational. It must be construed as a type of social practice, in the sense that it reflects and forms structure. Structure, which in its conventional formulation tends to be understood as largely material and external to the situations it constrains, is now defined so as to encompass ideas as well as resources. It is also envisaged as emerging out of, even as it impinges upon, social interactions.

There are, however, two additional concepts that have held a place in the conceptual pantheon of the social sciences and about which we have thus far said little: ideology and hegemony. To what extent are structures ideological, or, to put it differently, to what extent do structures embed power? How does the distribution of resources and relative access to legitimating cultural schemas produce and preserve social inequality and relative powerlessness? A related question concerns the extent to which structures are hegemonic. By hegemonic we mean not only that structures embed power, but that the operation of power in and through structures is obscured, remaining unquestioned and unrecognized.

While there is still much that is contested about the nature and meaning of ideology, there is considerable consensus over what it is not. Few contemporary scholars would claim that ideology is a grand set of ideas that in its seamless coherence precludes all other ideas. It is not, in other words, a single giant schema that determines how and what people think. In fact, the most promising reformulations of ideology do not posit it as a body of abstracted ideas at all (neither static, coherent, nor otherwise). Rather, ideology is a complex process "by which meaning is produced, challenged, reproduced, transformed."[1] Construed as a process, ideology shapes social life, not because it prevents thinking (by programming or controlling people's thoughts) but because it actually invites thinking. Ideology derives from and reflects back upon shared experiences, particularly those of power; it is inextricably tied to practical consciousness.

Ideology can be understood to represent an intersection between structure and consciousness. If we use the term *consciousness* to name participation in the production of structures, *ideology* refers to the processes that produce a specific pattern in social structure. An ideology, as a structure, always embodies a particular arrangement of power and affects life chances in a manner different from that of some other ideology or arrangement of power. This means that ideology is not to be equated with culture or structure in general, or with social construction simply as an interactive process.

Thus, defined as a form of sense making that embeds power, ideology has to be lived, worked out, and worked on. It has to be invoked and applied and challenged. People have to use it to make sense of their lives. It is only through that sense making that people produce not only those lives but the specific structures and contests for power within which they live.[2]

The need to constantly remake the world derives from the fact that meanings are not fixed but are always dynamic. Steinberg notes that social meanings are dynamic in two related senses.

> First . . . meaning is never wholly fixed by the sign(s) used to convey it. Signs are polyphonic, and part of the process of producing meaning is contest over what they should mean in a given context . . . Second, the meanings produced by signs are relational; the meaning that can be expressed by any given sign is partly constrained by the larger discourse of which it is a part and the time and context in which it is produced.[3]

Because meaning and sense making are dynamic, internal contradictions, oppositions, and gaps are not weaknesses or tears in the ideological cloth. On the contrary, an ideology is sustainable only through such internal contradictions. These contradictions become the bases for the invocations, reworkings, applications, and transpositions through which structures (schemas and resources) are enacted in daily life. In short, contradictions and oppositions underwrite everyday ideological engagement, and thus ensure an ideology's vitality and potency.[4]

We have found that ideological contradictions appear at different levels. They occur between cultural schemas (legality as God and legality as gimmick; "before the law" and "with the law"). "Before the law" encompasses traditional conceptions of the ideal of the rule of law; and, as we said in chapter 4, there is a sense in which "before the law" is the story law tells of itself. The ideal embodied in this schema is one where the law attends to what is general and universal, ignoring individual variation and particularistic concerns. "Before the law" envisions legality animated by an aspiration for disinterested decision making and impersonal treatment. This normative dimension justifies legality; it makes claims about how parties to legal interactions, both professional and lay, should act. It also specifies why law should or should not be invoked, obeyed, or resisted. By contrast, "with the law" offers a view of law as a ground for strategic engagements orchestrated to win in competitive struggles for social position, wealth, and power. "With the law" offers, in contrast to the self-proclaimed idealism of "before the law," a pragmatic, perhaps vulgar, account of the routine practices of biased, differentially endowed, and fallible actors. Rather than a sacred space of reason and objectivity, the rule of law in this opposite schema is a game in which partiality is legitimated and power is tamed but not eliminated.

The contradictions of legality exist not only between the schemas of legal consciousness but also within each schema. The schema "before the law" incorporates not only the ideal of the rule of law but also an account of the material constraints of formal organizations. It is not, therefore, entirely an idealized conception of legality but a story of how bureaucratized procedures both enable and limit what is done and what can be done, what is possible and what is not possible. The hierarchy of offices and specialization of tasks, characteristic of the formal bureaucracy, creates a sequence of action linking investigation and fact finding to judgment and then to implementation and execution across widely dispersed places and persons. This spatially and temporally coordinated activity creates the broad embrace that is named as the law. At the same time, people describe this network as constraining, frequently confining legality's reach.

Similarly, the schema we refer to as "with the law" incorporates not only a pragmatic account of social practice, but also a normative aspiration. Here, people expressed a justice claim that, although not the same as the ideal of objective rationalized law embodied in "before the law," is nonetheless a conventionally recognized account of legal processes and justice. In this schema, people emphasize the value of participation and agency. They respect the law's procedures, including the technicalities, that ensure the opportunity to be heard and the capacity to give voice to individual claims and opposing interests. This may be experienced as litigiousness, but it is also revered as self-governance and a civil right. This normative claim is associated with a recognition that individuals can shape the content of the law. Of course, this also means that people with more resources will have greater success in gaining access, having their voices heard, and determining the outcomes of legal processes.

Contradictions may also exist within a single representation. For instance, if we examine one of the most familiar representations of a deified view of law, the image of Justice Blindfolded, we find that it carries a suppressed reference to legality as partial, corruptible, human, a game. Evoked in the idea of a blindfolded justice, indeed lurking underneath that blindfold, is an idea of justice whose sight must be incapacitated in order to remain impartial. The impartiality of justice thus coexists with, indeed relies on, its negation.[5]

Similarly, we have noted that the same person may express vastly different understandings of law. In fact, contradictions were not simply expressed at different points in interviews or in regard to different events or experiences. In many instances, they were articulated within a single account, or even utterance. For example, the statement that the law is "just a gimmick" (and its variants) seems to acknowledge the law as a game (or gamelike). At the same time, through the inclusion of "just," it voices an aspiration that it be otherwise.

One woman with whom we spoke explicitly juxtaposed the law with God. *"I, most of the time, leave the justice up to God. But I know my rights too."* Thus, Barbara McNulty hedges her bet on divine justice with the trump of her legal rights.

Of course, the different images of legality that might be contained within a single statement do not necessarily find equal expression. One image tends to prevail over the other, even while it relies on the subordinate or suppressed theme for its intelligibility. In a previous chapter we quoted a woman who, in describing a dispute with a plumbing contractor, gave an account of why she didn't sue.

> [We] could have sued, really . . . There was enough to sue about
> but, I really . . . I'm not litigious. I mean there was no way I was
> going to pay a lawyer, you know, it was probably about two thou-
> sand dollars' worth of plumbing work and the lawyer would
> have cost me more. (Martha Lee)

On the surface, and dominating the interpretation of this account, the statement seems to express a calculating orientation toward the law, one that imagines it as an arena for pursuing self-interest, a game. Read more closely, however, the short narrative conceals a contradiction. After asserting, for example, that "there was enough to sue about," Martha Lee finally concludes the opposite: "the lawyer would have cost me more." If we are not to dismiss this apparent contradiction as merely sloppy calculation, we need to recognize that the two statements are actually about two different visions of legality. The first vision (indexed by the statement that she had "enough to sue") refers to an envisioned legality that protects one from certain losses or injuries understood independently from cost-benefit calculation. It is a conception of law as a protection of rights. Notably, she did not say that she suffered "a lot," or simply that she lost "two thousand dollars," but instead, she described her loss as "enough to sue," indicating that her assessment of the loss was dependent upon some legal definition. In defining what was enough to sue, Martha Lee did not simply calculate the costs of legal representation and compare it to the amount of probable monetary damages. Had she done this (given her calculation of legal services), she clearly would have rejected the idea that she had "enough to sue." Thus, the second statement ("the lawyer would have cost me more") concedes that were she to turn to law to find the very protection or remedy that she believed that law offers, she would lose. This account is discursively similar to descriptions of the law as "just a gimmick." It acknowledges the gamelike quality of law even while it implies that it should be (and perhaps is) more than that.

Martha Lee's self-assertion ("I'm not litigious") also illustrates her contradictory view of legality. Her claim not to be litigious may be read as revealing as much about Martha Lee's view of law as of herself. Litigiousness, in her own denial of it, signifies a negative individual trait and a higher purpose for law, one that goes beyond the pursuit of self-interest. Law may be a game, but one should not play it too often.

These ideological contradictions are often signaled by the various colloquial qualifications people make. "I'm not litigious, but . . ." "The jury was manipulated but the system works." The oft-heard preamble to a racist or prejudicial statement "I am not prejudiced, but . . ." also illustrates the expression of such ideological contradictions within a single statement.[6] While we might be tempted to dismiss such qualifications as self-serving, to do so would be to miss the larger point: the self is served by the disclaimer because it is ideologically necessary to express tolerance even while committing prejudice.

Moreover, the embedded oppositions make such statements invulnerable to challenge. In part, their invulnerability derives from the

In this way, law is understood to be separate from and elevated above ordinary life and commonplace affairs.[9]

However, a hegemonic legality is not achieved by simply removing law from everyday life through its various concepts, abstractions, and definitions. A parallel but opposite effect must also be achieved for legality to become hegemonic. At the same time that legality is constructed as existing outside of everyday life, it must also be located securely within it. Legality is different and distinct from daily life, yet commonly present. Everyday life may be rendered irrelevant by a reified law, but the relevance of law to everyday life is affirmed by the gamelike image of law. In the gamelike thread of hegemonic legality, law is available as an aspect of social relations in which one can deploy the resources and experiences of everyday life to gain advantage through its special rules and techniques.

Fitzpatrick, citing Lévi-Strauss, describes modern law as mythic insofar as it achieves this dual effect whereby the sacred breaks through to, and exists within, the profane.

> Figures are created in myth mediating between the diverse planes or sites in opposition. Heroes or monsters straddling the chaos and order will often have a parent who is divine. Thus, Gilgamesh of Mesopotamian myth was two-thirds divine and one-third human. The Church is of this earth but also Christ's mystical body . . . [A]ll mediating figures "must retain something of that duality" . . . namely an ambiguous and equivocal character.[10]

Specifically, the openness or generality of legal concepts—their metaphoric availability—enhances investment in the categories, allowing the sacred to break through to the profane. Because, as Lévi-Strauss reminds us, myths retain an openness (or something short of completeness), different readers or audiences can see in the same image or term diverse meanings. For example, by employing the language of rights to describe a relationship, we deny the complexity, ambiguity, and contradictions of social experience that are referenced by the term "right." Claiming a legal right, a person crystallizes experience in a set of abstractions that invoke connection and deference that have been empirically unavailable, hence the need to invoke the legal claim of right. Nonetheless, the label "right" authorizes and legitimates the imagining of association and community that is denied in practice.

In his analysis of liberal law and capitalism, Balbus argues that legality's hegemonic character derives from this same tension between the general and the particular. He claims that the generalized categories of liberal law, part of its transcendent quality, constitute one of its primary mechanisms of domination by being, in effect, beyond question. The specific forms of liberal law (open textured terms stated as principles or ideals), Balbus argues, reproduce the essential characteristics of capitalism in what he calls the "commodity form of law." In both capitalism and liberal law, generalized media of signification and exchange (e.g., money, individuals, rights) are used to obscure, and thus distort, the concrete and specific variation within those categories.[11]

Thus, it is precisely because law is what it is and what it is not, both general and particular, both here and not here, sacred and profane, something to stand before and to play with, that it is hegemonic. Of course, to discuss the matter in this way—that is, to counterpoise particular and concrete experience to general abstraction—is to reproduce the very ideological processes that we describe. That is to say, to oppose particularistic experience of persons and groups against general collective truths and abstractions constructed to contain those experiences is to presuppose that the two levels of reality are, in fact, separate and autonomous from one another. In doing so, we produce the very same radical and irreconcilable division that sustains the hegemonic and mythic view of law.

Resistance as Reconciliation

In fact, the division between the general and particular, as an ideological effect, is temporary and tentative. The same contradictions and openings that underwrite the operation of hegemony also make possible counterhegemonic readings and constructions. The recognition of these contradictions (i.e., that law is both a transcendent realm of rule-bound authority and yet available to resourceful skilled players), is, as we discussed in the previous chapter, at the heart of resistance. Counterhegemonic tactics depend on an appreciation of the way these dual threads work, molding legality's power to shape particular experiences. Resistance, then, consists of comparing the incomparable, reconciling the irreconcilable.

If legality is hegemonic to the degree that it effaces the connections between the particular and the general, resistance realizes those connections, making manifest the relationship between what C.

Wright Mills calls biography and history.[12] This is accomplished by understanding experience as part of an encompassing cultural, material and political world that extends beyond the local. To say this another way, resistance involves a recognition that power is not something that is removed from and merely enframes social relations, but that power is something that circulates in and through everyday interactions. Resistance recognizes that legality's power rests on its ability to be played like a game, to draw from and contribute to everyday life, and yet exist as a realm removed and distant from the commonplace affairs of particular lives.

According to Dorothy Smith, the relationship of the local and particular to general social relations is not merely a conceptual or methodological issue. Identifying the general in social relations or law is not simply a matter of establishing typicality or merely categorizing like cases. Rather, the relationship between the particular and general is a property of social organization, more precisely, the way the particulars are arranged and connected. What makes the recognition of this connection between the general and the particular possible is the mutually constitutive relationship between them; what makes it counterhegemonic or resistant is the fact that the relationship is so often obscured and taken for granted. Recognizing the duality of hegemonic legal consciousness, and acting on this recognition, challenges not only the illusory opposition between the particular and the general, but the hegemonic power that maintains that opposition as well.[13]

What, then, are the conditions that might generate such counterhegemonic accounts of legality? Can we identify the circumstances that encourage people to recognize the relationships among personal experience, local practices, institutions, and authority. Based on a reading of our data and of others' accounts of resistance, we suggest three conditions that are associated with counterhegemonic consciousness: social marginality, recognizing the world as socially constructed, and storytelling.

Motive: Social Marginality

First, and perhaps most obviously, social marginality is related to counterhegemonic consciousness. By definition, it is the marginal (the poor and working class, the racially and ethnically stigmatized, physically and mentally disabled persons, women, children, and the elderly) whose lives and experiences are least likely to find expression in the culturally dominant schemas and who have most restricted access to resources. To state the obvious, those who are most subject to power are most likely to be acutely aware of its operation.

In our accounts of resistance, it is abundantly clear that race, gender, and class—conventional and powerful indicators of relative powerlessness—were associated with a resistant consciousness of law. A disproportionate number of the stories of resistance—the acts of masquerade, inversions, and colonization of time and space— were practiced by persons of color, by women, or by unemployed and marginally employed working-class men. These persons must constantly confront the contradictions inherent in our common culture. Bess Sherman and Aida Marks encounter the gaps between our narratives of helping and social responsibility and the experiences of humiliation and degradation that sustain those narratives. And Mike Chapin, the unemployed working-class father, sadly perceives the fault lines between the American dream and his inability to support his family through his skilled occupation.

In recounting the stories parents told about the first time they were informed of their child's disability, David Engel describes the significance of social marginality. These parents of disabled children daily confront the limitations of what is socially defined as "normal" and "abnormal." As these parents watch their child embody and enact much that is defined as "normal," they experience the insufficiencies and contradictions of these socially defined, and enforced, categories.[14]

In stories about the initial confrontation with the professionals' account of their child's condition, parents recall their world shattering into a number of oppositions. Their child was defined in opposition to other children, their dreams for their child in opposition to his or her predicted future, and their wishes for their child's education in opposition to the recommendations of professionals. Yet these origin myths, the stories in which their encounter with the physician is told and retold, are, Engel claims, narratives of resistance. As stories, they rewrite the past in ways that subvert expert authority and validate their child's life. In juxtaposing the doctor's original insensitivity and pessimistic diagnosis with present accounts of their child's achievements, these stories deny the scientific knowledge and power of the professionals. Moreover, by depicting the initial fallibility of the physician, the stories enable parents to question and resist the authority of educational professionals in the present. "Retelling stories," Engel writes, "is a way to triumph over the *particularities* of historical time, to escape pain and frustration of day-to-day events and to affirm instead the lasting truths embedded in the mythical accounts of these first encounters between parents and professionals"[15] (emphasis ours).

The lack of correspondence between dominant cultural meanings and the lives of powerless persons can be discerned in the patterns that emerged in the numbers of problems and the kinds of problems respondents reported. Social marginality played a significant role in shaping the legal needs of respondents and the perceptions of available legal responses. For example, women reported significantly more problems or instances of trouble than did men. Females reported on average sixteen problems, while males reported only thirteen problems in response to a consistent set of probes. The overall number of problems reported by our respondents is of course only one relatively global measure of legal need, and relying on this single measure could obscure important information regarding the character of that need.

Women, however, also reported different kinds of problems. They were more likely to relate problems about noise in the neighborhood, fights among children, inability to obtain access to a child's school record, and having a child expelled from school, as well as differences with spouses about child rearing practices, alimony, being hit by a spouse, and drug use in the family.[16] Women also reported significantly more consumer problems than did men. These problems included not being able to return purchases, having problems with mail-order purchases, door-to-door salespersons, credit cards and creditors, mortgages, and repairs of appliances. In addition, women reported larger numbers of problems having to do with sexual harassment by colleagues and bosses, as well as discrimination in pay.

Race also seems to affect the sorts of experiences and problems people reported. Although there was no significant variation in the number of problems among different racial groups, there was variation in the kinds of problem situations. In general, minorities were significantly more likely than whites to experience poor police protection, police harassment, housing problems, and problems involving children, as well as problems with insurance, utilities, and creditors. Not surprisingly, minorities were also more likely than whites to report problems with schools failing to teach about their culture and to experience discrimination in renting apartments, buying homes, and getting jobs.

With a few notable exceptions, the most frequently reported problems identified by women and racial minorities are precisely those situations that are most likely to be defined as minor, trivial, or personal (i.e., not legal matters). They concern the recurring mundane interactions and disputes that punctuate daily life. Conspicuously absent from the list are the kinds of problems that are likely to involve large sums of money or property and therefore likely to end up in general-jurisdiction courts.[17] Thus, the problems experienced by socially marginal persons failed to find expression within the dominant legal narratives and structure.

Referring to this process of defining or excluding situations as part of "the conceptual culture of legality," Shamir describes the form of modern law as "a praxis of extracting and isolating elements from the indeterminate and chaotic flow of events [i.e., everyday life] and bounding them as fixed categories."[18] The product of such conceptualism is an interpretive grid that is then reimposed upon the world. In his account of the indigenous Bedouin of the Israeli Negev, he shows that the consequence of such an imposition can result in more than irrelevance. "[T]he resistance of law to elements that escape its conceptual grid results in the annihilation of the actions, movements, and histories of people who do not fit the frame."[19]

To a large extent, the imposition of existing legal categories and concepts upon the lives of women, racial minorities, and other less powerful persons results in a similar radical misalignment. To illustrate this point, many black respondents described situations in which they believed they had experienced discrimination. But they expressed reluctance to claim the situation was discriminatory. Recognizing the inability of legal concepts to sufficiently capture their experience, they often resigned themselves to silence. In many instances, nonwhite respondents suggested that the meaning of people's words were ambiguous, their intentions vague, and outcomes (such as not receiving service in a restaurant or getting a job interview) overdetermined. The fact that social interaction is chaotic and indeterminate means that these experiences did not "fit the frame" of legal discrimination. When an act fell outside of the legal "grid" that defines discrimination, many persons found it difficult to assess the significance of that act, attribute motive to others, or even calculate their injury.

After months of trying to reinstate his license, Raymond Johnson described what he called "harassment" from officials at the Registry of Motor Vehicles. When asked why he thought the harassment occurred, Raymond Johnson paused and said,

> *I really don't know for sure . . . Because I have not seen any of these people face to face. [Pause] Now they have all of my statistics. I mean, they know I'm black. I really at this point cannot even speculate.*

Another man, after having been a vice president and national sales manager for a liquor distributor for fourteen years, was turned down for another sales job on the grounds he lacked experience. When asked if he thought this might have to do with his being black, George Kofie turned the question back to the interviewer: "I don't know. You have to tell me. I'll leave it up to you to make that decision."

Raymond Johnson summed up the difficulty of interpreting such events as discrimination. Telling us of an experience in which he received medical treatment only after a great deal of difficulty, he told us, "They didn't refuse." He concluded, "But it was just the way they went about doing it. You could tell. Their attitude, the way they talked, the way they looked, you know."

The differences in the kinds of problems experienced by women and racial minorities, no doubt, reflect differences in the shape of daily life, as well as the resources available to different groups. They are the kinds of problems about which Roscoe Pound wrote, at the turn of the century, when he first articulated the fear that accumulating and unremedied little injustices erode citizens' faith in law and the legal system.[20] When people fail to see their experiences and needs reflected in law, or find legal remedies unavailable, unhelpful, unreliable, they are more likely to turn other means, such as the acts of resistance we described. Being subject to power, they are unable to accept the reified description of law as its entirety; yet, without adequate resources, they are unable to engage its ritual contests.

Means: Recognizing the World as Socially Constructed

Of course, as much of human history confirms, marginality alone is not sufficient for challenging the hegemonically constituted world. Although many find themselves in less powerful positions than others, they may not interpret situations as unfair or discern opportunities for change and remedy. In fact, much of modern life is organized in ways that make power less visible or make it seem necessary and efficient. The ability to claim injustice, to attribute responsibility to powerful others, and to imagine alternatives is hampered by the routinization of historic inequities and systems of representation that objectify subjective judgments.[21]

For example, bureaucracies divide responsibility and obscure causality and intention so that the locus of power is difficult to identify. Intersecting layers of institutional interest and expertise govern more and more of daily life and individual lifetimes, so that outcomes are difficult to assess as unfair. National and multinational institutions lift social activity from localized contexts and spread social relations across large distances of time and space so that the opportunities for action and intervention seem minimal. As technology and bureaucracy obscure the relays of power, contemporary life demands a high level of trust in the orderly and safe functioning of organizations and mechanisms that are unseen and often unknown to ordinary people.[22] Thus, to the extent that the world is understood to operate by invisible mechanisms for which no human power is seen to be responsible and that must be trusted and relied on for minimal engagement in social life, the room for claims of injustice or resistance are reduced.

The second condition for generating resistance, therefore, involves understanding how the hegemonic is constituted as an ongoing concern. Perceiving a concealed agenda and knowing the rules enhance the possibilities of intervention and resistance. We earlier defined resistance as opportunistic, taking advantage of openings within the face of power to escape, if only momentarily, its effects. For this to occur, one must recognize opportunity when it comes along.

White's story about Mrs. G. provides a poignant example of the recognition of power.[23] Mrs. G. is an African American woman who, defying her lawyer's advice, explained to a welfare hearing officer that among the life necessities on which she spent an unreported insurance payment were Sunday shoes for her children. Prior to this hearing, Mrs. G.'s attorney had explained to Mrs. G. the legal rule that would allow her to keep the unreported payment: if the money had been spent on life necessities, it would be considered unavailable for income and would not have to be returned to the welfare office. It was agreed that Mrs. G. would testify that the money had been spent on furniture, food, sanitary napkins, and everyday shoes for her children. Yet during the hearing, when asked how she had spent the money, Mrs. G. replied that she had used it to buy Sunday shoes.

Mrs. G.'s story was resistant because it wasn't scripted. Mrs. G. broke the rules of legal rhetoric, "the unwritten rule that told her to speak like a victim if she wanted to win," and refused to remain silent within the categories provided by the welfare office.[24]

This act of resistance was enabled, however, by Mrs. G.'s understanding of the simple fact that it was a script she was supposed to follow. White tells us,

> When I explained the necessities story, Mrs. G. said she might get confused trying to remember what all she had bought with the money . . . I reminded her that we didn't have to tell this story at the hearing, and in fact, we didn't have to go to the hearing at all. Although I was trying to choose my words carefully, I felt myself saying too much. Why had I even raised the question of which story to tell? It was a tactical decision—not the kind of issue that clients were supposed to decide. Why hadn't I just told her to answer the questions that I chose to ask?[25]

Rather than simply scripting Mrs. G., Lucie White informed her that it was a script. Rather than concealing the socially constructed nature of the proceeding, she empowered Mrs. G. to participate in that construction.

In the stories of resistance that we heard, respondents revealed their understandings of legal scripts. Knowing how legal power operated enabled them to turn it to their advantage in ways not formally permitted. Nell Pearson kept the lawyer on the telephone in order to get the insurance company to spend the fifty dollars they refused to compensate her for the losses from her car accident. She explained her tactic to us by saying that she understood well how lawyers bill their time. Aida Marks was able to move her son Ronald from what she believed was a substandard, perhaps discriminatory, hospital, because she removed his medical charts and was able as a consequence to move Ronald. She knew that the medical professionals would act only when they had written instructions to follow, and without hospital charts the medical professionals had no interest in Ronald. Becoming aware of the negotiated character of social reality, people are thus able to enter the negotiations themselves, acting tactically to promote their own agendas, agendas that are not expressed in the official scripts.[26]

Opportunity: Telling Stories

A third and final condition for generating resistance concerns the interactive conditions that enable recognition of the connection between history and biography. This insight is, we argue, most often a result of a particular type of storytelling. The accounts or narratives that people tell do more than relate events. They also make moral claims and to be intelligible must be related within conventional idioms and vocabularies of motive.[27] While many stories are themselves hegemonic, helping to sustain the legitimacy of the taken-for-granted world, resistant stories are a potent means through which individual lives and experiences are able to transcend the immediate and personal in such a way as to become socially meaningful and potentially transformative.

Social structures, in defining and organizing social interaction, can create both a common opportunity to narrate and a common content to the narrative. The experience of sharing stories thus has the potential to reveal the collective organization of power and legality. For example, the consciousness raising groups of the 1960s, which some have argued generated at least one branch of the contemporary feminist movement, illustrates this condition for the production of counterhegemonic accounts of power. In this historical example, a particular structure of female oppression—postwar domesticity—geographically and socially restricted the lives of middle-class women. Ironically, it was these very forms of restriction that generated the opportunities for storytelling and the content of the stories. In short, women who were bound together in their domestic duties, isolated from the world, work, and politics, ended up around kitchen tables sharing accounts of their personal experiences. The circulating stories allowed women to perceive a commonality of experience that revealed the operation of politics in their daily lives.[28] As R. W. Connell points out, in this case, structure contained the conditions for its own subversion.[29]

To cite another example, *The Autobiography of Malcolm X* describes the missionary work of the Nation of Islam within American prisons, where Nation ministers encourage storytelling by African American inmates. The stories would, collectively, reveal the structural causes of their imprisonment.[30] As this example suggests, total institutions such as prisons, mental hospitals, ghettos, and concentration camps are fertile grounds for the generation of subversive stories. The very nature of modern disciplinary power—restricting movement and association—ironically produces precisely the sorts of opportunities for subversive storytelling that are the basis of resistance.

Of course, stories are told and shared outside of total institutions and consciousness-raising groups. Storytelling among neighbors, friends, and coworkers enabled Bess Sherman and Mike Chapin to narrate stories against the law. Bess Sherman told us that she discussed the difficulties she was having getting SSI compensation with neighbors and fellow church members. It was in the context of these conversations, in which others shared their own experiences and advice, that Bess came to understand that legal representation and having connections (being "familiar") were important resources in determining outcomes. She also recognized as a result of these conversations, however, that she could not deploy these resources ("Bess ain't got no money"). Although Bess characterized her storytelling (and hearing) as simply "working off the nerve part," she also expressed an acute understanding of power and her relationship to it.

Notably, and of particular relevance to both the form and content of his accounts, Michael Chapin used his union membership as a template by which to understand and interpret whether corruption is a case of injustice or merely incompetence. He referred to his union experiences to assess the possible success of organizing opposition (in the neighborhood about proposed condominiums, at the union hall about nonunion contractors, at the schools about testing all, not just some, children). He has been a union member since he began working; his coworkers on the site and in the union hall form the audience for many of the stories he tells repeatedly. His wife tells him that with his stories and complaining "he bites the hand that feeds him." Mike Chapin replies, "Because the hand is rotten."

Storytelling is a conventional form of social interaction, among the ways we come to know each other, encounter the larger world, and learn about its organization. As such, storytelling also presents opportunities to display ourselves, a means by which people can assert a particular identity. Stories become moments for celebrating independence and power, as well as recounting pain, misfortune, or injustice. In other words, people tell stories with diverse interests, motives, and purposes in mind. The stories are always told, however, within interactional contexts.

In presenting an account to an audience, subjective experiences are translated into a common vernacular, employing culturally plausible interpretations (regarding character, motive, actions, and outcomes), and thus offer a particular definition of the situation. Stories are always collaborative productions, particularly when the tale is told in a face-to-face interaction. Elements of the story may be interrogated. The narrative may be interrupted as the audience provides additional examples from personal experience or demands more detail or greater elaboration. Finally, the definition of the situation that is claimed by the teller might be affirmed, amended, or rejected.

In the very act of telling, our experiences become objectified. First, recounted experience is objectified in the Meadian sense that tellers become audience to their own tales (and witnesses to their own experiences). Stories also objectify experience as they change in the course of interaction to reflect the experiences and interpretations of others. Through this process, the stories of particular individuals and specific events seem to transcend the subjective, particular, and personal.

In addition, stories are rarely told only once. We rehearse and retell our stories in interaction after interaction: with friends, coworkers, family, even strangers. With each telling, in fact, we may be more likely to tell again. As the story is elaborated and amended to more successfully compel, persuade, amuse, or enrage, we are emboldened to repeat it. Our narratives are emergent then, both within a given interaction and across many interactions. And with each interaction, meaning is made and remade collectively.

Thus we can say that stories are socially organized phenomena whose production, meaning, and effects are not solely individual but collective. Even the most personal story relies on and invokes collective narratives—symbols, linguistic formulations, structures, and vocabularies of motive—without which the personal would remain unintelligible and uninterpretable.

By telling stories to each other we claim more than each other's attention. A crucial part of the definition of the situation that the storytellers offer (whether they be inmates in prisons, housewives around kitchen tables, Millie Simpson, Nell Pearson, or Rita Michaels) is a particular construction of the moral universe and of legality. The storytelling encounter has the potential to collectivize that moral claim and its account of legality. As we mentioned above, stories do not exist outside of or prior to the context in which they are expressed but are, in effect, produced and communicated interactively with that social context.[31] The stories people tell do not merely reflect existing schemas and resources. They are not merely inserted into the consciousness-raising group, the prison, the family dinner, the neighborhood poker group, or the interview situation. Rather, the interaction is constructed in part by the stories told there. Storytelling is thus part of the constitution of its context.

Thus, by narratively taking a stance against the law, our respondents not only reveal their understandings of power and identity, they actively construct legality along with their particular identity. By recalling moments when they faced overwhelming power, and how they found and exploited cracks in legality's institutional facade, people enact conceptions of self that insist on human agency and dignity. In these counterhegemonic stories, with their reenactments of resistance, people insist on putting a human face and scale to legal institutions. In a sense, the stories of resistance, by recognizing and reconciling the dual threads of legality, create a middle distance[32] between the conception of generalized reified legality and competitive games orchestrated through legal forms.

Because legality is an ongoing production that is created anew daily, rather than a fixed and external entity, personal engagements, in the fact and in the retelling, have the capacity to reproduce as well as challenge legal hegemony. To the degree that people tell stories that make visible and explicit the connections between particular lives and social organization, they may be liberatory. By telling stories to each other, we make larger moral claims than simply explaining our predicaments. Through our storytelling, we (re)create the commonplace experiences of law.

CHAPTER EIGHT

Consciousness and Contradiction

cŏmm′on, a. (-er, -est). **1.** Belonging equally to, coming from, or done by, more than one, as *our ~ humanity, ~ cause, ~ consent.* **2.** Belonging to, open to, affecting, the public, as *~ crier, jail, alehouse, nuisance* . . . **3.** Of ordinary occurrence, as *a ~ experience* (*~ or garden,* sl., of the familiar kind); ordinary, of ordinary qualities, as *~ honesty, no ~ mind;* without rank or position, as *~ soldier, the ~ people;* of the most familiar type, as *~ nightshade, snake.* **4.** Of inferior quality; vulgar. **5.** (Math.) Belonging to two or more quantities, as *~ factor, multiple* . . .

cŏmm′on, n. Land belonging to a community, esp. unenclosed waste land; (*right of*) ~ . . . as *~ of pasturage;* . . . *in ~ ,* in joint use, shared; *in ~ with,* in the same way as (*in ~ with all sensible people* . . .)

The Concise Oxford Dictionary of Current English,
5th edition

We began this book with the hope of better understanding the power and durability of legal institutions in American society. This is, after all, a nation governed by the longest-lived democratic constitution in history, a nation of more lawyers, more novels, movies, and TV stories about law, and more litigation than perhaps any other. But if the law seems to dominate public and private life in America, the public reception of law is nonetheless ambivalent and law's power incomplete. Although law seems to be an "obsession" in American society, "gobbling up absolutely everything in its path,"[1] it was unclear when we began our research how the law, simultaneously revered and reviled, managed to sustain this power.

The signs of law's power and reverence are numerous. From *Dred Scott v. Sanford* (1856) through *State of Tennessee v. John Scopes*

(1925), *Brown v. Board of Education* (1954), *Roe v. Wade* (1973), to *People v. Simpson* (1994, 1995), American society has enacted its most divisive conflicts through legal processes. After all, what is a more telling expression of the power of law, and judges as the guardians of law, than *United States v. Nixon?* Under court order, Richard Nixon, president of the United States, deferred to congressional investigators by delivering the evidence that led to his removal from office. In this case, a judicial decision toppled a popularly elected administration without invoking any additional sources of authority or power. With respect to ordinary lives and affairs, law seems no less prodigious or powerful. The sheer number of lawyers and the consequent volume of litigation demonstrates a willingness to use law and implies confidence in the usefulness of law for life's important, as well as trivial, matters. Certainly, the law has a "mighty presence" in American society.[2]

Yet there are other signs that Americans may be less deferential to legal power than these indicators suggest. The surfeit of lawyer jokes conveys some sense of the public's contempt for the law's agents.[3] Politicians routinely are elected to public office by running against the law. Promising to roll back the regulations, rights, and entitlements built up over nearly a century of modern governance, recent electoral campaigns have emphasized the inadequacy of lawmakers, the Constitution, and government. The message is clear: law does not work. "Too many lawyers, too much law, and too much litigation" describes some of the current disaffection. There is a "sense of social unease, something gnawing at the consciousness of some part of the public": all is not right in the house of the law.[4]

It appeared to us, then, as we set out on this work, that Americans reserved their greatest hopes and expressed their sharpest criticisms about the same thing: the law. Having collected dozens of stories from hundreds of people, and then having analyzed and synthesized those thousands of accounts, what have we discovered about the relationship between legal consciousness and legality? Why and how are legal institutions durable and powerful components of American society? Recognizing the various ways in which legality holds a common place in American society, we believe, sheds some light on these questions.

> **cŏmm'on**, a. (-er, -est). **1.** Belonging equally to, coming
> from, or done by, more than one, as our ~ *humanity,* ~
> *cause,* ~ *consent.* **2.** Belonging to, open to, affecting, the
> public, as ~ *crier, jail, alehouse, nuisance* . . .

To begin, legal consciousness is common in the sense that it is collective. As a collective construction, consciousness is, as we indicated in chapter 2, not reducible to what individuals think about the law. Legal consciousness is not a set of opinions about the law. Rather, we have argued, legal consciousness is a process. Consciousness is participation—through words and deeds—in the construction of legal meanings, actions, practices, and institutions. As individuals express or enact their consciousness, they draw from and contribute to legality. As persons appropriate from the common repertoire of legal schemas and resources, they are constrained by what is available, by legality as it has been previously enacted by others. Thus, the stories of law are not infinitely various; each person does not invent an independent and unique conception of legality. Indeed, we found limited variation in the interpretive schemas emplotted within the stories of the more than four hundred people we interviewed. People relied on culturally available narratives of law to interpret their lives and relationships. At the same time, however, as storytellers with different audiences and purposes, people adapted, elaborated, and sometimes transformed those common narratives of law. They combined elements of different schemas with scraps of their own biographies to forge distinctive accounts of events and relationships.

Both legal consciousness and legality are objective phenomena. They are observable and interpretable. Their objective status derives from the fact that consciousness and structure are collectively produced and experienced. Legality is durable and powerful because it is experienced as objective and external, impervious to and constraining the desires of particular human beings.

> **cŏmm'on**, a. (-er, -est) . . . **4.** Of inferior quality; vulgar.
> **5.** Belonging to two or more qualities, as ~ *factor, multiple*
> . . .

Legality is also common because it is imperfect. As people told us their stories of child rearing, career development, and community life, as well as of traffic accidents, divorces, and home repair disasters, they produced contradictory representations of legality. People simultaneously combined normative aspirations for justice through law with accounts of law's meanness, its flaws, and its failures. Thus, our respondents enacted the dialectical structure of legality, a structure composed of both ideals and practices, normative aspirations and grounded understandings of social relations. The contradictory quality of legality is evident in the oppositions between the schemas of legal consciousness—"before" and "with the law"; the contradictions are also apparent within each schema.

Although each schema emphasizes a different normative value and provides a different account of the social organization of law, together as an ensemble they cover the range of conventional experiences of law. Because legality has this internal complexity—among and within the schemas—legality can be a hegemonic structure of society. Any particular experience or account can fit within the diversity of the whole. Rather than simply an idealized set of ambitions and hopes, in the face of human variation, agency, and interest, legality is observed as both an ideal and a space of practical action.

In an important sense, we have moved beyond conventional distinctions between ideals and practices, law on the books and law in action. We do not have to treat the contradictions within and among the multiple schemas of legality as a flaw to be remedied or a site to be managed. Indeed, we argue quite the contrary. One of the conclusions of this study is that the distinction between ideal and practice is a false dichotomy. Legality is composed of multiple schemas, and each of the schemas of legal consciousness emplots a particular relationship among ideals and practices, revealing their mutual interdependence. The persistently observed gap is a space, not a vacuum; it is one source of the law's hegemonic power.

cŏmm′on, . . . *in* ~ , in joint use, shared . . .

Legality is a durable and powerful structure because it is not exclusively legal. The schemas we call "before," "with," and "against the law" are exemplified by archetypes—bureaucracies, games, and just making do—that also characterize other structures of society. Sharing schemas and resources among different institutions and structures creates supplements that can be appropriated for legal purposes.

One is never before only the law because any legal matter is also a matter about something else. The "double institutionalization of law" that Bohannon so aptly named thirty-two years ago described law itself as a supplement, a doubling of social normativity and institutionalization.[5] Everyday life occurs as interactions among friends, among colleagues, among family members, between consumers and merchants. These relationships are the raw materials out of which disputes and legal cases emerge. Even where dispute or conflict is absent, which is most often, these interactions are grounded in normative expectations infused with legal language and concepts. As social actors and interactions become subjects of legal definition and regulation, they also retain their nonlegal character. Those familial, emotional, medical, or economic aspects may be reshaped by legal action, but the nonlegal aspects are not entirely erased. They are, in this sense, the raison d'être of the legal action and persist as a residue or supplement to legality.

These nonlegal supplements that legality shares with other institutions and structures and the residues of nonlegality that attach to legal actions are equally apparent in professional and lay actions and settings. Thus, the accounts of lawyers as friends, confidantes, and advisors to their clients are legion. The description of police as peacekeepers helping lost children, preceding motorcades through the city, and calming fearful elders concerned about noisy neighbors complements their formal role as crime fighters. These nonlegal considerations that occupy lawyers, judges, police, and regulators of all sorts are not extraneous to legality but resources that enable and buttress the production of legality as a structure of society. Legality, and law as a formal expression of legality, is continuous with the lived experience of everyday life because in doing legal work, professionals and nonprofessionals also do other things.

> cŏmm'on, a. (-er, -est) . . . 3. Of ordinary occurrence, as *a ~ experience* (*~ or garden*, sl., of the familiar kind); ordinary, of ordinary qualities, as *~ honesty, no ~ mind;* without rank or position, as *~ soldier, the ~ people;* of the most familiar type . . .

Finally, legality is a durable and powerful structure of American society because it is ordinary and has a common place in daily life. The character of the connection between legality and ordinary experience was brought home to us one day as we were stuck in a major traffic jam. We were returning from New Jersey, where we had been conducting interviews for this study. Sitting in the traffic on the expressway from Logan Airport to the tunnel into Boston, we noticed the degree of compliance, and perhaps complacency, among the drivers in what was certainly a frustrating situation. It seemed to us that the traffic jam symbolized the degree to which this is a society suffused with legality. The cars were registered, the drivers licensed, the traffic was in lanes whose size, construction, and marking are determined by law. Cars were sorted in lanes according to instructions inscribed on various signs: one lane for taxis, another for personal cars. As we watched the cars crawl toward and approach the tollbooth, the drivers' arms would emerge offering the stipulated toll. Having paid the toll, the cars disappeared into the tunnel.

There was very little that happened on that road that had not at some time been specified by law. And, although the thousands of people sitting in their cars that day, and the millions who drive along that road throughout the year, follow instructions about lanes, speed, tolls, licensing of cars, and themselves, this legal regulation is only rarely a matter of active contemplation and calculation. Typically we become aware of the law and our relationship to it only when the formal law—and the violence embedded in it—makes an appearance. Our pulse quickens at the sight of a police cruiser or the sound of a siren. At that moment, we scrutinize our own behavior and status in regard to the law's intentions and powers. Most of the time, this legal regulation is taken for granted, without consideration or challenge.

At the same time that the law appeared to be orchestrating the scene at the mouth of the tunnel, there was a great deal that was going on that seemed distant from the law-as-rules. While the law seemed to govern virtually everything, there was nothing it completely or totally regulated. People did not simply observe rules about right of way. At times, they would forgo their right of way to let another driver into the traffic, demonstrating their own sense of fairness or courtesy. Others blatantly violated such norms, enacting their own sense of daring or entitlement within the structure of rules defined by "the law." Paying the toll became an opportunity to voice a grievance or, for some, to share a pleasantry. In the lanes of traffic, tollbooths and drivers, somewhere in the intersection of rules and their enactment, emerged legality in the routine of ordinary everyday life.

Research Methods: On Secrets and Wizardry

I wish he would explain his explanation.

LORD BYRON, *Don Juan*

Reality is just like water, it's liquid and mobile, but it can only be compressed a little by using a great deal of force.

HARRY MULISCH, *The Discovery of Heaven*

At the end of her book *Uncoupling*,[1] Diane Vaughan includes a methodological appendix entitled "On Telling Secrets to a Stranger." She begins her account by observing that in the course of being interviewed people share what are often intimate details of their lives with a complete stranger (the researcher). Vaughan then frames her discussion of her methods in terms of the relationship that exists between researcher and subject.

In our own methodological accounting, we would like to appropriate, but modify, Vaughan's image. Rather than present ourselves as the strangers to whom secrets are told, we would like to suggest that herein you the reader are the stranger, and we are the tellers of secrets. For a methodological appendix is much like the climactic scene in *The Wizard of Oz* when the curtain is yanked aside and the wizard is revealed to be an old man frantically pulling levers and pushing buttons. It is, in other words, within such appendices that we reveal that knowledge, like law and wizardry, is socially constructed from the ground up.

A Research Narrative

This research began almost a decade ago when the New Jersey Supreme Court Task Force on Minority Concerns asked us to look at the differential use of law by white and nonwhite citizens. Our explicit research goals were first, to describe the number and kinds of potential legal problems people experienced; second, to identify what people did about these situations, specifically to determine the role of the law in citizens' repertoire of responses to these problematic events; and third, to see if there were differences by race in either the number and kinds of problems people experienced or their use of legal services. In seeking answers to those specific albeit important questions, we started to ask other questions regarding the meaning and role of law in the lives of citizens. And over the course of the next eight years, we (along with nearly one hundred other people in various capacities, including interviewers, coders, data analysts, and transcribers) explored this question.

Data Collection

The study used in-depth face-to-face, interviews with just over 100 persons in each of four New Jersey counties (total n = 430). The counties were selected for variation in racial composition, population density, and socioeconomic status. Using the U.S. Census data for 1980, four counties in New Jersey were purposively selected: Bergen, Essex, Hudson, and Camden. Bergen and Essex are the largest and most dense New Jersey counties with approximately 850,000 persons in each county. They differ from one another, however, by the percentage of the population that is nonwhite or Hispanic. Bergen County is less than 4 percent African American and less than 4 percent Hispanic, while Essex County is over 37 percent African American and 9 percent Hispanic. Essex County is also more economically diverse, containing communities with the highest and lowest median incomes. Hudson and Camden Counties are moderate sized (with approximately 500,000 persons) but with varied minority populations and local cultures. Camden County is in the southern part of the state, removed from the culture of metropolitan New York, with a mix of both urban and rural communities. Hudson County has the largest Hispanic population in the state in both proportion and number.

The data set was created using multistage cluster sampling. Within each county, census blocks stratified by race were randomly selected. From these clusters of census blocks, households were randomly selected for interviewing. Finally, individuals were interviewed within households.

Interviews were conducted in person, usually in the respondent's home. We (Silbey and Ewick) conducted approximately one-quarter of the interviews ourselves. The remaining interviews were conducted by an ethnically and racially diverse team of male and female interviewers, each of whom received approximately sixteen hours of training and periodic follow-up supervision.

Interview Format and Content

The interview was designed by synthesizing both the methods and substantive foci of previous studies of legal mobilization, attitudes, and consciousness. It specifically replicated portions of the instruments used in prior research.[2] Respondents were asked about ordinary, daily events and transactions, what they perceived as disruptions in those exchanges, and how they responded. We inquired about a range of situations and relationships, including consumer purchases and sales, housing, neighborhood and community matters, medical services, relations with educational and public institutions, and work and employment, as well as family and emotional connections. Questions also included standardized indexes used to measure knowledge of law, experience and familiarity with courts and legal institutions, perceptions of legal authorities and legal procedures, mastery of English, and basic demographic data.

Open-ended questions were placed throughout the interview, beginning with inquiries about respondents' attachments to their local community. We asked respondents to indicate ways in which they are the same or different from their neighbors and to name what they like or dislike about the community in which they live. Here, respondents were able to identify themselves in terms of their values and lifestyles. These questions were followed by a very long series of probes about ordinary events, whether the respondent had been troubled by any of these or any like those named, how often and when they happened, what the respondent did or did not do, the relationships between the parties, the circumstances, and the outcomes. When respondents asked what we meant by trouble or bother, interviewers were instructed to reply "anything that was not as you would have liked it to be, or thought it should be." In each instance, respondents were asked to account for their actions and interpret the situation and their own and others' responses. This was followed by an open-ended conversation about one particular incident. Respondents were also asked to describe in detail their experiences and reactions to any encounters with legal actors or other third-party counselors or intervenors. During this part of the interview, respondents were asked to describe events, to assess responsibility, to suggest motives, to identify grievances, to interpret their own and others' actions, and to make judgments about typicality and variance. We used nonanalytic, colloquial terms throughout.

The resulting survey was extensive and comprehensive; the interview booklet ended up being more than eighty pages and the interview itself took between 1½ to 5½ hours, with an average of 2¾ hours.

Qualitative Analysis

The data initially consisted of a completed interview booklet in which closed-ended responses were recorded and open-ended answers summarized by the interviewer and a cassette tape of each interview. In order to examine more fully how people think and talk about law, we received additional funding from the National Science Foundation to have a subset of the original 430 interviews transcribed. Eventually, 141 interviews were transcribed and analyzed qualitatively.

Analysis of the transcribed interviews was the longest and most cumbersome part of the process. Faced with more than ten thousand pages of transcription, much of it about the mundane, trivial, and particularistic details of individuals' lives, we were overwhelmed by the sheer amount of information and, to be honest, its apparent meaninglessness. Initially, without clear analytic categories or a sharp interpretive framework, we were not sure how to proceed.

The plan we finally developed involved each of us first reading through approximately twenty-five of the transcribed interviews and identifying themes that appeared recurrently. Based on that initial reading of interviews, we identified approximately forty themes, which we defined and labeled with one-word mnemonics. For instance, many persons mentioned time, either the amount of time it took for things to happen or the time they had to spend in pursuing solutions to their problems. Any reference to time, whether it was an explicit use of the word or an allusion to time that was embedded in a longer narrative, was coded [TIME]. Among other themes were forms of inscription that we coded as [PAPER]. References to paper could be expressed explicitly or allusively. For example, Aida Marks mentioned her green card without using the word *paper*. We also noted the circumstances when people accepted some state of affairs without action or response although they had defined the situation as unsatisfactory or a problem [ACCEPT]. We noted the circumstances under which people described themselves as taking initiative, standing up against others, seeing themselves as active shapers of the situation [ASSERT]. We also noted the moments when people demanded to see supervisors or someone in authority [TOP]. Often people talked about bureaucracies and bureaucrats [BUR]. Some of the codes were less abstract and simply named particular legal actors, such as the police [COPS], judges [JUDGE], or lawyers [LAWYERS].

Having defined more than forty codes, we each then read through all 141 interviews, inserting the codes wherever appropriate. Each transcript was also read a third time by one of two research assistants. Thus, each transcript was read at least three times, and often more than that. As a result of these readings, some of the original codes were eliminated or collapsed with others, and other codes were added. These handwritten codes were subsequently typed into the computer file of each transcription. By doing this we were able to search efficiently through all the interviews for any reference to "time" or "paper" or "police" or "property" and so forth. Thus, in addition to the complete interview transcriptions, we also generated a separate data source comprising files for each code or theme. In each file were all the identifiable references to a given theme as it appeared in any of the interviews. Pages containing the reference from the various interviews were collected in each file. In order to preserve the context for the reference, two or three surrounding pages were also copied and included in what we came to call the theme files.

In addition to the entire transcript and the theme files, each interview transcript was summarized by each reader in a three- or four-page synopsis. These condensations typically included any notes produced at the time of the interview (such as descriptions of its setting or characteristics of the respondent or any information not conveyed in the formal interview), a synopsis of the major stories or episodes related by the respondent, with particularly interesting quotations inserted, and any reactions, interpretations, or musings that reading the interview provoked in us. Thus, each interview could be approached in at least three ways: in its entirety; as portions of it appeared in files organized according to themes; and in our summaries.

From there our theorizing about legality and the analysis of the transcripts proceeded interactively. We did not begin the project with the theory fully elaborated in its current form. It developed out of an iterative process of data analysis and critical reflection about what we were finding in our respondents' comments. Thus, the models of legality and legal consciousness that we developed were produced both deductively and inductively, working with existing theoretical and empirical literature and the data we collected.

At first, we read the transcripts to identify moments when legal images, metaphors, terminology, or concepts were invoked. We also looked at the specific references to formal legal actors, private and public. In addition, we paid careful attention to what we thought were moments of silence, that is, references to events that could be made legal matters (within already existing conventional legal doctrine and practices) but where there were no such explicit references. We collected these legally silent accounts and juxtaposed them with the ones where explicit legal interpretations were announced to compare the alternative portraits. When explicit statements about the law appeared, for example, we asked ourselves, What makes the law appear to be lawlike to this person at this moment? What do our respondents say when they associate some situation or incident with law and how does this differ from the moments of silence?

As we read the transcripts, the repeated allusions to God, to bureaucracy, to games, to play, and to tricks and subterfuges emerged as prominent themes. These themes encompassed most of the variation in our respondents' allusions to law. We do not mean to suggest that there are no other allusions, references, or associations in these transcripts. We do believe, however, that these schemas were the most common and often repeated, and we could not identify any other imagery or theme that was similarly present in the transcripts. These themes were echoed in so many stories, across such varied persons and situations, that we became convinced that they are common features of legality within the lives and experiences of ordinary Americans.

Once we identified these themes, we explored our respondents' accounts to try to identify the narrative structure and social circumstances in which the different conceptions of law arose. Eventually, we organized the references by the schemas; we then looked at each collection separately. For example, as we looked at references to the lawlike character of events, we noticed that respondents described something remote from their daily lives; respondents made claims about the difference between going to law and what they did most of the time. When we put all these references together, it seemed that there were associations being made between the law's objectivity, its capacity to operate through relays of officers and agencies, the ways law is constrained by rules that limit discretion, and its segregation in specifically designated physical places and buildings. Moreover, it seemed that these four categories covered most of the references to the lawlike character of law. They cumulated to construct an image of law as external.

As we looked at the references we had assembled about the gaming qualities of the law and the experience of law as a contest, we again noticed that we could group the references along four dimensions. Originally, our categories were substantive. For example, in the bureaucratic schema people talked about the objectivity of law while in the gaming conception, people emphasized partiality and self-interest. Then, with unusual excitement, we began to work to see if we could find a relationship between the descriptions of the game and the descriptions of law as bureaucracy. At some point, we noticed that the indicators of the gaming schema could be interpreted as variations of the categories identified in the reified, or bureaucratic, lawlike vision of law. When respondents described the ways in which formal positions and rules limited what could be done in the name of law, we realized that they were describing constraints. When they described the demand that law produce resolutions and that these resolutions be uncertain or unknown beforehand, we saw that respondents were describing another form of constraint. Similarly, objectivity and partiality represented alternative normative values. From these descriptions, we developed the schema of legality as game.

The Respondents

In defining and selecting a sample, care was taken to ensure that the results of the research would approximate the demographic composition of the state. Because the task force was interested in how race and class operated to effect legal use, we needed to ensure that the sample included sufficient numbers of racial and ethnic minority citizens to be able to make comparisons among racial and ethnic groups. With these goals in mind, the 1980

Table 1   Selected Demographic Characteristics

Characteristic	New Jersey*	Sample (N = 402)	Transcribed Sample (N = 141)
Median Family Income	$47,589	$40,000–$49,999**	$40,000–49,999
Gender			
Male	48%	53%	52%
Female	52	47	48
Race***			
White	79.3%	76.9%	70.9%
Black	13.4	17.3	24.1
Asian	3.5	1.5	2.8
Other	3.7	4.2	2.1
Hispanic Origin	9.6%	7.4%	6.2%
Education			
No high-school diploma	23.0%	10.8%	7.9%
High-school diploma	31.4	19.6	19.4
Some college	22.6	18.6	22.3
College degree	23.1	51.0	50.4

*All New Jersey data are from the 1990 U.S. census.

**Income was measured ordinally in the survey.

***In the interview, race and ethnicity were measured separately. Thus, persons were asked in a separate question whether they had Spanish or Hispanic origins.

census was used to create a multistage, stratified cluster sample. The completed survey yielded 403 usable surveys. The population surveyed approximates well the demographic characteristics of New Jersey in 1990 (see table 1).

The subsequent selection of 141 interviews to be transcribed (interviews that serve as the basis of our analysis in this book) was purposive rather than random. We wanted to preserve the demographic representativeness of the original sample, but we were also concerned with two additional factors: the richness of the interview and our own knowledge of the person and the context of the interview interaction. For these reasons, the resulting subsample of transcribed interviews, while approximating the demographic profile of the entire sample, is drawn disproportionately from the approximately one hundred interviews completed either by Silbey or Ewick.

Table 1 compares the demographic profile of the sample of transcribed interviews with the entire sample and both of these samples with the entire state of New Jersey. As this comparison reveals, the interviewed sample and the transcribed sample correspond well to one another. They also accurately reflect the income and race composition of the state, although both samples contain higher percentages of nonwhite respondents. In addition, the two

Table 2   Frequencies of Problems Reported

Group	Mean Number of Problems Reported	Statistical Significance
Race/Ethnicity		
White	14.6	
Black	14.5	N.S.
Hispanic	12.9	
Other	12.0	
Gender		
Male	13.0	
Female	15.8	p < .001
Family Income		
$0–$29,900	14.0	
$30,000–$59,000	15.2	N.S.
$60,000 or more	14.0	

N.S. = The results were not statistically significant.

samples include a slightly larger percentage of men and a substantially higher percentage of college graduates than the state census reports among New Jersey residents generally.

Of the 100 situations about which we asked, people reported that they had experienced an average of 14 problems with the number ranging from 0 to 62. The average number reported by our respondents did not vary significantly by race/ethnicity or by socioeconomic class. As we indicate in chapter 7, the only variable that was shown to be significantly related to the number of situations defined as problems was gender. Females reported on average 16 problems, while males reported 13. (See table 2.) This difference in the number of problems was also reflected in differences in the types of problems reported by men and women. (See table 3.) Significant variation in the types of problems was also observed on the basis of socioeconomic indicators (table 4) and race/ethnicity (table 5).

A Final Note on Storytelling

As we indicated, we wanted to preserve the voice of our respondents. Of course, voices are mediated in many ways, and it is a romantic notion that they might appear in some pure, untampered form. The question becomes to what degree, and in what ways, do we tamper with them?

First, we had to make self-conscious editorial decisions about quoting respondents. In presenting quotes from respondents we had to make a decision as to how and when to edit what they said. People tend to speak in a less structured, more rambling manner than they write. They say "you know"

Table 3   Reported Problems by Gender

Reported Problem	Male	Female
Noisy neighbors*	47.6%	58.1%
Kids playing/fighting***	24.1	37.2
Mail order purchases**	22.7	39.3
Cannot return merchandise**	15.2	25.7
Credit card error*	29.5	39.5
Creditor problems*	13.2	20.5
Landlord did not repair*	24.1	36.8
Mortgage in default*	3.6	9.7
Received less pay than others*	14.8	24.3
Employer owes back pay*	14.8	8.5
Injured on job**	33.3	20.6
Sexually harassed by coworker***	1.9	9.5
Sexually harassed by boss***	1.0	11.6
Denied access to school record*	1.3	7.1
Child expelled or suspended*	10.0	19.7
Registry of Motor Vehicle problems*	25.8	17.3
Childrearing problems*	9.7	18.4
Drinking problems*	9.1	16.2
Spouse or child abuse*	4.8	10.5
Alimony/child support problems***	0.5	8.5
Drug problems*	7.2	13.3

Note: This table displays only those problem situations that showed statistically significant difference by gender.

   *$p < .05$.

   **$p < .01$.

   ***$p < .001$.

frequently, occasionally use an inappropriate word, mispronounce words, speak with distinctive accents. In the face of this variation, one possibility was to reproduce literally the words as they were spoken (or heard). This choice, while avoiding problems of censorship, produces other problems. Often it is difficult and tiresome to read these unedited quotes. It can take several pages of transcript to complete what is one paragraph with interruptions, elisions, "ums," "uhs," "you knows," edited out.

We finally decided on the following rule. We would "clean up" our respondents' language, but only minimally. We would edit no more than we had to in order to achieve clarity and retain what we honestly believed to be the meaning of an account. We would write "going to" instead of "gonna," "have to" instead of "hafta." We would eliminate any speech that seemed distracting and unrelated to the intended meaning, for example a series of "ums," and "you knows." We decided, in short, to eliminate for purposes of clarity and readability any gratuitous language. If someone said "you know"

Table 4   Reported Problems by Socioeconomic Status

Reported Problem	Socioeconomic Status		
	Low	Middle	Upper
Noisy neighbors*	58.8%	59.8%	42.6%
Kids playing/fighting**	43.4	25.9	22.2
Credit card error**	25.9	33.6	46.3
Creditor problems*	25.0	11.6	14.8
Threatened for joining union*	4.5	11.7	3.7
Fired or laid off*	19.8	23.2	10.3
Injured on job**	40.5	23.2	17.8
Sexually harassed by boss*	7.3	0.9	10.3
Benefits cut off/changed**	3.5	8.0	0.0
Drinking problems*	16.8	12.6	5.6
Kin works too much*	21.2	34.2	36.4
Kin spends too much time away**	11.5	12.5	26.2

Note: This table displays only those problem situations that showed statistically significant difference by socioeconomic status.
   *$p < .05$.
   **$p < .01$.

Table 5   Reported Problems by Race/Ethnicity

Reported Problem	Race/Ethnicity		
	White	Black	Hispanic
Kids playing/fighting*	26.2%	34.3%	46.7%
Problems with fences*	12.0	9.0	6.7
Credit card error*	38.7	24.2	20.0
Recent insurance problems**	32.6	37.3	13.3
Creditor problems**	14.0	31.3	13.3
Utility bill errors*	37.1	52.2	50.0
Landlord did not repair*	26.8	29.3	36.8
Assessment problems*	30.5	13.0	17.6
Filed grievance against employer**	10.2	25.8	26.7
Injured on job*	26.1	39.4	24.1
School did not teach about culture**	2.9	15.4	4.3
Poor police protection**	13.3	28.4	30.0
Police harassment*	9.1	17.9	3.3
Kin works too hard*	31.7	13.4	23.3
Discriminated against in getting a job**	12.0	28.4	23.3
Discriminated against in buying a home*	1.1	7.6	3.3
Discriminated against in renting an apartment**	4.2	13.4	6.7
Discriminated against in getting service at hotel/restaurant**	6.7	19.4	3.3

Note: This table displays only those problem situations that showed statistically significant difference by race/ethnicity.
   *$p < .05$.
   **$p < .01$.

five times, we might omit, for purposes of quotation, four of them. Occasionally we have left in a malaprop or a grammatical error. In these cases, we
believed the language revealed something relevant about the speaker.

Second, in writing the narratives that punctuate the chapters (e.g., those
of Rita Michaels, Dwayne Franklin, Bess Sherman), we obviously selected
and structured the subjects' stories in order to tell our own. We collected the
pieces that were distributed throughout the transcript. This admission now
brings us full circle. Ours is a story of legal consciousness, our respondents'
stories often were not. Respondents told us their stories for a variety of reasons. In some cases, they did so to persuade us that they were right and
someone else was wrong. Sometimes, they shared recollections with us to be
funny or amiable. Still others believed they were just relating the facts of
the episodes they were describing. Consistent with the cultural-constructivist
approach we outlined in chapter 3, we wanted to mediate the tension between the sociologists' interpretive role and the preservation of our respondents' meanings. We wanted to avoid completely translating respondents'
stories into data (more as we present them in the analytic sections). We
sought to preserve as much as possible of their stories and words, although
we do not reproduce the transcript in its entirety and sequence. In writing
our stories then, we tried to retain the integrity and meaning of the original
account while pursuing our own project.

Who's Who in the Text

Janet Briarly is a single, twenty-seven-year-old lapsed-Catholic white woman living with two roommates in an apartment complex. She is a college graduate and is employed as a systems coordinator earning $35,000.

Michael Chapin is married and has two young children. He is thirty-four years old, Italian American, and Catholic and says that he attends religious services less than once a year. Before he was laid off from doing carpentry and construction work, he worked thirty-five hours a week and often worked overtime. His wife is currently working thirty-three hours a week as a registered nurse. Michael's personal income is between $25,000 and $30,000 and total income for the family is between $50,000 and $60,000 a year.

Ray Civian is a fifty-four-year-old African American Baptist man working as supervisor of labor for the Board of Education in Essex County. He has some education above the college level and works sixty hours a week. His personal income falls between $40,000 and $50,000. He lives with his wife, who is employed as a special-education teacher. Their total family income is $60,000 to $75,000.

Janet and John Collier were interviewed together. John is a thirty-two-year-old white male working as a machine specialist for sixty hours a week. He is a high school graduate and earns $35,000 to $40,000. Janet is a vice president of a shirt company. Their total family income is over $75,000, and they live with their infant in a small suburban development of single-family homes in Essex County. He is a regular participant at the local Presbyterian church.

Jesus Cortez is a sixty-one-year-old Puerto Rican Catholic housepainter living with his wife in Newark. He chose not to identify with any racial group. He received a tenth-grade education and earns $20,000 to $25,000 a year.

Carol Dealy is a thirty-eight-year-old married black woman with three children under the age of seventeen. She is a college graduate and works forty hours a week as a schoolteacher, while her husband is an unemployed fork lift operator. She makes close to $13,000 a year. The total family income is between $20,000 and $25,000. Carol Dealy attends Pentecostal services several times a week in a suburb of Camden in southern New Jersey.

Claire Delorey is a sixty-two-year-old interior designer. She lives with her husband, a real estate broker, and their two grandchildren in northern New Jersey. She is white, has two years of education beyond college, and earns $60,000 to $75,000 annually.

Joseph Dimato is a thirty-four-year-old white male who makes a living as a hair stylist and salon manager. He refers to his profession as "prostitution" because he "serves women." He is divorced, lives alone, and works forty to fifty hours a week. He is a high school graduate and earns between $35,000 and $40,000 a year. Joseph is Catholic, attending services once or twice a year.

Paul Dyson is sixty-three years old, married, Catholic, and a father of a young child under the age of twelve. He is the president of his own truck driver personnel company. He has a law degree and used to practice law, although he has been out of the profession for the past twenty years. His income is more than $75,000. Paul's wife is a law office secretary. She works part time for seven months out of the year.

Andrew Eberly is a consultant on employee benefits. His personal earnings exceed $75,000 a year. Andrew is fifty-one years old, white, married, and is a high school graduate. His wife works as an executive secretary. They do not have any children living at home. Although he identifies himself as a Catholic, Andrew Eberly rarely attends church.

Jane Elliot is a fifty-three-year-old divorced black woman. She has a twelfth-grade education and now works full time as a program clerk in a VA hospital. Her income was between $17,500 and $20,000 a year. She lives in Irvington in a relatively new row house with her daughter, who is a student at Rutgers University. Jane Elliot is a Baptist, attending church infrequently.

Laura Flanagan is a sixty-seven-year-old public school secretary. She is widowed and lives alone. Working thirty hours a week, she earns between $20,000 and $25,000 a year; however, with Social Security benefits and her late husband's pension, her total income falls between $35,000 and $40,000. She is white and Catholic, attending Mass every week.

Alan Fox is a white, forty-five-year-old lawyer. He is Jewish and lives with his wife (an elementary school teacher) and two teenage daughters. The family income exceeds $125,000 a year.

Dwayne Franklin is a black Muslim who works as a welfare investigator. He is divorced and lives with his mother, father, sister, and two children in a well-kept two-family row house. Dwayne is a thirty-nine-year-old college graduate and makes $25,000 a year.

John Ganter is an advertising salesman who lives with his three adult children. He is a fifty-three-year-old divorced Catholic college graduate. Working just under forty hours a week, he earns between $50,000 and $60,000 a year.

Ambrose Grant, a forty-five-year-old African American male, earns a living as a government disability analyst. He is married, is a college graduate, and makes $30,000 a year. His wife is a psychologist. The total family income falls between $60,000 and $75,000. Ambrose says that he used to be Jewish but now attends an Episcopal church two to three times a month.

Claudia Greer is a fifty-year-old licensed practical nurse with two years of college education. Her husband is a civil servant working for the city of Camden; he is African American. She describes herself as black, with some Native American background. She is a religious woman, attending services weekly as a minister and praying continuously, she says.

Allen Horner is an attorney and lives with his wife, who does not work. He is white and earns more than $75,000. Allen attends Catholic Mass several times a year.

Odette and John Hurley are married and live with their two children, who are over the age of eighteen. John is forty-seven years old, white, and is a high school graduate. He works fifty-five to sixty hours a week as a data processing manager. Odette is a substitute teacher as well as a part-time mall information booth worker. Total income for the Hurleys is between $40,000 and $45,000. He says he is affiliated with no religion but goes to religious services several times a year.

Ralph Jeffers is thirty-four years old and married and lives with his wife, teenage child, and dog. He is a college graduate and now works as a technical recruiter. His work is less time consuming than his wife's job as a real estate agent. Despite the time disparity, her reported income was one half of Ralph's $45,000 to $50,000. Ralph and his family attend Catholic church two to three times a month.

Raymond Johnson is thirty-five years old, single, and black and lives alone. He graduated from one of the New Jersey state colleges in the southern part of the state, where he lives and has worked as both a purchasing agent and data processor. Because he was unemployed at the time of the interview, his personal income was only $8,000 to $10,000 for the year. Although he says he is technically Baptist, he attends both Presbyterian and Baptist services several times a week.

Shirley Joslin is a forty-five-year-old married white woman who lives with her husband and three children, all of whom are over eighteen. With her two years of college education, she used to work as a library technician but is currently disabled and unemployed. When working, she and her husband both earn about $20,000 a year. She is an active member in the local Catholic parish.

Joan Kinsler is a thirty-three-year-old white female. She is married and does not have any children. With three years of college education, she is currently employed as a dental hygienist. Her husband is a salesman for a plumbing supply company. Together, their family income is close to $75,000. Joan is Catholic and goes to church every week.

Susan Kligfield is a thirty-six-year-old white female with no children who is now living with another adult. Susan has one year of education after college and works as a software engineer. Her partner is also a software engineer; both of them work forty-hour weeks. She earns $50,000 to $60,000. She describes herself as Protestant but never participates in religious services.

George Kofie is married. He has one year of college education and works sixty hours a week as a realtor. George is fifty-two years old and African American and attends Baptist church services once or twice a year. His personal earnings fall between $17,500 and $20,000; his wife, a clerical worker, makes more than twice as much as he does. Their total income is close to $60,000 a year.

Martha Lee is a twenty-eight-year-old real estate associate with one year of education beyond the college level. She describes herself as white and adds that she is one-eighth Spanish. Martha is married to a Wall Street trader; she has no children. She earns $25,000 a year; the total family income is $60,000 to $75,000. She is Catholic but rarely attends Mass.

Jamie Leeson is forty years old and has never married. He lives alone, is self-employed, and works anywhere from five to forty hours a week. Jamie has one year of education above the college level and earns between $40,000 and $50,000 a year from periodic jobs in various social-service capacities and managing family investments.

Don Lowe is a fifty-year-old plant manager. He is married and has two children living at home. He usually works at least fifty hours a week; his wife is not employed. His personal income is between $60,000 and $75,000. He is white and Catholic and never attends religious services.

Jules Magnon is married and has an eight-year-old daughter. He is forty-seven years old and white and immigrated from France. Jules works fifty to fifty-five hours a week managing a hospital department of nuclear medicine. He has eight years of education beyond college and earns $40,000 to $50,000 a year. He is Presbyterian and attends services about once a month.

David Majors is married with two children under the age of six. He is a thirty-year-old white male with a high school education. He works forty hours a week as a warehouse receiver earning between $25,000 and $30,000 a year. His wife is a customer service representative and earns roughly the same income. He says he is Catholic but never goes to church.

Aida Marks is a fifty-nine-year-old African American woman with eight children. She is a high school graduate and worked at a hospital aide until she lost her job because of a disability. Her husband was employed in the postal services but is retired. Total family income for the year ranged between $6,000 and $8,000. Aida is Catholic and goes to church every week.

Barbara McNulty is a fifty-six-year-old associate dean for international students at a New Jersey college with three years of education beyond college. She is married and earns an annual personal income of $20,000 to $25,000. Her husband is a school psychologist. Barbara is a devout Presbyterian, attending services several times a week.

Rita Michaels is an office manager and works approximately fifty hours a week. She is fifty-three years old, divorced, and self-supporting and lives with her two college-age sons. She is a high school graduate, and her annual income is $34,000. She is white and attends Catholic religious services several times a week. Rita Michaels has lived in her present house for the past fifteen years.

Doris Milford is single and lives in a household with two other adults. She is forty years old, a nonobservant Catholic, and black. She works forty hours a week as a security guard and earns $20,000 to $25,000 a year. Doris completed three years of college.

Christopher Mitchem, an eighty-year-old black male, has lived with his wife in the same house in Camden for the past thirty years. He is retired from the Campbell Soup Company. His wife used to be a domestic worker and is now also retired. Christopher completed a seventh-grade education and earns under $20,000 a year. He is Catholic and attends church every week.

Louis Napier works a minimum of fifty hours a week as a receiving manager. He is a thirty-five-year-old married white male and has three young children. He makes $25,000 to $30,000 a year. His wife works thirty-six hours a week as a registered nurse; the total family income is $60,000 to $75,000. Louis is a high school graduate; he attends Catholic church every week.

Jay Oren is a twenty-eight-year-old black male from Jersey City. He works full time as an accountant. He is a college graduate and his reported income is between $17,500 and $20,000. Jay is single and lives alone. He attends an Episcopal church two to three times a month.

Nell Pearson is a writer and married to a public-interest lawyer. Previously she was an administrator of several NEA projects. She is forty-five years old, has four years of education above the college level, and now earns less than $2,000 per year; the total family earnings, however, fall between $60,000 and $75,000. She is adamantly antireligious and never attends any services.

Sima Rah is a thirty-three-year-old Vietnamese-Indian woman who works forty hours a week as a special-education teacher. She is divorced and lives with her three children. She has four years of education beyond the college level and now makes between $25,000 and $30,000 annually. Sima is Hindu and attends religious services nearly every week.

Charles Reed is forty-seven years old, living with his wife and three young daughters in an affluent suburb of Newark. He is an independent investor and venture capitalist, as well as a part-time high-level commissioned employee of a reinsurance company. His wife has a small independent dress business that she operates only several months a year out of their home. He is a college graduate with an income of several hundred thousand dollars a year. He is Protestant.

Carolyn Robinson is a fifty-one-year-old white married female living in a small suburban town in Essex County. With three years of college education, she is employed in the customer service department of a national corporation. Her husband is out of work; he was previously an art director for an advertising firm. Carolyn's reported income is just under $20,000. She is formally affiliated with the Dutch Reform Church but never attends religious services.

Maryann Sayer is a forty-year-old nonobservant Catholic white female, living with her four children. She completed ninth grade. She is separated from her husband, who is employed by a telephone company. She makes $24,000 to $26,000 as a bus driver working thirty hours a week.

Bess Sherman is a black woman over the age of sixty-five, has never married, and lives alone. Bess has lived in the same building for the past twenty-six years. Now retired, she used to work on an assembly line at an umbrella plant. She has a tenth-grade education. Bess identifies herself as Presbyterian and attends church several times a week.

Ann Shields is a forty-nine-year-old white female living with her two children. She is a college graduate. Currently she is retired, but her husband works fifty-five to sixty hours a week as a real estate developer. Their total family income exceeds $75,000. She is Catholic and attends religious services every week.

Amy Shull, a white Presbyterian, lives in a household of three, including one adult child, in a small suburban development in southern New Jersey. She is a forty-four-year-old high school graduate working twenty-two hours a week as a Dictaphone typist for $6 an hour. Her husband is a machine operator.

Sophia Silva is a sixty-year-old white female and lives with her husband and two adult children. She has one year of education beyond college. Currently, she is not employed, but she used to be a teacher. Her husband is an architect and planner who works more than seventy hours a week. The family income exceeds $75,000 annually. Sophia describes herself as Catholic and attends Mass two to three times a month.

Millie Simpson has never married and lives with her teenage son. She is a forty-five-year-old African American woman, has a high school diploma, and works thirty-seven hours a week as a domestic worker. Her income is about $18,000 a year. She is Baptist and is an active and involved member of her church.

Scott Smetona is a sixty-six-year-old married white male residing in a small town in southern New Jersey. He is now retired but used to work as quality control technician in the electronics division of RCA. His wife works about twenty-five hours a week as a nurse. He has two years of college education. His personal income, which comes strictly from Social Security, is about $9,000, but the total family income is $20,000. He is Lithuanian Catholic and attends services every week.

Bradley Spears is married and has no children. He is a school administrator, and his wife works full-time as a manager. Together, their annual income exceeds $75,000. He is forty-eight years old and white, attends a Unitarian church, and has completed eight years of education beyond the college level.

Nikos Stavros is separated and lives in a household of three, without children. As a programmer and analyst working forty hours a week, he earns up to $50,000 a year. Nikos has two years of education above the college level. He describes himself as Greek Orthodox, attending church about once a month.

Michelle Stewart is a thirty-three-year-old white woman. She is single and has lived alone since she was sixteen. A college graduate, she works in sales management. Her annual income is above $75,000. Michelle Stewart came from a family situation marked by alcoholism, domestic violence, and sexual abuse. Although not formally affiliated with any religious group, she attends some form of religious service two to three times a month.

Jane Sullivan has four children and is currently unemployed. When working, Jane is a psychiatric social worker with a master's degree; she specializes in drug and alcohol abuse counseling. She is white and Catholic and attends church about once a month. Her husband is an attorney; when she was working, the total family income was over $75,000. This interview was conducted by the pool at her country club.

Leroy Tanner is a white, sixty-nine-year-old retired pharmacist. He is divorced and lives alone in a small apartment in Union City. Leroy Tanner has one year of education above the college level and says that he speaks Italian in addition to English. Most of his total household income of $6,000 to $8,000 comes from Social Security payments. He observes no religion.

Diana Taylor, a thirty-one-year-old African American woman, is a licensed practical nurse with one year of education above the college level. She works more than forty hours a week and makes $20,000 to $25,000, about the same amount that her husband earns as a quality control specialist for Sony Corporation. They have three children under the age of twelve. The Taylors live in a suburban housing development. She describes herself as nondenominational Protestant attending services two to three times a month.

Ben Thompson is a forty-five-year-old single black male who lives with one other person. He attends Baptist church several times a year. He works forty hours a week and earns between $40,000 and $50,000 annually as the director of a hospital food service; total household income is between $60,000 and $75,000. Ben Thompson reported that he was frequently stopped by the police and has been a victim of racial discrimination throughout his professional career.

Robert Tisdell, a forty-nine-year-old white man, is married and lives with his three children. He states that he is Catholic but never attends religious services except for weddings and funerals. He is a college graduate and works around forty-four hours a week as a director of maintenance. His wife is a doctor's assistant and receptionist. Family income falls between $50,000 and $60,000.

Steven Wager is a seventy-four-year-old black divorced man who works several hours a week as an accountant. He lives alone in a run-down section of Newark. He is Ba'hai and attends religious services about once a month.

Joan Walsh is forty-three years old, white, and married with two children, one of college age. She works up to twenty-four hours a week as a librarian. Her husband is a technician at a telephone company. She has one year of college education. The total family income is between about $60,000 and $75,000. Joan Walsh and her family live in a wealthy suburb. The Walshes inherited the house in which they live from Joan's family, and she reported a sense of "not fitting in." She is Catholic but never attends Mass.

Stanley Warshawsky is seventy years old, white, and married. He has three years of college education. Prior to his retirement, he was employed as a design engineer. His wife used to work as a beautician but was recently laid off. Stanley and his wife live in a suburban development of ranch houses. He flies airplanes for a hobby. He is a lapsed Catholic, with an annual income of $50,000 to $60,000.

Olive Washington is a divorced fifty-one-year-old black female. She lives in Camden in a household of three and makes a living caring for a handicapped child. Two of her six grown children have spent time in prison. She has an eleventh-grade education. Her income for the year was between $15,000 and $17,500.

Arthur Williams is sixty-seven years old and married and has no children. He works fifty to sixty hours a week as a self-employed entrepreneur. His annual income is above $75,000. Arthur lives in an affluent suburb of Newark. He is Jewish and attends religious services once or twice a year.

Gretchen Zinn is fifty years old and white. She has four children. She has three years of education beyond college. Although she is not currently employed, she is trained as a psychiatric social worker and in the past worked as a drug and alcohol abuse counselor. Her income last year was between $30,000 and $35,000, and the total family income was just over $75,000. She is Catholic and attends services about once a month.

Chapter One

1. The names of all our informants have been changed.
2. Scott 1990.
3. De Certeau 1984.
4. Hartsock 1990, 172.

Chapter Two

1. There is a large and continually growing body of literature describing the social organization of law and legal practices. Rather than name hundreds of studies that could be legitimately cited here, we refer readers to the *Law and Society Review* and *Law and Social Inquiry*, journals that routinely publish such research; see also *Law and Policy; Studies in Law, Politics and Society; Journal of Law and Economics; Journal of Legal Studies; Crime, Law and Social Change: An International Journal; Yale Journal of Law and the Humanities; Social and Legal Studies: An International Journal; The International Journal of the Sociology of Law; Legal Studies Forum; American Journal of Legal History; Law and History Review; Law and Philosophy; Philosophy and Legal Affairs; Justice System Journal; Journal of Law and Society* (formerly *British Journal of Law and Society*); and *Law and Human Behavior.* See also Abel 1996; Black and Mileski 1973; Cotterrell [1984] 1992; Friedman 1975; Friedman and Macaulay 1969, 1993; Kidder 1983; Lempert and Sanders 1986; Turkel 1996; Vago 1997 for compilations and presentations of empirical studies of law. We use the phrases *law and society* and *socio-legal* to refer to this tradition of research and body of scholarship.
2. Sudnow 1965.
3. Felstiner, Abel, and Sarat 1980–81; Galanter 1983, 1986, 1996; Hensler 1994; Kritzer 1980–81, 1989; Kritzer, Bogart, and Vidmar 1991; Kritzer, Vidmar, and Bogart 1991; Trubek et al. 1983.
4. See Federal Judicial Caseload Statistics, 1996; National Center for State Courts, 1996. In our survey, 430 New Jersey residents described to us over 5,803 incidents that could have become matters of formal legal complaint. Only 14 percent of the reported problems led to legal action (calling police, contacting a lawyer, or complaining to a government agency). Even fewer led to litigation beyond the inquiry stage. See Silbey et al. 1993.
5. O'Brien 1997.

6. Sarat and Felstiner 1995.

7. Merry 1990.

8. Yngvesson 1993.

9. Hartog 1993.

10. Hartog 1993, 107.

11. Sarat and Kearns 1993, 55. See also Silbey and Sarat 1987, 172–74.

12. Eighty percent of our 430 respondents reported having been in an American courtroom. Although almost 50 percent reported having been a plaintiff or defendant in some action (ranging from traffic cases or divorce proceedings to major criminal prosecutions), only 6 percent of our respondents reported being a party to a major civil suit. Four percent of the respondents reported having been a party to a small-claims action. This pattern was consistent across racial/ethnic groups.

13. Silbey et al. 1993 provides the quantitative analysis of the interviews, some of which is reproduced and summarized in appendix A.

14. Llewellyn and Hoebel 1941.

15. This research project builds on a long sociological tradition of collecting stories as a means of understanding the lived experience of everyday life. For example, classic works of the Chicago school of sociology relied on informants' stories to construct their accounts of urban processes: see Abbott 1992; Park, Burgess, and McKenzie 1925. Contemporary studies of family, community, and professions often solicit life stories in the context of in-depth interviewing (e.g., Rubin 1976, 1979; Hochschild 1983, 1989; Imber 1986; Vaughan 1986; Stacey 1990; Cuba 1987; Cuba and Longino 1991; Hummon 1990; Cushman 1995. Van Maanen (1988) has written about the various ways fieldworkers represent those accounts while constructing their own story.

16. Mishler 1986; Bruner 1986, 1990; Sarbin 1986; Pillemer 1992; Pillemer et al. 1995; Ewick and Silbey 1995.

17. See Ricoeur 1984, 1985, 1988.

18. Todd and Fisher 1986, 1988; Reissman 1993.

19. For this distinction between stories as object, method, and product of inquiry, and for additional examples of the use of narrative as a device for understanding legality, see Ewick and Silbey 1995. Also see Bellow and Minow 1996 for an effort to use stories about law as a means of teaching about law; see Brooks and Gewirtz 1996 for examples of reading law as narrative.

20. Galanter 1974.

21. Dewey 1981, 186.

Chapter Three

1. Lawrence Friedman distinguishes lawyer's law ("ideas, problems, or situations of interest to legal theorists") from the law or legal system that includes, in his account, both legal acts ("rules and regulations of the mod-

ern state, the processes of administrative governance, police behavior") and legal behavior ("including the work of lawyers in their offices, advising clients"). In other words, Friedman (1985, 29) rests his accounts of law and the legal system on a definition that includes both the official acts of formal legal agents and the unofficial acts of these officials. Our conception of legality expands the compass further to include the "ideas, problems, or situations of interest" to *unofficial* actors as they take account of, anticipate, or imagine "legal acts and behaviors." Philip Selznick (1995, forthcoming 1997) seems to worry that by blurring the line between legal and nonlegal institutions, legal sociologists may undermine the normative value of recognizing an analytic distinction between law and society and consequently fail to attend to their integration. This integration, Selznick says, may not be fully understood but it is what Lon Fuller "had in mind when he recoiled from the phrase 'law *and* society' . . . [and] preferred the phrase 'law *in* society.'" We note that our use of the term *legality* is not meant to conjure necessarily normative connotations of a single social good but rather, as we have suggested and will explain further below, a property of social relations embodied in cultural schemas and resources embracing several normative claims.

2. We have gone to some length in this discussion to unsettle and deconstruct the law part of the "law and society" couplet. We have spent much less time unpacking the society side, however. As Ronen Shamir has reminded us in correspondence, this approach runs the risk of leaving intact (and thus reifying) society. We have tried to minimize this risk by using the phrase "social relations" rather than "society." Furthermore, by focusing our empirical attention on everyday life, we are also hoping to convey our understanding that society, like law, is local, concrete, and emergent.

3. Wolff 1969, 5.

4. Unger [1975] 1981, 39, 40.

5. Lind and Tyler 1988; Tyler 1990; see also Tyler et al. 1997, MacCoun and Tyler 1988; Sarat 1977; Vidmar and Miller 1980.

6. Chambliss and Seidman 1982, 70.

7. Balbus 1973, 6.

8. Some of this literature has focused on "false consciousness," or the inability of subjects, especially members of the working class, to perceive their true interests or recognize opposing interests. See Hunt 1985, Balbus 1973 for discussion. There are other structuralist and Marxist theorists, however, who do not treat cultural symbols as superstructural residues. Althusser, for example (1971), suggests that cultural symbols, or ideologies, are both material and relatively autonomous; hence culture and ideology are more than just a residue. In this sense, the distinction between base and superstructure is overdrawn and cultural products themselves participate in the production of self and social reality.

9. Socio-legal scholarship has generated numerous studies of legal con-

sciousness, some of which also attempt to understand the role of consciousness and cultural practice as communicating factors between individual agency and social structure. They work from what is sometimes called a constitutive perspective (Hunt 1993), describing the processes by which law participates in the articulation of meanings and values in everyday life. Attention is directed to the local contests over signification within different and competing discourses that extend from the most sublime to the most mundane areas of life. For studies of everyday American legal consciousness, see, for example, Henry 1983; Greenhouse 1986; Macaulay, 1987; Bumiller 1988; Conley and O'Barr 1990; Sarat 1990; Merry 1990; Engel 1991; Villmoare 1991; Tucker 1993; Engel 1993; Yngvesson 1993; Sarat and Kearns 1993; Greenhouse, Yngvesson, and Engel 1994; McCann 1994; *Law and Society Review* 1994; Sarat and Felstiner 1995; Brigham 1996.

10. Bourdieu 1977, 1990; Giddens 1984, 1990, 1991; Swidler 1986; Fantasia 1988; Sewell 1992; Steinberg 1991, 1996, forthcoming 1998.

11. Sewell 1992.

12. Giddens 1984, 21.

13. Steinberg 1991.

14. Steinberg 1991, 277.

15. Sewell 1992.

16. Sewell 1992, 13.

17. Sewell 1992, 4.

18. Currie 1968.

19. We have tried to minimize the use of the word *citizens* to avoid a connotation that only people holding citizenship participate in the construction of legality. We more often use the words *individual, person,* or *people.*

20. We should probably mention that much of the physical world is also a product of social construction. For example, the composition and shape of the land, the trees, and the air are, in part, products of human action. Even human bodies are the results of human action. Only in the narrowest sense, for example, can the shape of a nose be entirely a product of nature, i.e., outside a social world. The aesthetics of noses, its associations with ethnic identity, its role in opening or closing occupational opportunities is entirely a matter of social determination. Moreover, the aesthetics of noses helps shape courtship patterns, opportunities for sexual reproduction, and consequently the genetic possibilities for shaping a nose.

21. Engel 1991.

22. According to Searle 1995, 60, an emergent property is "a property that is explained by the behavior of the elements of [a] system; but it is not a property of any individual elements and it cannot be explained simply as a summation of the properties of those elements. The liquidity of water is a good example: the behavior of the H_2O molecules explains liquidity but the individual molecules are not liquid." Neurath (1959, 199, 201) has likened

this emergent quality of social structures to the process of rebuilding a boat plank by plank while still keeping afloat. "There is no way of taking conclusively established pure protocol sentences as the starting point of the sciences. No tabula rasa exists. We are like sailors who must rebuild their ship on the open sea never able to dismantle it in dry-dock and to reconstruct it there out of the best materials."

23. Henry 1987, 98, citing Attenborough.

24. Bourdieu and Wacquant 1992, 9.

25. Giddens 1984, xxiii, 41–110.

26. Fantasia 1988, 12.

27. Bourdieu 1977; Swidler 1986.

28. Wittgenstein 1953.

29. The obvious omission among this prepositional triad is outside the law. Imagining what such a form of consciousness might look like, it would seem to require an understanding and enactment of self and social relationships as completely distinct from and absent legality. We decided, on empirical and logical grounds, that this category is null. Even the most emphatic renunciation of legality and legal means (as one might hear among religious groups or politically subversive factions) define themselves (and their non-use of law) in relation to the law, deriving their identity by holding the law at bay, so to speak. For example, see Greenhouse 1986; Bumiller 1988. Furthermore, because we do not define consciousness as a completely subjective state such persons or groups, if only to be comprehensible and recognizable, would necessarily have to rely upon the culturally available schemas and resources. Since many of these are legal, and are shared with other institutions, the actors would, indeed could, not be construed as outside the law.

30. Goffman 1963, 9.

31. Billig 1995, 73.

32. Converse 1964; Nie, Verba, and Petrocik 1979. For a contemporary rejoinder, however, see Zaller 1992.

33. Billig et al. 1988.

34. Bakhtin 1981.

35. Ewick and Silbey 1995.

36. Swidler 1986; Potter and Wetherall 1987.

37. Billig 1995, 72.

38. Scott 1988.

Chapter Four

1. Berger and Pullberg 1965, 201.

2. One of the distinctive features of modernity may in fact undermine processes of reification. Giddens, for example, suggests that "the dynamism of modernity" derives in part from "the reflexive ordering and reordering of social relations in light of continual inputs of knowledge affecting the actions

of individuals and groups" (1990, 17). This increasing self-reflexivity under-mines the capacity of organizations, institutions, and social structures to be perceived as trans- or suprahuman. Recognizing that institutions are prod-ucts of human action and knowledge directly challenges the possibilities of reification, although some modern knowledge practices (e.g., actuarial prac-tices and grading systems) may nonetheless quite independently cloak their human constitution.

3. See appendix A for a fuller description of our research methods, including the way in which we developed these dimensions as categories of analysis. Although the dimensions seem to encompass a wide spectrum of social interaction, they are nonetheless unlikely to be exhaustive, and any judgment about their comprehensiveness and generality will depend on em-pirical work in other social domains and on other social structures.

4. Giddens 1984, 30.
5. Mills [1940] 1959.
6. Reichman 1986; Simon 1988.
7. Cover 1986, 1611.
8. Lipsky 1980; Silbey 1981.
9. Shamir 1996.
10. Greenhouse 1989, 1641.
11. Greenhouse 1989, 1643.
12. Thompson 1967, 61.
13. Lakoff and Johnson 1980.
14. Katsch 1989, 36.
15. Clifford 1988, 329.
16. Clifford 1988, 329.
17. De Certeau 1984.
18. De Certeau 1984, 140.
19. Bumiller 1990, 133.

Chapter Five
1. McCann 1994; Merry 1990; Yngvesson 1993.
2. McIntyre 1983 argues that rationality cannot be limited to means-ends relationships, and thus focusing on this dualism ignores other forms of rationality. For example, a narrative provides an account of causality and change over time with a set of characters and relationships. The narrative is rational, but the rationality inheres in the unfolding of a series of actions and possible oppositions over time, where change is understood and explained in terms of time and relational context rather than narrowly defined means and ends. Neither the substantively rational, the narratively rational, nor the moral practice can be subsumed under a simple instrumental conception of rationality. Habermas 1984 also sees means-ends (purposive and instrumen-

tal) rationality as merely one form; he identifies communicative rationality, based on subject-subject relationships rather than subject-object relationships, as an alternative.

3. Kairys [1982] 1990; Singer 1984.

4. Leff 1978.

5. Leff 1978, 1000.

6. Goffman 1961b.

7. Goffman 1961b, 27.

8. Leff 1978.

9. Like the shopkeeper who sells the toothpaste, the law is not merely an arena within which they might seek their interests but a party to the contract of sale. The schema grounds legality in the here and now while implying—without naming—the existence of a gameskeeper (state) that offers legality in the marketplace. This notion of the state as a symbolic purveyor of legality is, of course, not an unfamiliar notion (see Marx [1843] 1975).

10. Herbert Packer (1968) provides an extended analysis of the relative advantages and disadvantages in different conceptions of the legal game in criminal matters.

11. Goffman makes the distinction between the game and the gaming encounter. The rules of the game specify the orchestration of the formal encounter, while the enacted play generates independent effects and responses, such as emotional intensity and elation. Similarly, the rules of legal play define the legitimate moves in legal games and the effort to exclude irrelevancies; nonetheless, much empirical research on legal processes has shown that irrelevancies of material circumstance do in fact matter and affect the enactment of play—the gaming encounter—and its outcomes.

12. Leff 1978, 1001. Similarly, Tyler (1990) and Lind and Tyler (1988) claim that citizens evaluate the legitimacy and justice of law on its procedures rather than its substantive outcomes.

13. Mnookin and Kornhauser 1979; Cooter, Marks, and Mnookin 1982; Silbey and Bittner 1982; Silbey and Merry 1986.

14. Macaulay 1963.

15. Ellickson 1991.

16. Sarat and Kearns 1993, 47.

17. Harvey 1989, 219.

18. Goffman (1961b) also notes that the ability to lose oneself in the spontaneous activity of the game creates the possibilities of fun, elation, and solidarity among the players. The failure to participate fully in the game, to make irrelevant what the game excludes, erodes the possibility of creating a shared world in the game.

19. De Certeau 1984, 140.

20. Durkheim 1965, 53–54.

21. Hartog 1985.

22. *People v. Harriet,* New York Judicial Repository, 265, cited in Hartog 1985.

23. Hartog 1985, 932.

24. Hartog 1985, 930.

25. Galanter 1992.

26. Friedman 1985; Glendon 1991; Kagan 1992; Burke 1996.

27. Provine 1986; Seron 1996; Kritzer 1998.

28. Galanter 1992, 20.

Chapter Six

1. This account is taken from Korstad 1980. It is coincidence that Theodosia Simpson has the same last name as the pseudonymous Millie Simpson.

2. In *Belated Feudalism,* Karen Orren (1991) argues that much of what constitutes the modern American liberal state, especially the freedom to contract in labor relations, was "achieved in America . . . only through the initiatives of the labor movement in the late nineteenth and early twentieth centuries, and was finally ushered in as part of the processes of collective bargaining instituted by the New Deal."

3. "The subject is that which suffers, is subjected and which endures resistance and frustration; it is also that which attempts subjection of hostile conditions; that which takes the immediate initiative in remaking the situation as it stands." Dewey 1981, 184.

4. Gurr 1970; Gamson 1975; Tilly 1978; Moore 1978, Fantasia 1988.

5. Comaroff 1994, xi.

6. Goodman 1978.

7. Goffman 1961a.

8. De Certeau 1984.

9. De Certeau 1984; Scott 1990.

10. Goffman 1961a, 305.

11. Gordon 1993, 142.

12. Scott 1990, 273.

13. This feature of resistance presents a particularly difficult issue for students of the phenomenon who take seriously the issue of consciousness. Given the ambiguity and deniability that often accompanies such acts, it is often difficult to ascertain with any certainty the intentions of the resister (Calavita 1996). One solution, although admittedly a partial one, is to rely on the retrospective accounts of the act, when presumably the dangers or risks of revealing one's intention are lessened. Other indications of intent and consciousness might be found in the narrative context in which it is told. In other words, does the account of resistance narratively position the resister against a powerful opponent, since, as Gordon's definition implies, re-

sistance will always entail some consciousness of opposition and power? Finally, the manner in which the account is communicated might also reveal the person's interpretation of the event. Is the act revealed in an offhand way or as an incidental detail to a different sort of narrative, a detail in which we as scholars might invest significance, but that the teller clearly does not? The tone of voice, expression, tempo, use of dramatic presentation all might indicate and display a consciousness of being up against someone or some organization.

14. De Certeau 1984.

15. Swidler 1986.

16. Wolf 1974; Gordon 1994; Bumiller 1988; Rollins 1985.

17. Hoodfar 1991.

18. Handler 1992; McCann and March 1995; Rubin 1995.

19. Gilliom 1997.

20. Handler 1992.

21. Goffman 1961a, 201.

22. Goffman 1961a, 201.

23. Ewick 1992.

24. See also Rose 1989; Garland 1985; Hunt 1990; Winter 1996.

25. Foucault 1979, 44.

26. Foucault 1980b, 151.

27. Dreyfus and Rabinow 1983, 146.

28. Simon 1988. For an analysis of the possibilities of identifying power and voicing justice claims under globalization, see Silbey 1997.

29. Mitchell 1990; Shearing and Stenning 1985; O'Malley 1993.

30. Gusfield 1981; Tilly 1991.

31. John and Janet Collier were jointly interviewed. Thus, we have stories from both husband and wife.

32. Bumiller 1988.

33. The organizational hurdles for mobilizing justice are often too high, keeping commonplace problems that may be disruptive and injurious beyond the compass of the law. Although small-claims courts were designed to address just these issues, some studies suggest that they have become more resources in the arsenal of organized business interests than they are accessible and cost-effective legal venues for individual plaintiffs. Those plaintiffs still have to overcome the hurdles and costs of obtaining enforcement of court orders. See Sarat 1976 and Yngvesson and Hennessey 1975.

34. For a discussion of the role of continuing relationships in law, see Macaulay 1963 and *Wisconsin Law Review* 1985.

35. Black 1983, 34.

36. Black 1983.

37. Garfinkel 1964, 250.

38. Schutz [1932] 1967.

39. Goffman 1959.
40. Rollins 1985.
41. De Certeau 1984, 29.
42. Simmel 1950; Parsons 1966.
43. Emerson 1983.
44. Petchesky 1987, 275.
45. De Certeau 1984, 23.

Chapter Seven

1. Barrett 1980, 97. For additional analysis of ideology from this perspective see Williams 1977; Silberstein 1988; Fine and Sandstrom 1993; Steinberg 1993; Silbey 1997.

2. Any struggle is ideological to the extent that it "involves an effort to control the cultural terms in which the world is ordered and, within it, power legitimized." Although the dominant ideology of any time or place will belong to the most powerful group, ideologies cannot not be so coherent and consistent that they can be exclusively attached to the interests of any one group. Reigning ideologies may, however "be protected, even enforced, to the full extent of the power of those who claim it for their own." (Comaroff and Comaroff 1991, 24).

3. Steinberg 1994, 512.
4. Billig et al. 1988.
5. Curtis and Resnick 1987.
6. Billig et al. 1988.
7. Van Dijk 1993.
8. Messick 1988, 641.
9. Yngvesson 1993.
10. Lévi-Strauss 1968, 226, quoted in Fitzpatrick 1992, 26.
11. Balbus 1977.
12. Mills [1940] 1959, 6.
13. Smith 1987.
14. Engel 1993.
15. Engel 1993, 797.

16. This pattern cannot be explained by the gender of the interviewer since we varied interviewers by gender and race across the interviews. Subsequent analysis of interviews by the gender or race of interviewer revealed no systematic difference in responses. See appendix A for a summary of these data, and Silbey et al. 1993 for a complete report of the quantitative analysis of these data.

17. By contrast, men were more likely than women to report having been injured on the job. The two problems that were reported more frequently by white respondents involved property transactions of some sort

(tax assessment problems and credit card errors). See generally Mayhew and Reiss 1969.

18. Shamir 1996, 233.

19. Shamir 1996, 235.

20. Pound 1906.

21. Shamir 1996.

22. Simon 1988; Giddens 1990. Even the most banal activity, such as drinking water from a faucet in one's home, demands trust in the responsibility, efficiency, and virtue of power. Drinking water requires a commitment to believing that each step in the process of collecting in reservoirs, processing to remove pollutants, and distributing the water through networks of tanks and pipes has been done so that indeed what flows from the tap is water and not a conveniently available toxin.

23. White 1990.

24. White 1990, 49.

25. White 1990, 29.

26. Scheff 1984.

27. Ewick and Silbey 1995.

28. Freeman 1979.

29. Connell 1987.

30. Malcolm X 1965.

31. Narrative existing outside of or prior to a social context is, according to Herrnstein Smith 1980, a Platonic ideal: "unembodied and unexpressed, unpictured, unwritten and untold," it is, ultimately, unknowable.

32. See Trow 1981 for a discussion of the destruction of the middle distance, or the human scale of experience, in American popular culture and mass media.

Chapter Eight

1. Friedman 1985, 3, 6.

2. Friedman 1985, 26.

3. In fact, when presenting a paper based on this research at the 1996 Glasgow meeting of the Law and Society Association, our references to New Jersey elicited the following joke: "Why does New York have all the lawyers and New Jersey all the garbage? New Jersey got to choose first!"

4. Friedman 1985; Glendon 1991; Kagan 1992; Burke 1996.

5. Bohannan 1965.

Appendix A

1. Vaughan 1986.

2. Mayhew and Reiss 1969; Yankelovich, Skelly & White 1978; Kritzer 1980–81; Merry and Silbey 1984; Goodman and Sanborne 1986; Bumiller 1988; Lind and Tyler 1988; Tyler 1990.

REFERENCES

Abbott, Andrew. 1992. From causes to effects: Notes on narrative positivism. *Sociological Methods and Research* 20:428–55.

Abel, Richard. 1995. *The law and society reader.* New York: New York University Press.

Adams, John. [1774] 1851. Novanglus. In *Works of John Adams, second president of the United States: with a life of the author, notes, and illustration,* edited by Charles Francis Adams. Boston: Charles C. Little and James Brown, 1–177.

Althusser, Louis. 1971. Ideology and ideological state apparatuses. In *Lenin and philosophy.* London: New Left Books.

Auden, W. H. 1976. Law like love. In *W. H. Auden: Collected poems,* edited by Edward Mendelson. New York: Random House, 208–9.

Bakhtin, M. M. 1981. *The dialogic imagination.* Austin: University of Texas.

Balbus, Isaac D. 1971. The concept of interest in pluralist and Marxian analysis. *Politics and Society* 1 (2): 151–77.

———. 1973. *The dialectics of legal repression: Black rebels before the American criminal courts.* New York: Russell Sage Foundation.

———. 1977. Commodity form and legal form: An essay on the "relative autonomy" of the law. *Law and Society Review* 11 (3): 571–88.

Barrett, Michelle. 1980. *Women's oppression today: Problems in Marxist feminist analysis.* London: Verso.

Beale, Joseph H. 1935. *A treatise on the conflict of laws.* 3 vols. New York: Baker, Voorhis.

Bellow, Gary, and Martha Minow, eds. 1996. *Law stories.* Ann Arbor: University of Michigan Press.

Berger, Peter, and Stanley Pullberg. 1965. Reification and the sociological critique of consciousness. *History and Theory* 4 (2): 196–211.

Billig, Michael. 1991. *Ideology and opinions: Studies in rhetorical psychology.* London: Sage Publications.

———. 1992. *Talking of the royal family.* London: Routledge.

———. 1995. Rhetorical psychology, ideological thinking, and imagining nationhood. In *Social movements and culture,* edited by Hank Johnson and Bert Klandermas. Minneapolis: University of Minnesota Press, 64–267.

————. 1996. *Arguing and thinking: A rhetorical approach to social psychology.* Cambridge: Cambridge University Press.

Billig, Michael, Susan Condor, Derek Edwards, Mike Gane, David Middleton, and Alan Radley. 1988. *Ideological dilemmas: A social psychology of everyday thinking.* London: Sage Publications.

Black, Donald. 1983. Crime as social control. *American Sociological Review* 48:34–45.

Black, Donald and Maureen Mileski. 1973. *The social organization of law.* New York: Seminar Press.

Blumberg, Abraham S. 1979. *Criminal justice: Issues and ironies.* 2d ed. New York: New Viewpoints.

Bohannan, Paul. 1965. The differing realms of the law. In *The social organization of law*, edited by Donald Black and Maureen Mileski. New York: Seminar Press, 306–17.

Bourdieu, Pierre. 1977. *Outline of a theory of practice.* Translated by Richard Nice. New York: Cambridge University Press.

————. 1990. *The logic of practice.* Translated by Richard Nice. Stanford: Stanford University Press.

————. 1994. *In other words: Essays towards a reflexive sociology.* Translated by Matthew Adamson. Stanford: Stanford University Press.

Bourdieu, Pierre, and Loïc J. D. Wacquant. 1992. *An invitation to reflexive sociology.* Chicago: University of Chicago Press.

Brigham, John. 1996. *The constitution of interests: Beyond the politics of rights.* New York: New York University Press.

Brooks, Peter, and Paul Gewirtz, eds. 1996. *Law's stories: Narrative and rhetoric in the law.* New Haven: Yale University Press.

Bruner, Jerome. 1986. *Actual minds, possible worlds.* Cambridge: Harvard University Press.

————. 1990. *Acts of meaning.* Cambridge: Harvard University Press.

Bumiller, Kristin. 1988. *The civil rights society: The social construction of victims.* Baltimore: Johns Hopkins University Press.

————. 1990. Fallen angels: The representation of violence against women in legal culture. *International Journal of the Sociology of Law* 18 (2): 125–42.

Burke, Thomas F. 1996. Litigation and its discontents: The politics of adversarial legalism. Ph.D. diss., University of California, Berkeley.

Byron, George Gordon, Baron. 1982. *Don Juan.* Edited by T. G. Steffan, E. Steffan, and W. W. Pratt. New Haven: Yale University Press.

Calavita, K. 1996. Review of *Contested states: Law, hegemony, and resistance*, edited by Mindie Lazarus-Black and Susan F. Hirsch. *Contemporary Sociology* 25 (1): 94–96.

Chambliss, William, and Robert Seidman. 1982. *Law, order, and power.* Reading: Addison-Wesley.

Clifford, James. 1988. *The predicament of culture: Twentieth-century ethnography, literature, and art*. Cambridge: Harvard University Press.

Collins, William Wilkie. [1873] 1980. *The woman in white*. Edited by Harvey Peter Sucksmith. Oxford: Oxford University Press.

Comaroff, Jean, and John Comaroff. 1991. *Of revelation and revolution: Christianity, colonialism, and consciousness in South Africa*. Chicago: University of Chicago Press.

Comaroff, John L. 1994. Foreword to *Contested states: Law, hegemony, and resistance*, edited by Mindie Lazarus-Black and Susan F. Hirsch. New York: Routledge, ix–xii.

Conley, John M., and William M. O'Barr. 1990. *Rules versus relationships: The ethnography of legal discourse*. Chicago: University of Chicago Press.

Connell, R. W. 1987. *Gender and power: Society, the person, and sexual politics*. Stanford: Stanford University Press.

Converse, Philip E. 1964. The nature of belief systems in mass publics. In *Ideology and Its Discontent*, edited by David Apter. New York: Free Press, 206–61.

Cooter, Robert, Stephen Marks, and Robert Mnookin. 1982. Bargaining in the shadow of law: A testable model of strategic behavior. *Journal of Legal Studies* 11:225–51.

Cotterrell, Roger. [1984] 1992. *The sociology of law: An introduction*. 2d ed. London: Butterworth.

Cover, Robert. 1986. Violence and the word. *Yale Law Journal* 95 (8): 1601–29.

Crozier, Michael. [1964] 1967. *The bureaucratic phenomenon*. Chicago: University of Chicago Press.

Cuba, Lee. 1987. *Identity and community on the Alaskan frontier*. Philadelphia: Temple University Press.

Cuba, Lee, and C. F. Longino Jr. 1991. Regional retirement migration: The case of Cape Cod. *Journal of Gerontology* 46 (1): S33–42.

Currie, Elliott P. 1968. Crimes without criminals: Witchcraft and its control in Renaissance Europe. *Law and Society Review* 3 (1): 7–32.

Curtis, Dennis E., and Judith Resnick. 1987. Images of justice. *Yale Law Journal* 96 (8): 1727–72.

Cushman, Thomas O. 1995. *Notes from underground: Rock music counterculture in Russia*. Albany: SUNY Press.

Davis, Kathy, and Sue Fisher, eds. 1995. *Negotiating at the margins: The gendered discourses of power and resistance*. New Brunswick: Rutgers University Press.

de Certeau, Michel. 1984. *The Practice of everyday life*. Translated by Steven Rendall. Berkeley and Los Angeles: University of California Press.

Dewey, John. 1981. *John Dewey: The later works 1925–1953*. Vol. 1, *1925*.

Edited by JoAnn Boydston. Carbondale: Southern Illinois University Press.

DiMaggio, Paul, and Walter Powell. 1991. *The new institutionalism in organizational analysis.* Chicago: University of Chicago Press.

Dreyfus, Hubert L., and Paul Rabinow. 1983. *Michel Foucault: Beyond structuralism and hermeneutics.* 2d ed. Chicago: University of Chicago Press.

Durkheim, Emile. 1965. *The elementary forms of religious life.* New York: Free Press.

Ellickson, Robert. 1991. *Order without law: How neighbors settle disputes.* Cambridge: Harvard University Press.

Emerson, Robert. 1983. Holistic effects in social control decisionmaking. *Law and Society Review* 17 (3): 425–56.

Empson, William. 1935. Legal fiction. In *Collected poems of William Empson.* New York: Harcourt, Brace, 26.

Engel, David M. 1991. Law, culture, and children with disabilities: Educational rights and the construction of difference. *Duke Law Journal* 1:166–205.

———. 1993. Origin myths: Narratives of authority, resistance, disability, and law. *Law and Society Review* 27 (4): 785–826.

Ewick, Patricia. 1992. Postmodern melancholia. *Law and Society Review* 26 (4): 755–63.

Ewick, Patricia, and Susan S. Silbey. 1992. Conformity, contestation, and resistance: An account of legal consciousness. *New England Review* 26 (3): 731–49.

———. 1995. Subversive stories and hegemonic tales: Toward a sociology of narrative. *Law and Society Review* 29 (2): 197–226.

Fantasia, Rick. 1988. *Cultures of solidarity.* Berkeley and Los Angeles: University of California Press.

Federal Judicial Caseload Statistics. 1996. Administrative Office of the United States Courts: Washington, D.C.

Felstiner, William L. F., Richard Abel, and Austin Sarat. 1980–81. The emergence and transformation of disputes: Naming, blaming, claiming . . . *Law and Society Review* 15 (3–4): 631–54.

Fine, Gary Alan, and Kent Sandstrom. 1993. Ideology in action: A pragmatic approach to a contested concept. *Sociological Theory* 11 (1): 21–28.

Fitzpatrick, Peter. 1992. *The mythology of modern law.* London: Routledge.

Foucault, Michel. 1979. *Discipline and punish: The birth of the prison.* New York: Vintage Books.

———. 1980a. *The history of sexuality.* Vol. 1, *An Introduction.* Translated by Robert Hurley. New York: Vintage Books.

———. 1980b. *Power/knowledge: Selected interviews and other writings 1972–*

1977. Edited and translated by Colin Gordon. New York: Random House.

Fowler, H. W., and F. G. Fowler, eds. 1964. *The concise Oxford dictionary of current English*. 5th ed. Revised by E. McIntosh. Oxford: Clarendon Press.

Freeman, Jo. 1979. The women's liberation movement: Its origins, organization, activities, and ideas. In *Women: A feminist perspective*. 2d ed. Edited by Jo Freeman. Palo Alto: Mansfield Publishing, 557–74.

Friedman, Lawrence M. 1975. *The legal system: A social science perspective*. New York: Russell Sage Foundation.

———. 1985. *Total justice: What Americans want from the legal system and why*. Boston: Beacon Press.

———. 1990. *The republic of choice: Law, authority, and culture*. Cambridge: Harvard University Press.

Friedman, Lawrence, and Stewart Macaulay. 1969. *Law and the behavioral sciences*. New York: Bobbs-Merrill.

Galanter, Marc. 1974. Why the haves come out ahead: Speculations on the limits of legal change. *Law and Society Review* 9 (1): 95–160.

———. 1983. Reading the landscape of disputes: What we know and don't know (and think we know) about our allegedly contentious and litigious society. *UCLA Law Review* 31 (1): 4–71.

———. 1986. Adjudication, litigation, and related phenomena. In *Law and the social sciences*, edited by Leon Lipson and Stanton Wheeler. New York: Russell Sage Foundation, 151–257.

———. 1992. Law abounding: Legislation around the North Atlantic. *Modern Law Review* 55 (1): 1–24.

———. 1996. Real world torts: An antidote to anecdote. *Maryland Law Review* 55 (4): 1093–1160.

Gamson, William A. 1975. *The strategy of social protest*. Homewood: Dorsey Press.

Garfinkel, Harold. 1964. Studies of the routine grounds of everyday activities. *Social Problems* 11 (3): 225–50.

Garland, David. 1985. *Punishment and welfare: A history of penal strategies*. Aldershot, U.K.: Gower.

Giddens, Anthony. 1984. *The constitution of society: Outline of the theory of structuration*. Berkeley and Los Angeles: University of California Press.

———. 1990. *The consequences of modernity*. Stanford: Stanford University Press.

———. 1991. *Modernity and self-identity: Self and society in the late modern age*. Stanford: Stanford University Press.

Gilliom, John. 1997. Everyday surveillance: An ethnography of computer monitoring in the lives of the Appalachian poor. In *Studies in law, poli-*

tics, and society, vol. 16, edited by Austin Sarat and Susan S. Silbey. Greenwich: JAI Press, 275–97.

Glendon, Mary Ann. 1991. *Rights talk: The impoverishment of political discourse*. New York: Free Press.

Goffman, Erving. 1959. *The presentation of self in everyday life*. New York: Doubleday.

———. 1961a. *Asylums*. New York: Anchor Books.

———. 1961b. Fun in games. In *Encounters: Two studies in the sociology of interaction*. Indianapolis: Bobbs-Merrill, 17–84.

———. 1963. *Stigma*. Englewood Cliffs: Prentice-Hall.

Goodman, Leonard H., and Sherry Sanborne. 1986. *The legal needs of the poor in New Jersey: A preliminary report* (submitted to the Legal Services Program of New Jersey). Washington, D.C.: National Social Science and Law Center.

Goodman, Nelson. 1978. *Ways of worldmaking*. Indianapolis: Hackett Publishing.

Gordon, Linda. 1976. *Women's body, women's rights: A social history of birth control in America*. New York: Grossman.

———. 1993. Women's agency, social control, and the construction of "rights" by battered women. In *Negotiating at the margins: The gendered discourses of power and resistance*, edited by Sue Fisher and Kathy Davis. New Brunswick: Rutgers University Press, 122–44.

———. 1994. *Pitied but not entitled: Single mothers and the history of welfare, 1890–1935*. New York: Free Press.

Gordon, Robert. 1982. New developments in legal theory. In *The politics of law*, edited by David Kairys. New York: Pantheon Books, 281–93.

Gosden, Christopher. 1994. *Social being and time*. Oxford: Blackwell.

Greenhouse, Carol J. 1986. *Praying for justice: Faith, order, and community in an American town*. Ithaca: Cornell University Press.

———. 1989. Just in time: Temporality and the cultural legitimation of law. *Yale Law Journal* 98 (3): 1631–51.

Greenhouse, Carol J., Barbara Yngvesson, and David M. Engel. 1994. *Law and community in three American towns*. Ithaca: Cornell University Press.

Gross, David. 1985. Temporality and the modern state. *Theory and Society* 14 (1): 53–82.

Gurr, Ted. 1970. *Why men rebel*. Princeton: Princeton University Press.

Gusfield, Joseph R. 1981. *The culture of public problems*. Chicago: University of Chicago Press.

Habermas, Jürgen. 1970. Toward a theory of communicative competence. *Inquiry* 13 (4): 360–75.

———. 1984. *The theory of communicative action*, edited by Thomas McCarthy. Boston: Beacon Press.

Handler, Joel F. 1992. A reply. *Law and Society Review* 26 (4): 819–24.

———. 1995. *The poverty of welfare reform*. New Haven: Yale University Press.

Hartog, Hendrik. 1985. Pigs and positivism. *Wisconsin Law Review*, no. 4: 899–935.

———. 1993. Abigail Bailey's coverture: Law in a married woman's consciousness. In *Law in everyday life*, edited by Austin Sarat and Thomas R. Kearns. Ann Arbor: University of Michigan Press, 63–108.

Hartsock, Nancy. 1990. Foucault on power: A theory for women. In *Feminism/post-modernism*, edited by Linda Nicholson. New York: Routledge, 157–75.

Harvey, David. 1989. *The condition of postmodernity*. Cambridge: Basil Blackwell.

Henry, Stuart. 1983. *Private justice: Towards integrated theorising in the sociology of law*. London: Routledge and Kegan Paul.

———. 1987. Construction and deconstruction of social control: Thought on the discursive production of state law and private justice. In *Transcarceration: Essays in the sociology of social control*, edited by John Lowman, Robert Menzias, and T. S. Palys. Aldershot, U.K.: Gower, 89–108.

Hensler, Deborah R. 1994. Why we don't know more about the civil justice system—and what we could do about it. *University of Southern California Law* (fall): 10–15.

Herrnstein Smith, Barbara. 1980. Narrative versions, narrative theories. *Critical Inquiry* 7: 213–36.

Hochschild, Arlie R. 1983. *The managed heart: Commercialization of human feelings*. Berkeley and Los Angeles: University of California Press.

———. 1989. *The second shift*. New York: Viking Press.

Hoodfar, Homa. 1991 Return to the veil: Personal strategy and public participation in Egypt. In *Working women: International perspectives on labor and gender ideology*, edited by Nanneke Reddift and M. Thea Sinclair. New York: Routledge, 104–24.

Howells, William Dean. [1885] 1983. *The rise of Silas Lapham*. New York: Penguin Books.

Hummon, David M. 1990. *Commonplaces: Community, ideology, and identity in American culture*. Albany: SUNY Press.

Hunt, Alan. 1985. Ideology of law: Advances and problems in recent applications of the concept of ideology to the analysis of law. *Law and Society Review* 19 (1): 11–37.

———. 1990. Rights and social movements: Counter-hegemonic strategies. *Journal of Law and Society* 17 (3): 309–28.

———. 1993. *Explorations in law and society: Toward a constitutive theory of society*. New York: Routledge.

Imber, Jonathan. 1986. *Abortion and the private practice of medicine*. New Haven: Yale University Press.

Kafka, Franz. [1937] 1982. *The trial.* Translated by Willa and Edwin Muir. New York: Alfred Knopf.

Kagan, Robert A. 1992. Adversarial legalism and American government. *Journal of Policy Analysis and Management* 10 (3): 369–406.

Kairys, David, ed. [1982] 1990. *The politics of law.* New York: Pantheon Books.

Katsh, Ethan M. 1989. *Electronic media and the transformation of law.* New York: Oxford University Press.

Kidder, Robert L. 1983. *Connecting law and society: An introduction to research and theory.* Englewood Cliffs: Prentice-Hall.

Korstad, Bob. 1980. Those who were not afraid: Winston-Salem, 1943. In *Working lives: The "Southern Exposure" history of labor in the south,* edited by Marc Miller. New York: Pantheon Books, 184–99.

Kritzer, Herbert M. 1980–81. Studying disputes: Learning from the CLRP experience. *Law and Society Review* 15 (3–4): 503–24.

———. 1989. Popular legal culture: An introduction. *Yale Law Journal* 98 (3): 1545–58.

———. 1991. Propensity to sue in England and the United States of America: Blaming and claiming in tort cases. *Journal of Law and Society* 18 (4): 400–427.

———. Forthcoming. *Legal advocates: Lawyers and nonlawyers at work.* Ann Arbor: University of Michigan Press.

Kritzer, Herbert M., W. A. Bogart, and Neil Vidmar. 1991. The aftermath of injury: Cultural factors in compensation seeking in Canada and the United States. *Law and Society Review* 25 (3): 499–543.

Kritzer, Herbert M., Neil Vidmar, and W. A. Bogart. 1991. To confront or not to confront: Measuring claiming rates in discrimination grievances. *Law and Society Review* 25 (4): 875–87.

Lakoff, Mark, and George Johnson. 1980. *Metaphors we live by.* Chicago: University of Chicago Press.

Law and Society Review. 1994. Symposium on Community and Identity in Sociolegal Studies. Vol. 28, no. 5.

Leff, Arthur Allen. 1978. Law and. *Yale Law Journal* 87 (5): 988–1011.

Lempert, Richard, and Joseph Sanders. 1986. *An invitation to law and social science: Desert, disputes, and distribution.* New York: Longman.

Lévi-Strauss, Claude. 1968. *Structural anthropology.* Harmondsworth: Penguin Books.

Lind, Allan E., and Tom R. Tyler. 1988. *The social psychology of procedural justice.* New York: Plenum Press.

Lipsky, Michael. 1980. *Street-level bureaucracy.* New York: Russell Sage Foundation.

Llewellyn, Karl N., and E. Adamson Hoebel. 1941. *The Cheyenne way: Conflict in case law in primitive jurisprudence.* Norman: University of Oklahoma Press.

Lukács, George. 1971. *History and class consciousness.* Translated by Rodney Livingstone. Cambridge: MIT Press.

Macaulay, Stewart. 1963. Non-contractual relations in business: A preliminary study. *American Sociological Review* 28:55–67.

————. 1987. Images of law in everyday life: The lessons of school, entertainment, and spectator sports. *Law and Society Review* 21 (2): 185–218.

————. 1989. Popular legal culture: An introduction. *Yale Law Journal* 98:1545–58.

MacCoun, Robert J. and Tom R. Tyler. 1988. The basis of citizens' perceptions of the criminal jury: Procedural fairness, accuracy, and efficiency. *Law and Human Behavior* 12 (3): 333–52.

Malcolm X. 1965. *The autobiography of Malcolm X.* With the assistance of Alex Haley. New York: Grove Press.

Marx, Karl. [1843] 1975. On the Jewish question. In *Karl Marx: Early Writings,* translated by Rodney Livingstone and Gregor Benton. New York: Vintage Books, 211–41.

Mayhew, Leon H., and Albert J. Reiss Jr. 1969. The social organization of legal contacts. *American Sociological Review* 34:309–18.

McCann, Michael W. 1994. *Rights at work: Pay equity reform and the politics of legal mobilization.* Chicago: University of Chicago Press.

McCann, Michael W., and Tracey March. 1995. Law and everyday forms of resistance. In *Studies in Law, Politics, and Society,* vol. 15, edited by Austin Sarat and Susan S. Silbey. Greenwich: JAI Press, 207–36.

McIntyre, Alasdair. 1983. *After virtue.* Notre Dame: University of Notre Dame Press.

Merry, Sally Engle. 1990. *Getting justice and getting even: Legal consciousness among working-class Americans.* Chicago: University of Chicago Press.

Merry, Sally Engle, and Susan S. Silbey. 1984. What do plaintiffs want?: Reexamining the concept of disguise. *Justice System Journal* 9 (2): 151.

Messick, Brinkley. 1988. Kissing hands and knees: Hegemony and hierarchy in shari'a discourse. *Law and Society Review* 22 (4): 637–59.

Miller, Peter, and Nikolas Rose. 1992. Political power beyond the state: Problematics of government. *British Journal of Sociology* 43:173–205.

Miller, Richard E., and Austin Sarat. 1980–81. Grievances, claims, and disputes: Assessing the adversary culture. *Law and Society Review* 15 (3–4): 525–66.

Mills, C. Wright. [1940] 1959. *The sociological imagination.* New York: Oxford University Press.

Mishler, Elliot G. 1986. *Research interviewing: Context and narrative.* Cambridge: Harvard University Press.

Mitchell, Timothy. 1990. Everyday metaphors of power. *Theory and Society* 19 (5): 545–78.

Mnookin, Robert H., and Lewis Kornhauser. 1979. Bargaining in the shadow of the law: The case of divorce. *Yale Law Journal* 88 (2): 950–97.

Moore, Barrington, Jr. 1978. *Injustice: The social bases of obedience and revolt*. New York: Pantheon Books.

Mulisch, Harry. 1997. *The discovery of heaven*. Translated by Paul Vincent. New York: Viking Press.

National Center for State Courts. 1996. *State trial court caseloads*. Williamsburg, Va.: National Center for State Courts.

Neurath, Otto. 1959. Protocol sentences. In *Logical positivism*, edited by A. J. Ayer. Glencoe: Free Press, 199–208.

Nie, Norman H., Sidney Verba, and John R. Petrocik. 1979. *The changing American voter*. Cambridge: Harvard University Press.

Nietzsche, Friedrich Wilhelm. 1974. *The gay science*. Translated by Walter Kaufman. New York: Random House.

O'Brien, David M. 1997. *Supreme Court watch: 1996*. New York: W. W. Norton.

O'Malley, Pat. 1993. Containing our excitement: Culture and the crisis of discipline. In *Studies in Law, Politics, and Society*, vol. 13, edited by Austin Sarat and Susan S. Silbey. Greenwich: JAI Press, 159–86.

Orren, Karen. 1991. *Belated feudalism: Labor, the law, and liberal development in the United States*. Cambridge: Cambridge University Press.

Packer, Herbert. 1968. *The limits of criminal sanction*. Stanford: Stanford University Press.

Park, Robert E., Ernest W. Burgess, and Roderick McKenzie. 1925. *The city*. Chicago: University of Chicago Press.

Parsons, Talcott. 1966. On the concept of power. In *Varieties of political theory*, edited by David Easton. New York: Free Press, 79–107.

Petchesky, Rosalind Pollack. 1987. Fetal images: The power of visual culture in the politics of reproduction. *Feminist Studies* 13 (12): 263–89.

Pillemer, David. 1992. Remembering personal circumstances: A functional analysis. In *Affect and accuracy in recall: Studies of "flashbulb" memories*, edited by Eugene Winograd and Ulric Neisser. New York: Cambridge University Press, 236–64.

Pillemer, David, Martha Picariello, Anneliesa Beehe Law, and Jill S. Reichman. 1995. Memories of college: The importance of specific educational episodes. In *Remembering our past: studies in autobiographical memory*, edited by David C. Rubin. New York: Cambridge University Press, 318–37.

Potter, Jonathan, and Margaret Wetherall. 1987. *Discourse and social psychology: Beyond attitudes and behaviour*. London: Sage Publications.

Pound, Roscoe. 1906. The causes of popular dissatisfaction with the administration of justice. Address delivered at the annual Convention of the

American Bar Association, Chicago, 1906. Reprinted by the American Judicature Society, n.d., 1–25.

Provine, Doris Marie. 1986. *Judging credentials: Nonlawyer judges and the politics of professionalism*. Chicago: University of Chicago Press.

Reichman, Nancy. 1986. Managing crime risks: Toward an insurance based model of social control. In *Research in Law, Deviance and Social Control*, vol. 8, edited by Steven Spitzer and Andrew T. Scull. Greenwich: JAI Press, 149–70.

Reissman, Catherine Kohler. 1993. *Narrative analysis*. Newbury Park, Calif.: Sage Publications.

Ricoeur, Paul. 1980. Narrative time. *Critical Inquiry* 7 (1): 169–90.

———. 1984, 1985, 1988. *Time and narrative*. Vols. 1–3. Chicago: University of Chicago Press.

Rollins, Judith. 1985. *Between women: Domestics and their employers*. Philadelphia: Temple University Press.

Rose, Nikolas. 1989. *Governing the soul: The shaping of the private self*. London: Routledge.

Rubin, Jeffrey. 1995. Defining resistance: Contested interpretations of everyday acts. In *Studies in Law, Politics, and Society*, vol. 15, edited by Austin Sarat and Susan S. Silbey. Greenwich: JAI Press, 237–60.

Rubin, Lillian B. 1976. *Worlds of pain*. New York: Basic Books.

———. 1979. *Women of a certain age: The midlife search for self*. New York: Harper and Row.

Sarat, Austin. 1977. Studying American legal culture: An assessment of survey evidence. *Law and Society Review* 11 (3): 427–88.

———. 1976. Alternatives in dispute processing: Litigation in a small claims court. *Law and Society Review* 10 (3): 339–75.

———. 1990. "... The law is all over": Power, resistance, and the legal consciousness of the welfare poor. *Yale Journal of Law and Humanities* 2 (2): 343–79.

Sarat, Austin, and William L. F. Felstiner. 1995. *Divorce lawyers and their clients: Power and meaning in the legal process*. New York: Oxford University Press.

Sarat, Austin, and Thomas R. Kearns, eds. 1993. *Law in everyday life*. Ann Arbor: University of Michigan Press.

Sarbin, Theodore R., ed. 1986. *Narrative psychology: The storied nature of human conduct*. New York: Praeger.

Scheff, Thomas. 1984. *Being mentally ill*. Hawthorne, N.Y.: Aldine Press.

Schutz, Alfred. [1932] 1967. *Phenomenology of everyday life*. Evanston: Northwestern University Press.

Scott, James C. 1985. *Weapons of the weak*. New Haven: Yale University Press.

———— 1990. *Domination and the arts of resistance: Hidden transcripts.* New Haven: Yale University Press.

Scott, Joan. 1988. *Gender and the politics of history.* New York: Columbia University Press.

Searle, John. 1995. The mystery of consciousness. *New York Review of Books.* 2 November, 60–66.

Selznick, Philip. Forthcoming. Legal cultures and the rule of law. In *The rule of law after communism,* edited by Adam Czarnota and Martin Krygier. Aldershot, U.K.: Dartmouth Publishing.

Seron, Carroll. 1996. *The business of practicing law: The work lives of solo and small-firm attorneys.* Philadelphia: Temple University Press.

Sewell, William H. 1992. A theory of structure: Duality, agency, and transformation. *American Journal of Sociology* 98: 1–29.

Shakespeare, William. 1905. *King Richard II: Shakespeare's Tragedy of King Richard II.* Edited by William J. Rolfe. New York: American Book Company.

Shamir, Ronen. 1996. Suspended in space: Bedouins under the law of Israel. *Law and Society Review* 30 (2): 231–57.

Shearing, Clifford D., and Philip C. Stenning. 1985. From the panopticon to Disney World: The development of discipline. In *Perspectives in criminal law,* edited by Anthony N. Doob and Edward L. Greenspan. Toronto: University of Toronto Press, 335–49.

Silberstein, Sandra. 1988. Ideology as process: Gender ideology in courtship narratives. In *Gender and discourse: The power of talk,* edited by Alexandra Dundas Todd and Sue Fisher. Norwood, N.J.: Ablex Publishing, 125–49.

Silbey, Susan S. 1980–81. Case processing: Consumer protection in an attorney general's office. *Law and Society Review* 15 (3–4): 849–910.

————. 1997. Let them eat cake: Globalization, postmodern colonialism, and the possibilities of justice. *Law and Society Review* 30 (2): 207–35.

————. 1998. Ideology, power, and justice. In *Power and justice in law and society research,* edited by Bryant Garth and Austin Sarat. Evanston: Northwestern University Press.

Silbey, Susan S., and Egon Bittner. 1982. The availability of law. *Law and Policy Quarterly* 4 (4): 399–434.

Silbey, Susan S., Patricia Ewick, Elizabeth Schuster, and Lisa Kaunelis. 1993. *Differential use of courts by minority and non-minority populations in New Jersey.* New Jersey: New Jersey Judiciary.

Silbey, Susan S., and Sally Engle Merry. 1986. Mediator settlement strategies. *Law and Policy* 8 (1): 7–32.

Silbey, Susan S., and Austin Sarat. 1987. Critical traditions in law and society research. *Law and Society Review* 21 (1): 165–74.

Simmel, Georg. 1950. Superordination and subordination. In *The sociology of Georg Simmel,* edited and translated by Kurt H. Wolff. New York: Free Press, 181–86.

Simon, Jonathan. 1988. Ideological effects of actuarial practices. *Law and Society Review* 22 (4): 771–800.

Singer, Joseph William. 1984. The player and the cards: Nihilism and legal theory. *Yale Law Journal* 94 (1): 3–69.

Skolnik, Jerome H. 1975. *Justice without trial: Law enforcement in democratic society.* 2d ed. New York: John Wiley.

Smith, Dorothy. 1987. *The everyday world as problematic: A feminist sociology.* Boston: Northeastern University Press.

Stacey, Judith. 1990. *Brave new families: Stories of domestic upheaval in late twentieth century America.* New York: Basic Books.

Steinberg, Marc. 1991. Talkin' class: Discourse, ideology, and their roles in class conflicts. In *Bringing class back in: Contemporary and historical perspectives.* Edited by Scott G. McNall, Rhonda Levine, and Rick Fantasia. Boulder: Westview Press, 261–84.

———. 1993. Rethinking ideology: A dialogue with Fine and Sandsrom from a dialogic perspective. *Sociological Theory* 11 (3): 314–20.

———. 1994. Dialogue of struggle: The contest over ideological boundaries in the case of London silkweavers in the early 19th century. *Social Science History* 18 (4): 504–41.

———. 1996. Discourse, identity, and class consciousness among nineteenth-century English workers: A dialogic perspective. *International Labor and Working-Class History* 49:1–25.

———. Forthcoming. *Fighting words: Working-class formation, collective action, and discourses in early nineteenth century England.*

Sudnow, David. 1965. Normal crimes: Sociological features of the penal code in public defender office. *Social Problems* 12 (3): 255–76.

Swidler, Ann. 1986. Culture in action: Symbols and strategies. *American Sociological Review* 51: 273–86.

Thompson, E. P. 1967. Time, work-discipline, and industrial capitalism. *Past and Present* 38:56–97.

Tilly, Charles. 1978. *From mobilization to revolution.* Reading: Addison Wesley.

———. 1991. Domination, resistance, compliance . . . discourse. *Sociological Forum* 6 (3): 593–602.

Todd, Alexandra Dundas, and Sue Fisher, eds. 1986. *Discourse and institutional authority: Medicine, education, and law.* Norwood, N.J.: Ablex Publishing.

———. 1988. *Gender and discourse: The power of talk.* Norwood, N.J.: Ablex Publishing.

Trow, George W. S. 1981. *Within the context of no context.* Boston: Little, Brown.

Trubek, David, Austin Sarat, William L. F. Felstiner, Herbert Kritzer, and Joel

B. Grossman. 1983. The costs of ordinary litigation. *UCLA Law Review* 31 (1): 72–127.

Tucker, James. 1993. Everyday forms of employee resistance. *Sociological Forum* 8 (1): 25–45.

Turkel, Gerald. 1996. *Law and society: Critical approaches*. Boston: Allyn and Bacon.

Tyler, Tom R. 1990. *Why people obey the law*. New Haven: Yale University Press.

Tyler, Tom R., Robert J. Boeckmann, Heather J. Smith, and Yuen J. Huo. 1997. *Social justice in a diverse society*. Boulder: Westview Press.

Unger, Roberto Mangabeira. [1975] 1981. *Knowledge and politics*. New York: Free Press.

Vago, Steven. 1997. *Law and society*. 5th ed. Upper Saddle River, N.J.: Prentice Hall.

van Dijk, Teun A. 1993. Stories and racism. In *Narrative and social control: Critical perspectives*, edited by Dennis Mumby. Newbury Park, Calif.: Sage Publications, 121–42.

Van Maanen, John. 1988. *Tales of the field: On writing ethnography*. Chicago: University of Chicago Press.

Vaughan, Diane. 1986. *Uncoupling: Turning points in intimate relationships*. New York: Oxford University Press.

Vidmar, Neil. 1981. Justice motives and other psychological factors in the development and resolution of disputes. In *The justice motive in social behavior: Adapting to times of scarcity and change*, edited by Melvin J. Lerner and Sally C. Lerner. New York: Plenum Press, 395–422.

———. 1984. The small claims court: A reconceptualization of disputes and an empirical investigation. *Law and Society Review* 18 (4): 515–50.

Vidmar, Neil, and A. Dittenhoffer. 1981. Canadian public opinion and the death penalty: The effects of knowledge on attitudes. *Canadian Journal of Criminology* 23:43–56.

Vidmar, Neil, and D. T. Miller. 1980. Social psychological processes underlying attitudes toward legal punishment. *Law and Society Review* 14 (3): 401–38.

Villmoare, Adelaide H. 1991. Women, differences, and rights as practices. *Law and Society Review* 25 (2): 385–410.

Weber, Max. 1947. *The theory of social and economic organization*. Translated by A. M. Henderson and Talcott Parsons. New York: Oxford University Press.

———. 1954. *On law in economy and society*. Translated by Edward Shils and Max Rheinstein. New York: Simon and Schuster.

———. 1958. The characteristics of bureaucracy. In *Max Weber*, translated and edited by H. H. Gerth and C. Wright Mills. New York: Oxford University Press, 196–244.

White, Hayden. 1987. *The content of the form: Narrative discourse and historical representation*. Baltimore: Johns Hopkins University Press.

White, Lucie. 1990. Subordination, rhetorical survival skills, and Sunday shoes: Notes on the hearing of Mrs. G. *Buffalo Law Review* 38:1–58.

Williams, Raymond. 1977. *Marxism and literature*. Oxford: Oxford University Press.

Winter, Steven L. 1995. The "power" thing. *Virginia Law Review* 82 (1996): 721–835.

Wisconsin Law Review. 1985. Symposium on Law, Private Governance, and Continuing Relationships. Vol. 1985, no. 3.

Wittgenstein, Ludwig. 1953. *Philosophical investigations*. Translated by G. E. M. Anscombe. Oxford: Basil Blackwell.

Wolf, Margery. 1974. Chinese women: Old skills in a new context. In *Woman, culture, and society*, edited by Michelle Zimbalist Rosaldo and Louise Lamphere. Stanford: Stanford University Press, 157–72.

Wolff, Robert Paul. 1969. Beyond tolerance. In *A critique of pure tolerance*, by Robert Paul Wolff, Barrington Moore Jr. and Herbert Marcuse. Boston: Beacon Press, 3–52.

Yankelovich, Skelly & White, Inc. 1978. Highlights of a national survey of the general public, judges, lawyers, and community leaders. In *State courts: A blueprint for the future*, edited by Theodore J. Fetter. Williamsburg, Va.: National Center for State Courts, 5–69.

Yngvesson, Barbara. 1993. *Virtuous citizens, disruptive subjects: Order and complaint in a New England court*. New York: Routledge.

Yngvesson, Barbara, and Patricia Hennessey. 1975. Small claims, complex disputes: A review of the small claims literature. *Law and Society Review* 9 (2): 219–74.

Zaller, John R. 1992. *The nature and origins of mass opinion*. New York: Cambridge University Press.

Zerubavel, Eviatar. 1981. *Hidden rhythms: Schedules and calendars in social life*. Chicago: University of Chicago Press.

INDEX

Respondents' names (all pseudonyms) appear in italics.

Abbott, Andrew, 272n. 15
Abel, Richard, 271n. 1, 271n. 3
actors (lay): approaches to consciousness of, 35–39; characteristics and capacities of, 132, 136–37, 150–52, 249; constraint on, 53, 76–77, 88–90; law mobilized by, 18–22, 77–78, 84, 86–87; marginality of, 234–38; meaning making by, 39–43; organizational hurdles for, 279n. 33; plea bargaining by, 147; vs. professional, 19–21, 22–23, 131, 152–53, 249, 272–73n. 1; roles manipulated by, 205–7; transformed into cases, 10, 214; variable consciousness of, 50–51, 226–30; violence and threats legitimized by, 201–4. *See also* agency; collective action; self-interest; social action
Adams, John, on government, 91
African Americans: and construction of legality, 6–7, 9; discrimination against, 70, 237–38; and legal engagement, 11–12, 13; role possibilities for, 206–7; structures subverted by storytelling, 241–42. *See also* race
against the law. *See* legality as resistance
agency: absence of, 9; denial in, 77–

82, 100, 106–7; located in players, 150–58; openings for, 9, 180–89, 204–20; and reification of law, 77–82; role of, 38–43, 106; and social construction, 29. *See also* resistance
Agricultural Packing and Allied Workers of America, 181–82
airplane accidents, 152
alcoholics, driving by, 210–11
Althusser, Louis, on cultural symbols, 273n. 8
animals, protection of, 173, 175
appliances, problems with, 58, 110, 154, 211–12, 218
arts, disputes in, 104, 155, 190–91
attorneys. *See* lawyers
automobile accidents: and insurance disputes, 152, 216; and legal consciousness, 67; responses to, 172, 180; responsibility for, 3–14, 62–63, 67; testimony on, 154; and time at court, 97. *See also* traffic citations
automobile companies: and contract law, 149–50; individuals' disputes with, 124–27, 134–35, 179

Bailey, Abigail, diary of, 21–22, 47
Bakhtin, M. M., on heteroglossia, 51

299

CPSIA information can be obtained
at www.ICGtesting.com
Printed in the USA
LVOW03s0812190118
562902LV00003B/10/P